The
BIRD
GARDEN

National
Audubon
Society

The

BIRD
GARDEN

STEPHEN W. KRESS

Foreword by Roger Tory Peterson

DORLING KINDERSLEY
LONDON • NEW YORK • STUTTGART • MOSCOW

A DORLING KINDERSLEY BOOK

Produced for
DORLING KINDERSLEY
by THE BOOKMAKER
10 Garrick Street, London WC2E 9BH

Designed by Peter Bridgewater, Ron Bryant-Funnell
Managing Editor Jemima Dunne
Managing Art Editor Philip Gilderdale
Production Fiona Wright
Editor Jill Hamilton
Horticultural Consultant Ray Rogers

First American Edition, 1995
2 4 6 8 10 9 7 5 3 1
Dorling Kindersley Publishing, Inc., 95 Madison Avenue
New York, New York 10016

Library of Congress Cataloging-in-Publication Data
Kress, Stephen W.
    The bird garden / Stephen W. Kress ; foreword by Roger Tory
Peterson. –– 1st American ed.
        p.   cm.
    At head of title: The National Audubon Society.
    Includes index.
    ISBN 0-7894-0139-8
    1. Gardening to attract birds –– North America.   2. Bird attracting –
– North America.   I National Audubon Society.   II. Title.
QL676.57.N7K74 1995
598' .072347 –– dc20   95-6748
                                                                CIP

Color reproduction by Bright Arts, Hong Kong
Printed and bound in the United States by R. R. Donnelley and Sons.

Contents

FOREWORD

NO SUBURBAN GARDEN *is without birds or butterflies, but by creative planning you can easily double the number of wildlife that may visit. The environmentally oriented gardener can enjoy not only red, orange, yellow, and blue flowers, but also birds of similar colors, such as cardinals, orioles, goldfinches, and jays.*

Attracting birds to the backyard is important. The state of the art has gone beyond the window feeder, the wren box, and the birdbath. This book opens new vistas. Rather than planting showy flowers

The golden-crowned kinglet

which please only the human eye, you can provide flowers that please both humans and birds. Within these pages you will find the secrets to creating backyard habitats that meet all of the needs of wild birds — food, water supply, cover, and nesting places.

This book is an important landmark, a volume for all of North America. In its pages are new ideas for improving backyard habitat, but do not hesitate to try your own ideas. There is no substitute for ingenuity and imagination. The birds themselves will decide if your experiments are valid.

ROGER TORY PETERSON

Prelude to a feast
Spring hawthorn blossom
is followed by greenish
yellow fruits.

INTRODUCTION

THE SINGLE MOST constructive step that anyone can take to assist wild bird populations is to improve the land for wildlife. Fortunately, it is within nearly everyone's capabilities to improve bird habitats by managing the land for important food, cover, and nesting plants. Such management is becoming vitally important because of the frightening loss of natural landscapes in the Americas.

Quality nesting habitat, migration stopovers, and wintering habitat for birds are all disappearing since the human population in North, Central, and South America has increased fivefold from 141 million in 1900 to more than 713 million in 1990. The spread of agriculture has devastated the forested areas of the Caribbean and Central America, leaving fragmented remnants of forests that were once vast. Such loss affects bird populations, since many birds of North America winter in the Tropics.

Serious habitat loss is not restricted to the Tropics though. Recent estimates predict that, by the year 2000, approximately 3.5 million acres in the United States and Canada will be covered with pavement for highways and airports, and an additional 19.7 million acres of presently undeveloped land, an area equivalent to the states of New Hampshire, Vermont, Massachusetts, and Rhode Island, will have been converted into suburbia.

CONTROL THE DEVELOPMENT

Development in North America is greatest along coastal regions where human populations are increasing at the fastest rates. For example, 7.9 million people lived in the Chesapeake Bay area of Virginia and Maryland in 1970, but that population is estimated to be 16.3 million by the year 2020. Such development can also devastate other important migratory stopovers, such as the chenier, a shrubby belt of vegetation along the Texas and Louisiana coasts, where cross-Gulf migrants find vital shelter and food after their epic spring flights. The coastal areas of Massachusetts, New Jersey, Virginia, southern California, and South Florida are especially important staging and migratory stopovers, but development pressures in these areas are severe. While paved parking lots and clear-cut forests are conspicuous losses

Fishy dish *A female belted kingfisher takes her prey to the safety of a tree branch where she beats it senseless and then throws it in the air before catching it in her mouth.*

Scarlet winner
Sumacs are colorful shrubs with showy seedheads. There are 16 species native to North America. They are an important backyard plant since they provide shelter for many birds.

of bird habitat, it is easier to overlook a greater problem – the replacement of native plant communities by monotonous groups of exotic and aggressive plants from other continents. So many Asiatic shrubs and vines and European weeds are now loose on the American landscape that native trees and shrubs providing a combination of food, nesting places, and shelter for birds are crowded out.

Bird gardeners seeking a more natural look to their property cannot assume that benign neglect of odd corners of the backyard will result in a most useful mix of plants, since the species likely to secure a roothold will usually prove to be exotic Asian invaders such as the multiflora rose, oriental bittersweet, or the dreaded kudzu. Ironically, many exotics are readily eaten and distributed by birds.

Fall splendor *The hairy, red fruits of the staghorn sumac provide valuable winter food for at least 98 species, as well as ornamental beauty in the yard.*

PLANT REQUIREMENTS

Just as birds have specific nutritional needs and requirements for shelter and nesting places, many plants require birds to distribute their seeds. The birds carry the seeds for the next generation of plants across the landscape, while the plants nourish the birds with sweet or fatty seeds at the right time of year. This helps the

birds' metabolism to grow new feathers and helps with the essential build up of fat reserves for long migratory journeys.

In the past decade there has been a revolution of awareness and interest in using native plants for gardening. There is a wider availability of native plants in local nurseries, but the backyard bird gardener must often look further. The recommended plant lists included in this book emphasize the choices of native plants. A careful selection of native plants adapted to your annual rainfall and soil will not only enhance the appearance of your yard, creating spectacular gardens with staying power against weather extremes, insects, and diseases, but can also benefit songbirds throughout the seasons. I hope this book will encourage a revolution among backyard gardeners to fuss less with the fluffy azaleas and straggly forsythia that offer little benefit to birds, and to give our native serviceberries, dogwoods, viburnums, and the other native bird-attracting plants a place in the backyard.

The opportunity to increase or restore wild bird populations rests on the ability of most species to replenish their numbers quickly. For example, a pair of American robins, which produces two broods each year, would leave 24,414,060 descendants in 10 years if all its young were to survive and reproduce. That in itself would prove an ecological disaster.

Small forager *The ruby-crowned kinglet is as small as the largest hummingbird. It forages for insects in the foliage of trees and shrubs.*

SURVIVAL MANAGEMENT

Obviously, such increases do not happen, but understanding the reasons that permit wildlife populations to increase or to shrink is the basis of good habitat management, and is essential knowledge for the bird gardener hoping to increase the variety of birds that visit the sanctuary of a backyard.

Habitat management is the key to any successful effort to increase wildlife numbers. The number of animals that can survive within any piece of habitat is determined by any one of several restrictions known as limiting factors. These usually include food, cover, water, and nesting sites, but other factors such as parasites, predators, display areas, or singing posts may also limit populations. The real challenge for those interested in increasing bird populations is to determine which of these factors keeps a given population from increasing naturally.

LIMITING FACTORS

When attempting to solve this puzzle, remember that limiting factors change from season to season. Food may limit numbers in

the winter, but not in the summer. Likewise, cover may be sufficient in the summer but not in the winter. Providing more nesting cover and food may be useless if your property lacks an adequate supply of open water or suitable nest sites. As soon as one limiting factor is identified and removed, another factor comes into play. If this one is then removed, the population will increase still further until something else limits growth. Eventually, social factors such as territoriality, will limit numbers, but even territory size is not a constant – most birds will reduce this for quality habitat.

Local breeding populations of birds such as song sparrows and gray catbirds serve as a source for new recruits to colonize improved habitat. Chance stopovers during migration are another source of colonists for your improved backyard. If the habitat meets the requirements of a particular species, bird numbers will eventually increase, since established pairs help attract others of their species, which then establish new territories on adjacent habitat.

A BIRD'S EYE VIEW

The bird habitat improvements presented in this book rest on the principle that bird populations will increase only when proper action is taken to remove limiting factors. Because the results of management efforts are often difficult to predict, careful planning is an extremely cost-effective way to increase your chances for success. The chapters are organized to help identify limits to bird population growth and to offer techniques and resources for improving bird habitats. In some cases, improving habitat by planting is slow, but for those with patience and an interest in using a variety of trees and shrubs, there will be a longer-lasting and sounder benefit to birds than can be achieved just by filling birdfeeders.

This book shows how to create and encourage native plantings in your backyard that provide food, cover, and nest sites for birds. The inclusion of artificial nest boxes and watering places can also make a great difference where scarce nest sites or water supplies deter birds from occupying habitat that is otherwise suitable. Of course, planting and creating water supplies for birds will also benefit other small wildlife creatures such as chipmunks, skinks, butterflies, frogs, toads, and salamanders.

IMPROVE THE PLANET

Human presence is so prevalent on earth that there are few places left where the course of nature is unaffected by our actions. This is especially true in large cities and in the suburbs. Without a concerted effort to improve and protect land for birds, the tragic loss of many of our native birds will continue as the more aggressive and generalist bird species, such as herring gulls, red-winged blackbirds, European starlings, and house sparrows, dominate many of the bird habitats "ecologically simplified" by the effects of decisions made by human beings.

Many of the world's great environmental problems certainly seem beyond our daily grasp, but the tendency toward monotonous landscapes is something that any property owner can decide to change. The urban or suburban backyard offers a great opportunity to improve a small patch of the planet for wildlife.

CREATE A HABITAT

Plant big trees with spreading canopies and create a leafy subcanopy with serviceberries, viburnums, and dogwoods. Lace this setting with vines and groundcovers that will remind a passing bird of its natural habitat. Encourage your neighbors to create a similar environment. A group of bird-landscaped backyards viewed from above – as migrants would see them – can offer ideal resting and feeding places, as well as safe nesting places, for summer visitors.

Birds brighten our lives with their song, color, and grace, but we must not take their existence for granted. If we each wish to leave a natural wildlife heritage for future generations as rich and varied as that which we know today, we must pursue a more active and responsible approach to the issues of conservation.

Making an effort to restore the ecology of our own gardens, while creating a useful habitat for birds, is an excellent place for us to start.

Constant food *During spring, it is essential for the parent bird, here an American robin, to be able to find enough food for itself and its offpsring.*

Chapter One

LANDSCAPING FOR BIRDS

Ripening fruit
These red dogwood berries make an attractive addition to a backyard.

Ornamental vine
At least 15 species eat the fruit of American bittersweet. The leaves of this vine turn an attractive yellow in fall.

REGARDLESS OF the total size of your property, one principle applies: the variety of bird species that regularly visit your backyard will increase with careful manipulation of both vegetation succession and physical structure. This chapter explains several bird management projects that are devised to meet the varied needs of birdlife for food, water, nest sites, and cover. The wise owner of an average-sized backyard garden area can increase the variety of vegetation by replacing an expansive, close-cropped lawn with more creative landscaping. If you choose plants that have high birdlife value and use them effectively in a good design, the backyard will be both easier to maintain and more alive with birds.

Ground hunter
The mockingbird often hunts for insects on lawns. It nests in shrubs, and sings from a high perch in trees.

THE RELATIONSHIP BETWEEN PLANTS AND BIRDS

BIRDS PERFORM an essential service to plants by carrying seeds away from the parent plant to other locations. Seed dispersal over a wide area is vital, because seedlings that germinate below their parent are usually doomed as a result of competition with each other and the parent for sufficient light and water. While some plants disperse their seeds by windborn parachute

place as the seed passes through the gizzard before being deposited in nitrogenous fertilizer, far from parent and sibling plants.

In the eastern deciduous forests, more than 300 species of plant have seeds that are dispersed by birds. Some of the more familiar species in this region include magnolias, cherries, gooseberries, serviceberries, roses, honeysuckles, viburnums, blueberries, and dogwoods.

ATTRACTIVE FRUITS

Because birds are important to plants, the plants have developed fruits that are attractive and conspicuous to birds. For example, the fruits of bird-distributed plants typically have single, hard seeds that are no more than three-fifths of an inch in diameter, the largest size that a seed-eating bird can swallow. Most bird-distributed fruits are bright red, a color that is attractive to birds. In contrast, orange, yellow, and green fruits generally signal unripe fruits with immature seeds. Some plants that rely on certain birds for seed

Red berries The bright color is an important signal for most birds that food is ready to eat. This highbush cranberry is a delicious gourmet treat.

(cottonwoods and willows), or helicopter-like samaras (maples), most trees and shrubs rely on birds as the ultimate disperser of their seeds.

Unlike rodents, such as squirrels and mice, which destroy seeds by chewing them with sharp teeth, birds swallow plant seeds intact. Seed germination is improved by the scarification (scratching of the seed coat) that takes

Essential seeds

The house finch feeds on seeds during the cold winter months, but will eat sweet fruits in summer.

Cover and food
American elder is an excellent choice for providing late summer food and nesting cover in moist areas.

Migrant birds usually stop for several days along their flight routes to eat certain foods. Trees and shrubs that produce fruits with high fat (lipid) content are attractive to birds at this time. Lipids have twice the energy value/unit weight as carbohydrates, and they help the birds build up essential deposits of subcutaneous fats, which permit them to stay airborn during the long flights. Magnolia trees, spicebush, flowering dogwood, and sassafras produce high-lipid fruits which birds consume.

In contrast, many plants that fruit in the fall and depend on birds bear low-lipid fruits. These plants include the wild rambling rose, viburnum, and hawthorn, whose fruits are usually not eaten until winter or spring.

dispersal appear to disregard the red color rule by having fruits that are blue, black, or white. Such plants may either develop red stems (like gray dogwood) or they display their fruits among red, orange, or yellow leaves that contrast with nearby vegetation. Virginia creeper, poison ivy, and wild grapes all depend upon birds to distribute their blue or white fruits. In these plants, enzymes prematurely break down the green chlorophyll in the leaves, which allows underlying yellow, red, and orange to show through.

The message for the bird gardener is to plant a variety of trees, shrubs, and flowers that will benefit birds throughout the four seasons. It is a worthwhile message.

Juniper berry *Only female juniper plants have the blue-black berry. It is a favorite food of many backyard birds, including the mockingbird.*

FRUIT FOR MIGRATION

The fruit of over 70 percent of bird-distributed plants ripens in the fall, which is just in time for migration. In New England, most shrub and tree fruits ripen in August and September, coinciding with the migration of the thrush and cedar waxwing. The same plants will have ripe fruits a month later in the Carolinas, providing migrants with continuous food on their southbound flight.

ANALYZING THE SITE

BEFORE ATTEMPTING to improve your property for birds, draw up an inventory to see which birds currently visit it. The location of the property – a built-up city, a busy town, a rural area surrounded by farmland – and its proximity to oceans, lakes, rivers, or streams will, to a certain extent, dictate the number and variety of species that visit. However, there is always something of interest in the backyard, and rare visitors can happen at any time, especially during the migratory seasons.

List the most numerous birds that visit, how many of each, and whether they are nesting in the backyard. Ideally, do this during each season. If you notice a shortage of birds during a season, when clearly there are a considerable number in the neighborhood, note the plants that they visit.

Lush planting *The levels of vegetation in this Californian garden provide good cover for many birds, and the fuchsia will attract nectar-eating birds.*

MAKE A GARDEN INVENTORY

Draw up a map of the existing features of your garden. Map the garden's plant communities, property borders, outbuildings, including the garage, greenhouse, and shed. Also include swampy areas, overgrown spots, lawn areas, changes in slope, birdfeeders, and nestboxes.

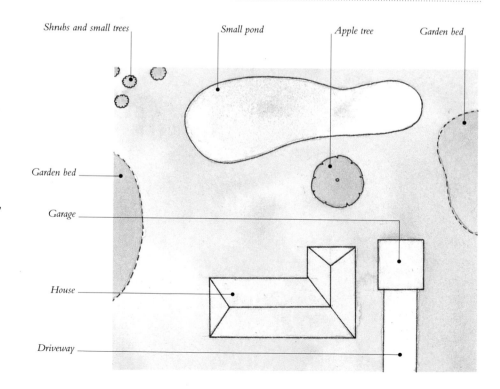

Shrubs and small trees

Small pond

Apple tree

Garden bed

Garden bed

Garage

House

Driveway

DECIDE WHAT TO GROW

With the inventory map complete, plan on paper what changes you might accomplish to improve the property for wildlife. The plan will depend largely on the size of the property and the time and finances available to you, but it will also vary according to the birds that you hope to attract. This, in turn, will help you decide which trees, shrubs, groundcovers, and vines should be retained and encouraged, and which should be replaced by plants that attract the birds of your choice. It is possible that your previously held views on gardening may have to change. For example, if you arc someone who pulls up every weed the minute it raises its "ugly" head, think about the consequences for birds.

The primary factor to bear in mind is that the structure of plant communities and their arrangement are the keys to successful bird-attracting through the seasons. Because of the abundant mix of food, cover, nest sites, perches, and other limiting factors, bird variety is greatest where two or more plant communities work in harmony in the backyard.

Lookout

Perched on a stem of blossom, a yellow warbler checks that the area is clear of predators.

COMPLETED GARDEN PLAN

The second stage is to prepare a final plan that outlines the structure and arrangement of plant communities in relation to the existing features. The white pine and dogwood trees create a small windbreak, and the cherry and crab apple trees, the elderberry shrub, and a few brambles provide cover and nesting sites. Weeds and grasses are planted in the bird food plot.

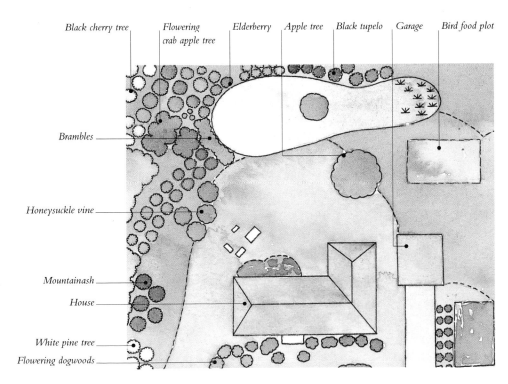

Black cherry tree · Flowering crab apple tree · Elderberry · Apple tree · Black tupelo · Garage · Bird food plot

Brambles

Honeysuckle vine

Mountainash

House

White pine tree

Flowering dogwoods

VEGETATION VARIETY

EVEN WITHIN the same habitat, each bird shows a strong preference for the specific elevation at which it feeds and nests. This is most apparent in forests, where some birds, such as tanagers and grosbeaks, sing and feed in the canopy level but nest in the subcanopy. Others, such as the chipping sparrow, may feed on the ground, nest in shrubs, and sing from the highest trees. These bird movements demonstrate that a multileveled planting design is important.

Backyard vegetation can be improved in various ways. Shade-tolerant shrubs such as dogwood, holly, and serviceberry, as well as honeysuckle and other vines, can be planted at the base of a large tree to improve food supplies and provide nesting

Multilevel flowers *The flowering currant 'King Edward VII' attracts many birds to the garden.*

places for birds. When you are selecting border plants, mix several different shrubs rather than choosing just one species. Also, select shrubs that fruit at different times to ensure a steady food supply. Varying levels can also be created by planting both tall and small, spreading shrubs, and a few bird-attracting groundcovers. This type of planting will ensure a variety of shape and density.

Adding levels to a plant community increases surface area by creating more leaves, stems, nooks, and crannies on which birds can nest, feed, and sing. Insects live on leaf and stem surfaces and, since most birds feed on insects for part of the year, these surfaces provide a good food source and nesting materials for birds.

Vertical view   Shrubby hedgerows are an effective way to increase the variety of birds that visit your backyard.

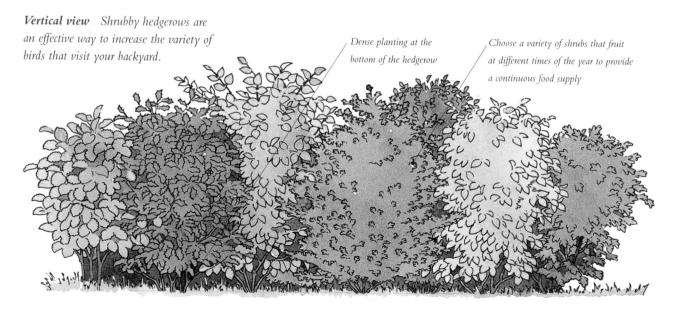

Dense planting at the bottom of the hedgerow

Choose a variety of shrubs that fruit at different times of the year to provide a continuous food supply

HEDGING

SHRUBBY HEDGEROWS are very important to birds. Their form and shape provide shelter from extreme summer and winter weather, and can be used as a secure nesting site. Hedgerows also create cover so that avian predators such as hawks will not be able to see their prey easily. If your hedgerow is planted wisely, birds will come to the profusion of insects and ripe fruits available throughout the year. Hedgerows create an effective windbreak, and provide a privacy screen from neighboring properties. Clusters or rows of shrubs can also be used to separate areas in a larger backyard, as well as adding a pleasing visual diversification.

A hedgerow is particularly important for bird populations in larger cities, or in rural areas where both agricultural methods and changes in the choice of the crops that are grown have resulted in the removal of numerous hedgerows. These are important to rural communities and their bird populations, and ought to be retained, or replaced, not only because of their value to birds, but also for other environmental reasons.

Bushy screen The remarkably bushy Ceanothus 'Gloire de Versailles' *is a favorite of many birds. It is a good choice for a border planting.*

THICKETS

Rapid-growing thickets thrive at the edges of woodlands. When these are planted next to fruit-producing shrubs, and both are swarming with insects, the thickets are very attractive to many birds. Thicket shrubs, for example, hawthorn, wild rose, juniper, mesquite, and raspberry, have well-armed stems that deter browsing rabbits and deer. These thickets also make safe nesting places.

Finally, avoid choosing invasive exotic plants that will almost certainly spread into adjacent land. Always consult your local plant nursery.

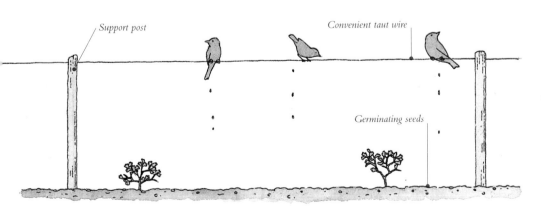

Economic hedgerow *A wire stretched across a tilled or dug-over plot of land allows a natural hedgerow to develop from seeds that drop to the ground in bird excrement.*

LAWN AND GROUNDCOVER

A SMALL, central patch of cropped grassy lawn is a practical way of viewing yard birds. The birds that regularly feed and make their nests in the surrounding trees and shrubs will venture onto lawns – especially if lured by feeders, birdbaths, and a small dust-bathing area. Yet, a simple expanse of cropped lawn is one of the most uninteresting habitats for birds that you can find in a backyard.

Leaf-litter This brown thrasher is one of many species that will forage for insects in fall leaf-litter.

too often missing from the manicured yard. Large areas of lawn make even less sense in a dry climate. It is preferable to plant groundcovers that have adapted well to local arid growing conditions.

FOOD SUPPLY

Perennials that produce berries in large enough quantities on a regular basis are a reliable food source for many birds. There are some low-growing, spreading plants,

GROUNDCOVER

While the robin feeds on earthworms and insects it finds in lawns, other birds, such as the white-throated and fox sparrows, and towhees, prefer feeding among fallen leaves, where they are able to scratch for insects. Such habitats, however, are

such as bearberry, bunchberry, cotoneaster, and creeping juniper, that are more useful to birds than others, such as Boston Ivy and periwinkle. Although many of these plants are an effective alternative to lawn (especially in shady areas), choose carefully in order to grow those that provide food.

Long grass A patch of grass left to grow longer is a good food source for birds throughout the year, as this male western bluebird has discovered in his hunt for earthworms.

LEAF-LITTER

EVEN ROBINS suffer if lawns are the only feeding habitat available in the garden. A variety of bird cover can be achieved by planting leafy borders at the edges of a patch of lawn, creating leaf-littered areas where birds can regularly feed. A patch devoted to tall native grasses also provides useful cover and litter for birds. *(See pages 166 – 167.)*

Overzealous gardeners rake away leaves, thus depriving ground-feeders of food. A good place to create a leaf-littered area is under shrubs and trees where grass grows poorly. Avoid raking this area clean on a daily basis and try to extend it several feet by adding a few inches of fallen leaves to the litter each fall. By spring, the accumulated leaf-litter should have become a rich soil, filled with earthworms and insects for migrants to eat.

Different cover *A selection of native grasses, planted under the canopies of larger trees, provides good cover, and a choice of foods, since the seeds of native grasses are attractive to a variety of birds.*

Green area Leafy shrubs, planted around a patch of lawn, provide good leaf-litter areas for resident and visiting birds.

ARTIFICIAL SLOPES

GROUND-FEEDING birds such as sparrows and towhees are attracted to abrupt changes in ground slope. In natural habitats, birds often forage along stream banks and rocky outcrops, and among tree roots, since these habitats have a wealth of crevices and crannies in which to dig and probe for hiding insects, worms, and other small-animal life. Breaks in elevation can be used to advantage when you design a landscape for birds.

Groundcover *The cotoneaster is an ideal deciduous shrub to plant on a slope since its foliage, flowers, and fruit provide food and cover for birds.*

Artificial slope changes can be created in a backyard by building a gently sloping soil mound, then adding a steep rock face. The rock face provides the tiny crevices used as hiding places by insects and earthworms.

Building a rock garden or a stone wall at the property boundary, and between two areas, for example between a rose garden and a kitchen herb garden, also provides an abrupt change in elevation.

On larger properties, the opportunities for creating varied slopes are even greater. In this situation, a bulldozer moves more earth than is possible with a small shovel and a wheelbarrow. The machine allows you to construct miniature cliffs that can be landscaped with groundcovers, shrubs, and rotting logs, which vary the terrain. It is important to create warm, south-facing slopes that will attract early spring migrants and cool, north-facing slopes where birds may forage for insects during the summer. Variations in the ground level combined with rock-faced water ponds *(see page 70)* are very attractive to birds throughout the seasons.

When choosing plants for these slopes, select a combination of evergreen, semievergreen, and deciduous groundcovers, and low-growing species that prefer well-drained soil. Plants that flower and fruit at different times of the year will bring a wider variety of species to the backyard.

Brambles

Steep rock fall

Create a slope *By constructing an artificial slope in the corner of a yard, you can attract wrens and sparrows, which forage for insects and other food.*

Log and leaves

DUST BATHS

MANY BIRDS, including pheasants, quail, birds of prey, sparrows, and kinglets, can be seen taking a vigorous dust bath. To them, it is a form of dry cleaning. They will often flutter around in the dust bath after water-bathing.

The function of dusting is not yet fully understood, but it may help rid the bird's body of parasites such as feather lice. Feather maintenance is the second most important activity, after feeding, that birds do on a daily basis.

A dust bath is another way to attract birds into an open space. Even a small yard can accommodate several square feet of dusting area. An area that measures 3 feet square provides enough space for several birds to bathe together. If too many sparrows decide to bathe at the same time, quarrels occur when they get in each other's way.

After ascertaining that there are no cats lurking in undergrowth, a bird settles itself in the dust bath. Its movements in dust are the same as

Grooming For a northern bobwhite, rolling about and shaking its feathers in dust is an exercise to dislodge feather parasites.

those it uses in water. A bird ruffles its feathers to fill them with dust, and squats in the dust bath with its tail fanned to ensure its belly is well covered, while flicking dust over its back. After shaking off any excess dust, the bird flies away, leaving small craters in the dust bath. This ritual body-dusting is usually followed by preening.

SUNBATHING

It is not quite clear why birds sunbathe. Sometimes you see them perched still in a sunny place to soak up the warmth of the sun on a chilly day. Yet birds will sunbathe with their wings spread out on the snow in cold but clear weather, and also lie in the sun on hot days, panting with their bills open in an attempt to keep cool. This behavior is mystifying to many ornithologists. Birds appear to be in a deep trance when sunbathing. The ornithological question is: are birds merely enjoying themselves, as humans do, or is this part of a feather-maintenance ritual?

Making a dust bath Excavate enough soil to create a dust bath about 6 inches deep. Line the edge with bricks or rocks. To make a suitable dust mix, combine $1/3$ each of sand, loam, and sifted ash.

CREATING WINDBREAKS

IN WINDY PROVINCES and in the prairie states, the existence of a windbreak is recognized as an important technique to protect soil, plants, animals, and buildings from the impact of wind. On a smaller scale, establishing a windbreak gives protection to a backyard and the edges of a property. If planted with birds and other wildlife in mind, a windbreak provide both protection from harsh winds and useful habitat. For most yards, a two- or three-row-deep windbreak is adequate, but for larger properties, one of six rows is preferable. The length of windbreaks is more important than width. Sacrifice the width to increase the length if space is a limiting factor.

Sheltered life
A spreading shrub, such as this flowering maple, on the outer edge of a windbreak provides both cover and shelter for many birds.

WINDBREAK PLANTINGS FOR NORTHERN STATES AND PROVINCES
(SOUTH DAKOTA AND POINTS NORTH)

Trees	Height (ft)		Shrubs	Height (ft)
Colorado spruce	80–100		Chokecherry	6–20
Austrian pine	70–90		Siberian peashrub	8–12
Bur oak	70–80		Saskatoon serviceberry	6–12
Scotch pine	60–75		Red-osier dogwood	4–8
Green ash	30–50		Silverberry	3–8
Common hackberry	30–50		Silver buffaloberry	3–7
Black willow	30–40		Snowberry	3–6
Downy hawthorn	15–25		Common juniper	1–4
Amur maple	10–20			

Wind-protection
A cedar waxwing feeds safely in the shelter of foliage.

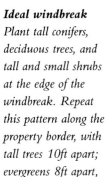

Ideal windbreak
Plant tall conifers, deciduous trees, and tall and small shrubs at the edge of the windbreak. Repeat this pattern along the property border, with tall trees 10ft apart; evergreens 8ft apart, and shrubs 6ft apart.

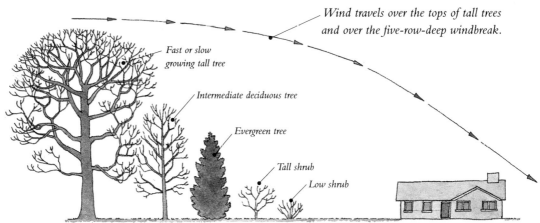

Wind travels over the tops of tall trees and over the five-row-deep windbreak.

Fast or slow growing tall tree

Intermediate deciduous tree

Evergreen tree

Tall shrub

Low shrub

Plant the tallest trees at the back and the lowest shrubs at the front edge. Vary the kinds of trees and shrubs within each row and select those that flower and fruit at different times of the year to encourage a variety of birds.

Mix fast-growing and slow-growing trees and shrubs in the windbreak to ensure the provision of cover over a longer period. Evergreen conifers provide seed crops and shelter from extreme weather; the deciduous trees provide food and nesting cavities, and the tall and low shrubs

provide additional nest sites and often abundant fruit crops. The establishment of a row of herbaceous cover on the edge of the windbreak provides both another source of food and nesting habitat for pheasant and quail (in country areas) and ground-feeding birds such as sparrows.

On the edges of larger properties, plant the larger conifers in a weaving row. This gives the windbreak a more natural appearance and avoids the creation of an open, parklike appearance under the larger, dominating conifer trees.

WINDBREAK PLANTINGS FOR CENTRAL PRAIRIE AND PLAINS STATES
(FROM NEBRASKA SOUTH TO NORTHERN TEXAS)

Trees	Height (ft)		Shrubs	Height (ft)
Black walnut	70–90		Blackhaw viburnum	12–15
Bur oak	70–80		American cranberry	6–15
Red mulberry	40–70		Saskatoon serviceberry	6–12
Eastern redcedar	40–50		Red-osier dogwood	4–8
Common hackberry	30–50		Silver buffaloberry	3–7
Flowering crabapple	15–30		Coralberry	2–5
Hawthorn	15–25		Common juniper	1–4
Osage orange	10–50		Prairie rose	1–2
Chokecherry	6–20			

Ground-feeder
The rufous-sided towhee is a seed-eater that also forages in foliage for insects.

SELF-SEEDING FOOD PATCHES

WILD PLANTS, such as ragweed, amaranth, lamb's-quarters, bristle, and panic grasses, are among the most important bird foods *(see page 166)*. Weed seeds are so abundant in the soil that there is usually an ample supply to grow as soon as the ground is tilled. Once a small patch of wild plants is established in your backyard, you will have a regular supply of seeds for future growth.

CREATING A FOOD PATCH

During the cold winter months, when food is scarce and birds require extra amounts to keep warm, they spend the greater part of the day searching for their food. It is the same during the long summer months, when nestlings must be fed regularly.

Rusty blackbird *This sociable bird is a common, ground-feeding bird of farmland, grassland, and other open habitats. It forages in large flocks.*

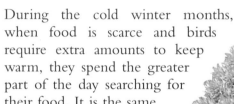
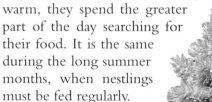

A ready-made food patch can help birds with this endless search and, at the same time, give the backyard birdwatcher the pleasure of watching the parent birds as they forage for and pick up the nutrient-rich seeds.

Farmers and the owners of larger properties may consider planting a more ambitious wild food patch. Consult the appropriate county Soil Conservation Service office for details about specific plant varieties that are best suited to your local conditions.

Useful weed *Members of the Amaranthus genus are prolific seed-producers – single plants are known to produce over 100,000 tiny seeds.*

FRUITING TREES AND SHRUBS

IT TAKES a wide variety of fruiting trees and shrubs to adequately feed wintering birds. To ensure that you are able to provide enough natural food, always select shrubs with a consideration of their food-producing abilities, as well as imagining how they will look with the rest of your garden's landscape design.

A clumped formation provides an attractive focal point, and works well in a bird garden. Plants of the same species are likely to fruit at the same time, making larger food supplies available. Ideally, you should plant several different clumps of trees or shrubs that provide food and cover throughout the four seasons, which means including both evergreen and deciduous plants in your final selection.

Trees such as mulberry and American holly have both male and female plants, requiring a close supply of pollen to ensure successful fruit sets. Planting at least five of each species also provides insurance that, if one or two should die, there will still be three or four that will survive.

Dwarf conifer *A low-growing shrub, such as the* Picea pungens *'Montgomery' above, provides good dense groundcover, especially when planted in clumps.*

Insect-eater *The garden shrubbery undergrowth is one of the habitats in which to find the chirpy white-throated sparrow. It visits gardens to search for insects and seeds that it finds in leaf-litter. Its whistling song is heard all year.*

Dense shrubbery *A corner of the backyard planted with several gray dogwoods will almost certainly guarantee the arrival of birds to feed and nest in the foliage. They are also a desired addition to a garden landscape design.*

SONGBIRD AND HUMMINGBIRD GARDENS

To enjoy the delightful sounds of songbirds in the backyard is not difficult. If you select garden flowers with a lot of seeds, you will be surprised at the variety of songbirds that will visit the garden bed.

SONGBIRD GARDENS

Many of the songbirds' favorite flowers belong to the sunflower family, and the seeds of these plants are eaten in large quantities by the goldfinch and house finch. The latter's pleasant voice can be heard at any time of year since this species visits backyard feeders in the winter and birdbaths all year.

One of the first signs of spring is the cheerful song of the northern cardinal. You may be lucky enough to catch a glimpse of the male's brilliant scarlet body in the leafy trees, shrubs, and vines as it searches for its food. The yellow warbler is a migrant bird which appears in the backyard in early spring. Its diet is made up almost entirely of insects, gleaned from the foliage of trees and shrubs, although it also eats ripe berries in late summer.

Who can ignore the northern mockingbird's dynamic personality? These birds are keen fruit-eaters, particularly during the winter.

PLANT SELECTIONS

Most of the plants listed in the chart below will grow during summer in moist soil throughout North America. Many require open, sunlit areas. Fertilize the soil monthly, following the instructions. Water, but do not soak roots, and mulch. Let the flower heads go to seed for fall and winter birds.

Purple beauty *This mainly summer-flowering buddleia shrub is also known as summer lilac and butterfly bush.*

BIRD-ATTRACTING FLOWERS FOR NORTH AMERICAN SUMMER GARDENS

Asters *(Aster* spp.*)*	Cornflower *(Centaurea cyanus)*	Plume cockscomb *(Celosia plumosa)*
Bachelor's button *(Centaurea hirta)*	Cosmos *(Cossmos* spp.*)*	Prince's plume *(Celiosa plumosa)*
Basket flower *(Centaurea americana)*	Crested cockscomb *(Celosia cristata)*	Rock purslane *(Calandrinia* spp.*)*
Bellflowers *(Campanula* spp.*)*	Dayflowers *(Commelina* spp.*)*	Royal sweet sultan *(Centaurea imperialis)*
Black-eyed Susan *(Rudbeckia* spp.*)*	Dusty miller *(Centaurea cineraria)*	Silene *(Silene* spp.*)*
Blessed thistle *(Carduus benedictus)*	Love-lies-bleeding *(Amaranthus caudatus)*	Sunflower *(Helianthus annuus)*
Calendula *(Calendula officinalis)*	Phlox *(Phlox* spp.*),* especially *P. drummondii*	Sweet scabious *(Scabiosa atropurpurea)*
California poppy *(Eschscholzia californica)*	Portulaca *(Portulaca* spp.*),* especially moss rose *(P. grandiflora)*	Tarweed *(Madia elegans)*
China aster *(Callistephus chinensis)*		Verbena *(Verbena hybrida)*
Chrysanthemum *(Chrysanthemum* spp.*)*		Zinnia *(Zinnia elegans)*
Coreopsis *(Coreopsis* spp.*)*		

PLANTS FOR HUMMINGBIRD GARDENS

Common Name	Latin Name	Type
Bee balm/Oswego tea	*Monarda didyma*	perennial herb
Butterfly bush	*Buddleia davidii*	shrub
Canada columbine	*Aquilegia canadensis*	perennial herb
Cardinal flower	*Lobelia cardinalis*	perennial herb
Citrus	*Citrus* spp.	tree
Coral bean	*Erythrina* spp.	tree
Coralbells	*Heuchera sanguinea*	perennial herb
Four o'clock	*Mirabilis jalapa*	perennial herb
Fuchsia	*Fuchsia* spp.	flowering shrub
Hibiscus	*Hibiscus* spp.	flowering shrub
Hollyhock	*Althea* spp.	perennial herb
Honeysuckle	*Lonicera dioica, L. ciliosa, L. sempervirens*	flowering shrub/ climbing vine
Indian paintbrush	*Castilleja* spp.	annual and perennial herb
Jewelweed	*Impatiens* spp.	annual herb
Larkspur	*Consolida ambigua*	annual herb
Lemon bottlebrush	*Callistemon lanceolatus*	shrub
Morning glory	*Ipomoea* spp.	annual vine
Penstemon	*Penstemon* spp.	perennial herb
Petunia	*Petunia* spp.	annual herb
Phlox	*Phlox drummondii* & spp.	annual and perennial herb
Salvia	*Salvia* spp.	annual and perennial herb
Scarlet runner bean	*Phaseolus coccineus*	cultivated legume vine
Trumpet vine	*Campsis radicans*	native vine
Weigela	*Weigela* spp.	flowering shrub
Zinnia	*Zinnia elegans*	annual herb

Seed supply *A lesser goldfinch searches for seeds in a group of sunflowers, one of the main sources of food for this songbird. At least 40 other species eat sunflower seeds.*

Wall climber *This slightly hardy fuchsia flowered currant represents an abundance of food to many songbirds. Its fruits are spherical and red. The plant flourishes when trained against a south- or west-facing wall.*

HUMMINGBIRD GARDENS

In the eastern states of the United States, the ruby-throated hummingbird is the only hummingbird, except for an occasional western or Caribbean stray. Hummingbirds are more common in the western and especially the southwestern states. At least 14 species are found in these states and some are regular visitors throughout the year.

Hummingbirds belong to the Trochilidae family. They are a brilliant exponent of flight, beating their wings up to 90 times a second. These tiny birds usually fly backward or hover as they take nectar and insects from bright tubular flowers. Anna's hummingbird probably consumes

SIZE 3¼"

Rufous hummingbird *This species nests farther north than other hummingbirds, flying up as far as Alaska and the southern Yukon.*

the most. It requires the nectar of about 1,000 blossoms a day, taken in through its thin bill and extendable tongue. Sometimes up to 20 or more rubythroats will frequent the same food patch, working it over for nectar and insects. Also, as each bird feeds, the flower's pollen settles on its head and is carried to the next bloom, assisting the plant's pollination process.

The sap from sapsucker holes is also taken, and all hummingbirds eagerly come to feed at sugar-water feeders. *(See pages 134 and 150 for information on specific species.)*

ATTRACTING HUMMINGBIRDS

Plant flowers that have brightly colored tubular flowers. Orange and red flowers are the most frequently visited, but hummingbirds will visit yellow, pink, purple, and even blue flowers. A clump of the same flower makes a conspicuous display; be sure also to choose plants that will provide a continuous display from spring to fall. Consult the plant list on the previous page and ask the nursery for plants of a specific color. Some trees and vines also attract hummingbirds.

Bee balm

Position a fountain mist *(see page 67)* near the flowerbed because hummingbirds like to bathe by flying swiftly through a fine mist, catching water in their feathers as they flit past. This activity also cools their minute bodies.

Bugle

Ruby-throated hummingbird *This bird, shown feeding on the nectar of a bleeding heart plant, migrates to Central America for the winter.*

Trumpet vine

Bush fuchsias

Columbine

SIZE
3½ – 4"

Anna's hummingbird *A resident of the Pacific seaboard, its diet includes the nectar of fuchsia, tobacco plant, and century plant flowers.*

CREATING A MULTILEVEL GARDEN

Build up layers of cascading plants on the side of your home by securing a trellis to an exterior wall located in the sun. Plant a trumpet vine, or one of the colorful climbing honeysuckles, and train the plants to grow up and over a wooden trellis. Place a selection of shrubs such as bush fuchsia and four o'clock, and fragrant low-flowering herbs like phlox, bugle, and Canada columbine below and in front of the trellis.

SIZE
3¾"

Black-chinned hummingbird *Similar to the ruby-throated hummingbird, the male has a black gorget with a violet band.*

31

Chapter Two

PLANTING ADVICE

YOU CAN buy bird-attracting trees and shrubs from your local specialized plant supplier, or from mail-order nurseries *(see page 169).* Important factors to the success of your bird garden are the selection of plants that tolerate the local climate and soil conditions, proper preparation of the planting site, and care after planting. There is an old gardener's adage that, if you have only $20 to spend on a tree, it is best to spend $1 on the tree, and the rest on preparing the area and on maintaining it afterward while the plant adjusts to its new location. This chapter offers advice on planting trees and shrubs that will give pleasure to both you and the birds.

Ground-feeder
An American crow prefers to forage for worms in rough lawn.

Garden tools
Made to take the hard work out of gardening, small tools are easy to handle and maintain.

Plant variety
Careful planning is required to achieve a display like this.

CHOOSING TREES AND SHRUBS

THE DECISION to buy a tree or shrub is an important one. Choosing a healthy plant is a process that ought to be approached meticulously.

You can purchase plants that are balled-and-burlapped, grown in a container, or bare-rooted. These different types may be obtained from local plant nurseries and garden centers, or from reputable mail-order nurseries. *(See pages 168–169.)*

Plants may be bought in a variety of sizes and at varying stages of growth. The advantage of an older tree is that it creates an impact on the backyard instantly. However, older trees are more expensive. Younger trees establish their root systems in a new site more quickly than do older trees, and this gives them a greater chance of survival.

Whichever type you buy, ensure that the tree or shrub has healthy top-growth and that its roots are free of disease and not damaged. Examine the branch and root systems of the plant to see if they are healthy.

BALLED-AND-BURLAPPED TREES

Deciduous trees over 10 feet tall, and many evergreen varieties, particularly palms of over 6 feet tall, are sold balled-and-burlapped. Nursery-grown plants are usually more expensive

Balled-and-burlapped tree *This is a good example of a balled-and-burlapped tree, where the root ball is firm and the covering is intact. Do not buy a potbound plant with protruding roots.*

than bare-root plants, but they have been transplanted and root-pruned more than once before they reach the plant nursery. These plants develop thriving root systems, which gives them a good chance of doing well after transplanting. A firm root ball and intact wrapping are essential if the tree or shrub is going to establish quickly in its new site.

CONTAINER-GROWN PLANTS

Many retail outlets, including supermarkets, sell plants grown in containers. These are more expensive than a bare-root or a balled-and-burlapped plant of a similar size. This is the preferred way of buying trees and shrubs that do not easily transplant since you do not disturb the roots as much.

When buying a tree or shrub, first remove it from its container, if possible, and look at the roots closely. If the plant's roots are potbound, or it has thick roots poking through the drainage holes, choose another plant. These potbound plants may not grow well even in good conditions.

Look closely at the root ball and, if the soil does not cling to the root ball when you take the plant from its container, its root system is not established. Choose another plant. The container should be large enough in proportion to the tree or shrub: the container's diameter should be at least a quarter of the plant's height. The potting

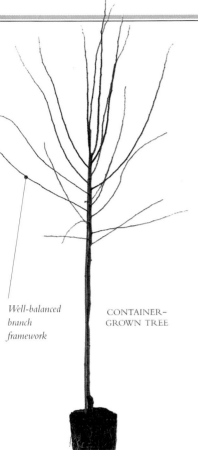

Well-balanced
branch
framework

CONTAINER-
GROWN TREE

Bad example
*Tightly wound,
congested roots mean
restricted growth.*

Good example
*This tree has a well-
established root system
and will grow well.*

Container grown *Before buying a tree,
remove it from its container, if possible,
and be sure to check the roots clearly.
Avoid trees with congested roots.*

directions. Many tiny roots is a good sign since
it means that the roots have been trimmed
annually. This encourages strong growth. Look
closely at the roots to check that they are not dry,
diseased, or damaged. The chances for successful
transplanting are high if the plant's roots do not
dry out. Do not buy trees or shrubs where all the
growth is on one side of the root ball, since these
plants will not adapt well to their new location.

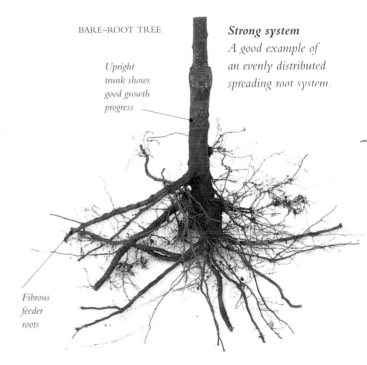

BARE-ROOT TREE

Upright
trunk shows
good growth
progress

Strong system
*A good example of
an evenly distributed
spreading root system.*

Fibrous
feeder
roots

mixture is also important since trees and shrubs
that are packed in soil-based potting mixtures
adjust to their new soil environments more
quickly than those grown in other mixtures.

BARE-ROOT PLANTS

Most trees and shrubs that are sold bare-root are
deciduous, grown in the open, and dug up with
almost no soil clinging to the roots. It is essential
to buy this type of tree or shrub in fall or early
spring when it is not in a growth phase. Look
closely at the tree or shrub to make sure it has
well-developed roots that spread evenly in all

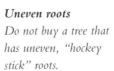

Uneven roots
*Do not buy a tree that
has uneven, "hockey
stick" roots.*

Tightly coiled roots
*The root system shown
here is not sufficiently
established.*

PLANTING TREES AND SHRUBS

IT IS IMPORTANT to provide a young plant with the best growing conditions. Climate, soil type, and the amount of light and shelter available all affect a plant's growth. Check that the plant will flourish in the temperature range, rainfall, and humidity levels of the chosen site. If spring frosts are common, choose plants that come into leaf late since frost frequently damages young growth.

Choose the best position for it, since the microclimate may vary considerably within the garden. In coastal areas, a sheltered site is preferable because sea-spray and salt-laden winds may scorch foliage and damage growth buds.

In particular, ensure that the trees you plant will not come into contact with overhead wires, or their roots with underground cables and pipes.

PLANTING A CONTAINER-GROWN TREE

1 Defining the area
Place the tree on the soil and mark an area 2 or 3 times the diameter of the root ball. Lift any sod or weeds. Dig a hole no deeper than the depth of the root ball.

2 Preparing the hole
With a good-sized gardening fork, roughen the sides, then the bottom, of the planting hole. Mix well-rotted matter with the soil.

3 Staking
If using just one stake, hammer it firmly into the hole, slightly away from the center and on the windward side of the hole.

4 Teasing out the roots
Place the plant on its side and carefully work it out of the pot. Tease out the roots without breaking up the root ball. Make sure you remove any weeds from the soil.

5 Holding up
Place the tree next to the stake and spread out its roots. Lay a long stake across the hole to check that the depth is correct.

6 Filling the hole
Add more topsoil, working it down the root ball, then build a ring of soil around the hole to form a moat to catch rain and water from the watering system or hose.

7 Pruning excess stems
Cut back any stems that are damaged and any long side shoots. It is a good idea to mulch 2 – 3in deep around the base of the young tree to retain moisture.

Mail-order nurseries and local plant nurseries sell bare-root trees and shrubs that have been root-pruned, and often stem-pruned, before being shipped to your door. Early spring and early fall are the best seasons to plant these bare-root deciduous trees and shrubs.

Summer is a stress period for many plants since water evaporates quickly, and in late fall there is not enough time for bare-root plantings to develop adequate winter root systems.

The method of planting bare-root trees and shrubs is similar to that used for container-grown plants. The general rule for balled-and-burlapped plants is that the hole should be twice as wide as the root ball. If planting in heavy clay soils, make the hole three times as wide. You can improve drainage in clay soils by placing the top of the root ball just above the clay soil, and covering the top with 2 to 3 inches of good topsoil, leaving an area about 1 to 2 inches wide around the stem. Water the plant well and mulch generously, and you will find this eventually improves the condition of the soil. Usually, medium to tall shrubs do not need staking in place, except for standards such as roses.

SOAKING PLANTS

The chances for successful transplanting are high if the roots of the plant do not dry out. When nursery stock is delivered, inspect the plants carefully. If the roots appear dry, immediately soak them in water for several hours before planting out. If it is too cold to plant out when your order arrives, unpack the plants, sprinkle the tops and roots with water, and cover the roots with damp peat moss and a layer of burlap or canvas. Keep the plants in a cool but frost-free environment until you are ready to plant them. If the weather is warm, and you are not ready to plant the trees or shrubs, dig a shallow trench in a cool, moist area of the garden in preparation for temporary planting, known as "heeling in."

PLANTING A BALLED-AND BURLAPPED TREE OR SHRUB

Preparation
Dig a hole 2–3 times the diameter of the root ball. Mix well-rotted matter with the soil. Place the plant in the hole and untie the wrapping.

Unwrapping
If the root ball is wrapped in plastic "burlap," remove the covering gently without disturbing the root ball. Back-fill, firm, and water.

HEELING IN

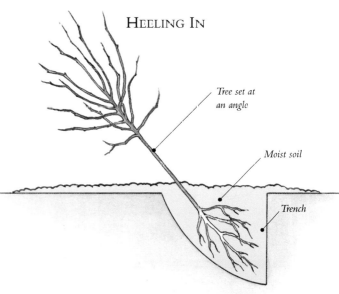

Tree set at an angle

Moist soil

Trench

Root care *Cut all strings and spread the plants out along the trench, making sure that you bury all the roots. Water thoroughly and tamp the soil firmly to reduce air pockets near the roots. Keep the soil moist until ready to plant.*

STAKING TREES

IT MAY BE necessary to add support to the trunk of a young tree or shrub since its new root system may require a few growing seasons before it is established.

Strong winds can damage a tree trunk, causing it to grow at an angle, so staking may be necessary to prevent this occurring.

SUPPORTING TREES

The method chosen to support the young tree depends on the type of tree and the planting site. Many old-fashioned gardeners still prefer to use a tall stake, pushed into the ground on the side of the prevailing wind. However, these days a shorter stake is often used because it allows the tree to move naturally in the wind so there is less chance of the trunk snapping. The depth of the stake in the soil is usually to about 18 – 20 inches. With flexible-stemmed trees use

Tall stake Drive in a single, tall stake before planting. Secure the tree to the stake using two padded or buckle-and-spacer ties.

Short stake This allows the young tree's trunk some movement; insert it so that only about 18in is seen above ground level.

a tall stake in the first year, then cut it shorter for the next growing season and, if the tree is established, you can remove it in the third season.

SHORT STAKES

To support a tree that has been grown in a container or is balled-and-burlapped, use a short stake and drive it into the ground at an angle, facing in the direction of the wind. This will easily clear the tree's root ball, even if you do this after the tree has been planted. Or, put two or three shorter stakes in the ground, evenly spaced around the tree and outside the root ball area. If the site is windy, insert one tall stake either side.

Secure large trees with guy ropes attached to short stakes. Cover these guys with hose lengths or white tape to make them more visible and to prevent someone tripping over them.

Angled stake Add a short stake after planting. Drive it into the ground at a 45° angle.

Two stakes Insert one stake on either side of the tree, and secure them to the tree with rubber ties.

USING GUY ROPES

Hose lengths
Cushion guys with hose lengths to prevent damage to the tree trunk.

U-bolts
The guys are secured at the stakes with U-bolts that can be adjusted.

Support team *Attach guy ropes made of multistrand wire or nylon rope to short stakes angled at 45° away from the tree. Space the guy ropes evenly around the tree and secure them to the stakes.*

SECURING TREE TIES

TREE TIES need to be extremely secure and last for several seasons, and also accommodate the girth of a tree as it grows. If ties do not accommodate the girth, they will cut into the bark and damage the tree.

Various types of commercial ties are available, or you can make them yourself

Buckle-and-spacer tie *This buckle is taut, but the spacer prevents bark damage.*

Rubber tie *If using a rubber tie without a buckle, nail it to the stake to prevent damage.*

using nylon webbing or rubber tubing. A spacer or padded tie in the shape of a figure-eight nailed to the stake will prevent the upright stake from

rubbing against the bark. If using a few stakes, tie the tree to these stakes with a wide, strong rubber or plastic strip.

When using the buckle-and-spacer type, thread the tie through the spacer, around the tree, and back through the spacer; buckle it so that it is taut but not so taut as to damage the bark. When using the tie without a buckle, nail it to the stake to prevent friction damage. Use galvanized nails to prevent rusting.

TRANSPLANTING WILD PLANTS

WILD TREES and shrubs have the advantages of being inexpensive, hardy to the area, and adapted to local soil conditions. They may also be more resistant to insects and disease. Always get permission from a landowner, and do not remove rare plants that are on the endangered or threatened species lists.

Plants growing in the wild often have roots and branches that are tangled with those of neighboring plants. The main roots may be few and widespread, making it difficult to transplant enough roots, so always select isolated plants. Choose the plant in early spring and move it to its new location in the following spring.

Root prune using a spade to make an 8-inch incision circling the tree about 2 feet away from the trunk. Do this in early spring so that the roots will branch during the following growing season, forming a compact, fibrous root system closer to the trunk or shrub crown. This gives the plant a better chance of transplanting well.

Early next spring, dig up the plant, taking as much soil as possible, and wrap the root mass in burlap. Plant in the new site, spread the roots naturally, and check that they are at the same depth as at the original site. Three-quarters fill the hole with soil. Water to eliminate air pockets. Fill gaps with loose soil. Build a shallow rim around the hole to help retain water. To keep the soil moist, cover the base of the plant with mulch 3 inches deep.

Afterwards, remove one-third of the branches near the trunk or main branches. Do not destroy the natural shape of the plant. Pruning reduces the amount of leaves and stems, balancing this part of the plant with the reduced root system.

CONSERVING WATER

AN IMPORTANT consideration in arid climates is the conservation of water for plants. Two inexpensive ways to conserve water are by using either a canvas soaker hose (left) or a water lance (right) that apply water directly to the roots of trees and shrubs. The water supply to a plant is limited by the size of its root system. The main limitation, though, is the rate at which the soil takes up the water. Soil absorbs only about $\frac{3}{8}$-inch of water per hour, so it is best to water slowly to ensure that water reaches deep in the soil. Spreading mulch over the planting hole improves deep rain penetration and minimizes evaporation. Many types of trickle and drip-feed irrigation systems are designed to conserve water and it is worth considering the cost-effectiveness of such systems, and the benefits to your plant.

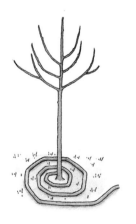

Soaker hose *In arid habitats, this implement is used to apply water directly to the roots of the tree.*

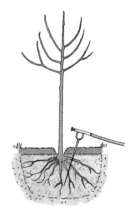

Water lance *An implement such as a water lance ensures that water goes directly to the root system.*

PROTECTING AGAINST PREDATORS

IN WINTER, when the tender buds, twigs, seeds, and other favorite bird foods are already eaten or buried under snow, mice, rabbits and deer often turn to the bark of young trees and shrubs. This stripping of the bark nips back new growth.

PROTECTIVE WRAP

To protect the tree from these hungry animals, surround the tree with chicken wire and hold the wire in place with a few stakes. Or, you can use spiral guards made of flexible plastic, or guards made from wire mesh or of heavy duty plastic. These are available from local garden centers. Biodegradable plastic-net tree guards are also available. These range in height from 2 to 6 feet. Ask the supplier about using a tree shelter on an exposed site.

Young plum *Without protection, this trunk is at the mercy of passing wildlife with a penchant for bark.*

To reduce the damage caused by mice and rabbits, pull straw mulch away from the trunks of new plantings during the fall, or wrap 1/4-inch hardware cloth around the tree trunk at least 2 feet higher than the average winter snow line.

KEEPING DEER AWAY

Deer are more difficult to keep away from trees and shrubs, since they become very bold at night and often browse on plantings in the suburbs. To discourage deer, spread dried blood, available from garden centers, and hair clippings around favorite plants. Fragrant soap in mesh bags, hung around trees or a shrubbery, will also repel deer. Apparently deer avoid areas where they pick up the smell of other mammals.

Secure guard
A barrier of wire netting is staked to the ground.

Firm support
A rigid plastic tree shelter is good for exposed hill sites.

Strong wrap
A tall, thick rubber or plastic stem guard is very effective.

Flexible guard
A spiral, wraparound guard is made from flexible plastic.

Chapter Three

NESTING STRUCTURES

S CARCITY OF suitable nest sites often prevents many birds from occupying what is otherwise excellent habitat. Providing artificial nest structures can increase the populations of a variety of birds, not just the species that are cavity-nesters. Even treetop-nesting species such as the great horned owl and the great gray owl will accept artificial nesting platforms. When these are designed to repel predators and resist destructive weather elements, they provide birds with a more secure nest than do natural sites. This chapter gives information on the construction of artificial nests from economical building supplies, and explains the importance of it becoming part of the natural habitat.

Nest egg
Two tiny hummingbird eggs are cushioned in a soft nest ringed with leaves.

Checking for predators
A male and female Cassin's finch check the area is clear before entering the nestbox.

Night owl
An eastern screech-owl in its nesting cavity.

BUILDING A STANDARD NESTBOX

YOU DO NOT need great carpentry skills to build nestboxes – most birds are not fussy about their housing – but certain techniques improve your chances of success. Neat joints, sealed with silicone, look better and reduce the chance of the nest getting wet in heavy rain. To avoid rusting, use galvanized nails and brass, or coated screws, hinges, and catches. The best building materials are 6-inch floorboard, ¾-inch white cedar, and thick exterior-grade plywood. Spruce, pine, and poplar woods are easy to work with, weather-tolerant, and will last for years.

ASSEMBLY

Follow the dimensions carefully and make sure you match each edge to its corresponding edge as shown in the photographs. Drill a small hole at the top and bottom of the back, to attach the box to a post or tree. Nail the sides to the base, then attach the back and front to these. Hinge the roof with waterproof material (inner tube rubber is ideal). Fix hooks and eyes to hold it shut. A metal plate placed around the hole will prevent predators from enlarging it.

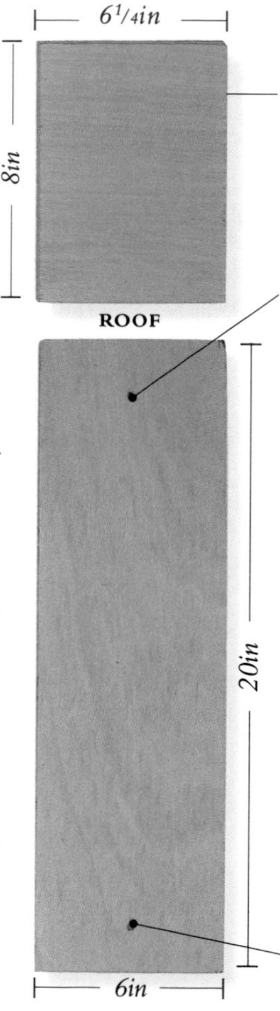

6¼in

8in

Beveled to butt up to the back

ROOF

Attachment hole

Attachment hole

Attachment hole

20in

6in

BACK

Attachment hole

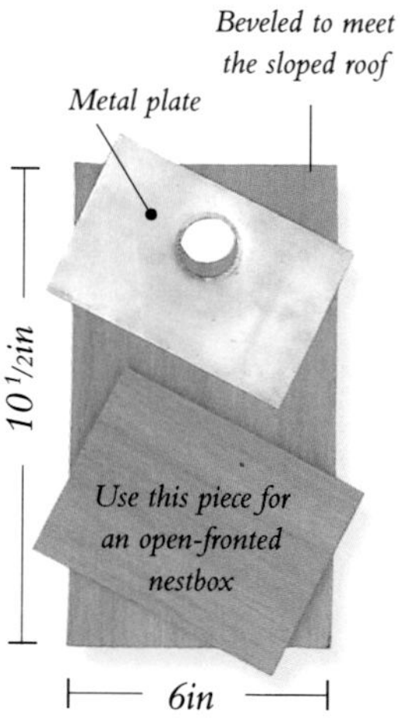

Beveled to meet the sloped roof

Metal plate

10½in

6in

ENCLOSED FRONT

Use this piece for an open-fronted nestbox

6¼in

73°

12¼in

6in

SIDE

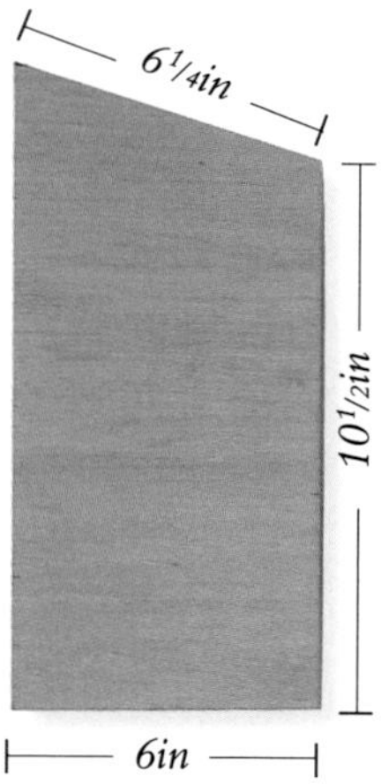

6¼in

10½in

6in

SIDE

Attachment hole

COMPLETED BOX

Hooks and eyes

Nails 1½in

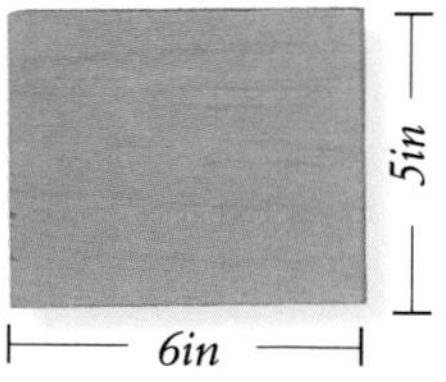

5in

6in

BASE

Webbing

Tacks

HELPFUL TIPS

● If the roof is not hinged, screw it down tight.

● Make the hole with an adjustable bit, or drill a circle of holes and join them up with a jigsaw.

● All wood must be treated with a nontoxic wood preservative.

SITING THE NESTBOX

The site of a nestbox is of primary importance in attracting birds that visit the yard in winter to stay through the breeding season. Some species will nest in secret corners of the yard and raise families if you place the nestbox properly. House wrens, chickadees, bluebirds, and other hole-nesting birds will move into a new nestbox. Ideally, a nestbox must be sited at least 5 feet above the ground, placed out of direct sunlight and heavy rain. The best way to secure a nestbox in a tree is to attach a wooden strut to the back and wedge the strut between the branches. See page 55 for protection against predators.

Entrance hole   Small holes, such as the cavities found in old trees, are usually in short supply in the yard. An enclosed box is a good substitute and appeals to a variety of small birds.

DIMENSIONS GUIDE (ENCLOSED NESTBOX)

The size of both the nestbox itself and the entrance is crucial in determining which birds use it, since different species are attracted to boxes of different dimensions. Follow the recommended sizes listed below and the appropriate species will use your nestbox.

	Floor area	Entrance hole	Height to hole	Comments
Chickadees	4 x 4in	$1^{1}/8$in	7in	Line with woodchips
Titmice	4 x 4in	$1^{1}/4$in	7in	Line with woodchips
Nuthatches	4 x 4in	$1^{3}/8$in	7in	Line with woodchips
House wren	4 x 4in	$1^{1}/8$in	7in	
Bluebirds	4 x 4in	$1^{3}/8$in	8in	
Tree swallow	5 x 5in	$1^{1}/2$in	5in	
Downy woodpecker	4 x 4in	$1^{3}/8$in	7in	Line with woodchips
Hairy and red-headed woodpeckers	6 x 6in	2in	10in	Place 12 – 20ft up, and line with woodchips
Northern flicker	7 x 7in	$2^{1}/2$in	15in	Line with woodchips

HOUSES FOR BLUEBIRDS

PEOPLE HAVE provided housing for bluebirds for at least 150 years, however, only in the past 40 years have declines in bluebird populations sparked an interest in using nestboxes to help increase their numbers. Research suggests that that eastern bluebirds have declined as much as 90 percent since 1940. The populations of western and mountain bluebirds have also declined but less dramatically than the eastern species.

The decrease in bluebird numbers coincides with regrowth of expansive farmlands into forests, widespread use of persistent pesticides, and the introduction of two serious nest competitors, the house sparrow and the European starling. Loss of traditional nest cavities in old apple orchards and wooden fence posts on larger properties are probably both contributing factors to the decreasing population.

THE RIGHT LOCATION

To help reverse this decline, an army of volunteers has been nailing together bluebird houses for the past several decades. To make monitoring them easy, the nestboxes are mounted along "trails" where the nest contents can be checked and the boxes can receive regular maintenance. Proper location of bluebird boxes is very important since

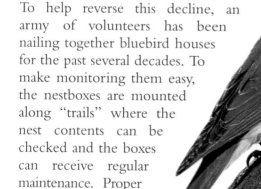

these birds rarely nest in urban or forested areas. They prefer open countryside, with a scattering of trees and undergrowth. Large lawns, pastures, golf courses, parks, and other open areas are their preferred habitats. This would suggest that birders owning large, wide open backyards stand a greater chance of encouraging bluebirds to visit, and perhaps nest on, their property.

CORRECT MOUNTING

Bluebird nestboxes should be mounted 3 to 6 feet above the ground, and because bluebirds are highly territorial, it is usually unproductive to mount nestboxes closer than 100 yards apart. The boxes should face and be within 50 feet of a tree, fence or other structure on which fledglings can perch after their first flight. This reduces the chances of the young birds landing on the ground where they are vulnerable to predators. The proper siting of nestboxes can also help minimize nest competition from house wrens, house sparrows, and starlings. House sparrows are the most serious nest competitor for bluebirds. Unlike starlings, which can be excluded by a 1½-inch entrance hole, house sparrows can use bluebird boxes and their persistence at renesting is legendary. By using smaller internal dimensions, you can discourage house sparrows. The nestbox on the opposite page, designed by Dick Peterson of Minneapolis, has proven to be successful at discouraging starlings.

Eastern bluebird *Feeders stocked with peanut kernels, raisins, and suet are attractive to eastern bluebirds when their natural food supplies are scarce.*

A BLUEBIRD NESTBOX

THE STEEP sloping roof and front reduce the floor space and thus the time-consuming gathering of nesting material. There is also less room inside for blowfly larvae to hide. Use ¾-inch-thick exterior plywood for the roof and sides, and 1-inch galvanized nails to avoid rusting.

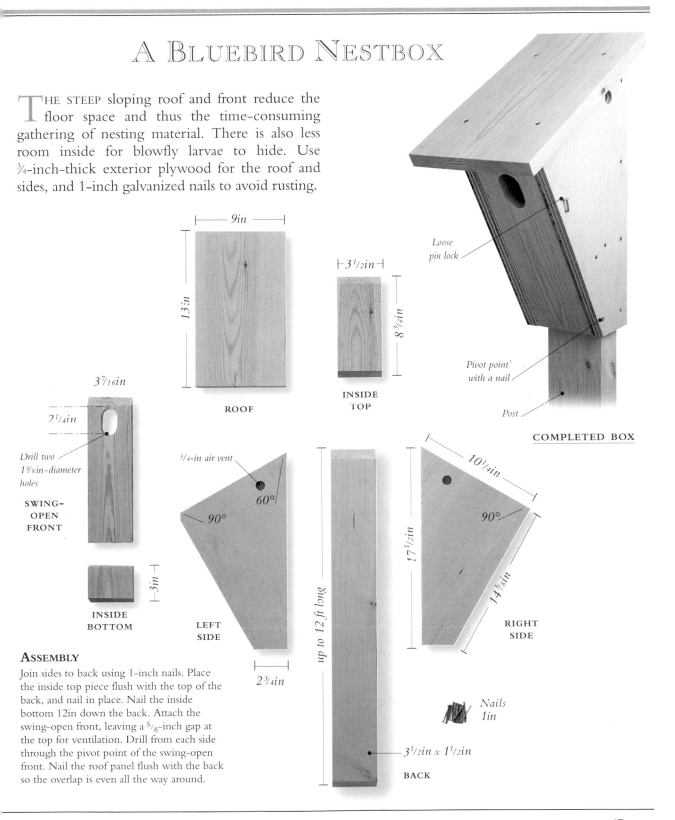

9in

13in

ROOF

3½in

8⅜in

INSIDE
TOP

Loose
pin lock

Pivot point
with a nail

Post

COMPLETED BOX

3⁷⁄₁₆in

2¼in

Drill two
1⅜in-diameter
holes

SWING-
OPEN
FRONT

INSIDE
BOTTOM

3in

¾-in air vent

90°

60°

LEFT
SIDE

2¾in

up to 12 ft long

17½in

10¼in

90°

14⅜in

RIGHT
SIDE

3½in x 1½in

BACK

Nails
1in

ASSEMBLY

Join sides to back using 1-inch nails. Place the inside top piece flush with the top of the back, and nail in place. Nail the inside bottom 12in down the back. Attach the swing-open front, leaving a ⅝-inch gap at the top for ventilation. Drill from each side through the pivot point of the swing-open front. Nail the roof panel flush with the back so the overlap is even all the way around.

47

THE PURPLE MARTIN

THESE DAYS, purple martins nearly always nest in artificial nesting structures, but it was not always that way for the species. Before the Europeans colonized North America, purple martins were known to make their nests in empty woodpecker-riddled snags, old tree trunks, saguaro cacti, and crevices in cliffs.

Multilevel living   What begins as a single purple martin colony in one house can expand to many families living under the same roof.

HABITAT

The species was probably rare in the vast eastern forests; their usual habitat was the open, grassy valleys along the edges of rivers, lakes, and seacoast marshes. The greatest purple martin populations in precolonial times were found in the partly forested central regions of North America, a large area that remains the heart of the purple martin's current population distribution.

Native Americans were the first people to lure purple martins to nest in artificial structures. They used to hang many dried gourds from trees near their villages in the hope that these would entice the birds to eat nuisance insect pests such as mosquitoes and flies. In the southeastern states, gourds are still a good way to provide housing for families of purple martins.

SOCIAL CREATURES

Because purple martins are highly social, they readily accept multiple housing units. As many as 200 pairs of purple martins have been known to

Feeding the young   *A female purple martin arrives on the balcony of this condominium with a large insect to feed to her young inside the structure.*

Collective housing   *This collection of martin gourds hangs in South Carolina low country. It is well located near small trees and shrubs that provide cover for circling purple martins.*

Hanging out gourds *Dry the gourd before cutting a $2\frac{1}{2}$-inch hole in the middle of the side. Scrape out the seeds, saving them for a new crop. Drill $\frac{1}{2}$-inch drainage holes in the bottom and a $\frac{1}{4}$-inch hole through the neck to attach a line with which to hang it. Replace used gourds each year.*

nest in the same house, with many of the adult birds returning to the same colony year after year. Multiple-unit martin houses offer several advantages over gourds. The thick wooden walls provide insulation, and the houses may be built with a central chamber that conducts heat up to the roof, where it disperses through ventilation holes. A porch may be added, to prevent young birds from fledging prematurely.

Aluminum martin houses offer birds all the advantages of wooden houses, and are also much lighter in weight. This reduces the chances of the house falling in strong winds and makes it easier to raise and lower it each season.

MOUNTING AND LOCATING

Martin houses should be mounted on top of a post approximately 14 feet tall. Position the mounting post in an open area, at least 15 feet away from overhanging tree limbs or buildings. Purple martins like to circle their colony, and they shun homes judged to be vulnerable to climbing predators. Placing the house near a pond is very popular. You can also mount a martin house on the roof of your house by building a base that fits tightly onto the apex.

CONTROLLING USURPERS

Since purple martins spend seven months of the year either going to, living in, or returning from their wintering habitat, their nestboxes are often used by house sparrows and starlings. To stop starlings becoming established paint the interior white. This also keeps the martins cool in hot weather. House sparrows are more difficult to discourage. To keep starlings and sparrows out of the nestbox, lower it in fall, clean and paint it in winter, and put it back up a week ahead of the purple martins' arrival date of the previous year.

Nesting instinct *The male takes as positive a part in collecting nesting material as the female. Here, a male arrives home with his welcome contribution.*

A MARTIN HOUSE

THIS DESIGN for a three-level condominium is best made of ½-inch-thick plywood but any quality treated exterior lumber will suffice. Use 1-inch nails, and you will need 4 hooks and eyes for each level. Assemble each internal partition first, then assemble the exterior side panels. Make the roof next, and then the support post. Paint the exterior of each level separately, using one coat of primer and two top coats. You may want to use waterproof wood adhesive as well as nails.

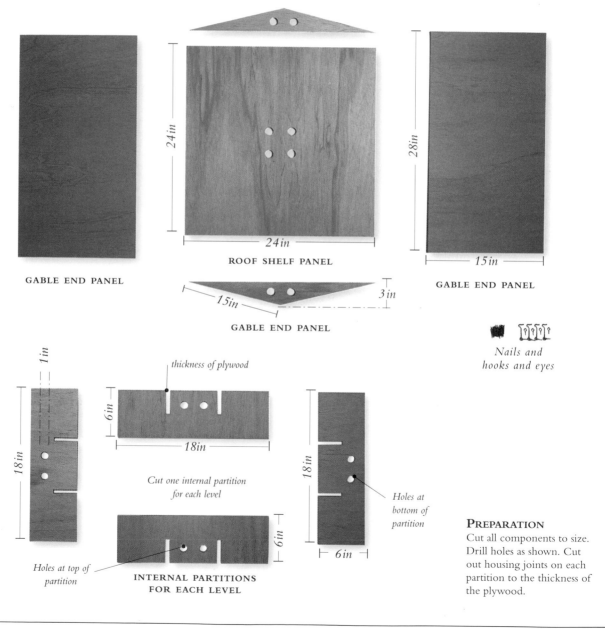

GABLE END PANEL

24 in

24 in

ROOF SHELF PANEL

28 in

15 in

GABLE END PANEL

15 in

3 in

GABLE END PANEL

Nails and hooks and eyes

1 in

18 in

6 in

thickness of plywood

18 in

Cut one internal partition for each level

18 in

Holes at bottom of partition

6 in

Holes at top of partition

6 in

INTERNAL PARTITIONS FOR EACH LEVEL

PREPARATION
Cut all components to size. Drill holes as shown. Cut out housing joints on each partition to the thickness of the plywood.

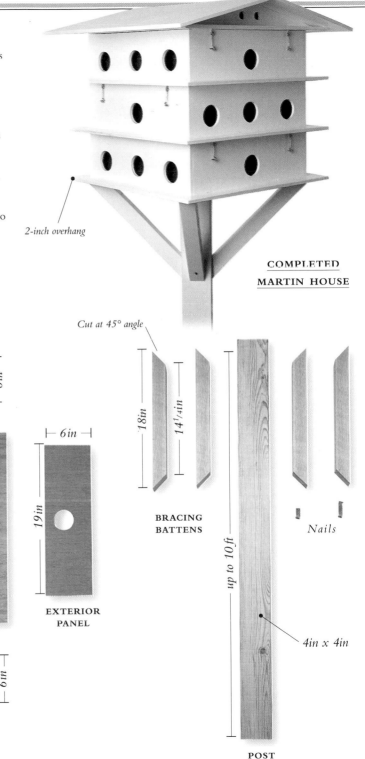

ASSEMBLY

1 Enclose the internal partitions with the 4 outside panels to make one level, using 1¼-inch nails. Check the box is square by measuring across the diagonals and adjusting corners until the measurements are the same.

2 Turn the box over, so it is upside down (ventilation holes will be at the bottom), nail a shelf panel to the box. Ensure the overhang is the same on each side. Repeat this process to assemble the second and third levels.

3 Make the roof by joining the roof panel to the gable end panels, set in 3 inches from the end of the roof panel. Turn the roof upside down and nail the shelf panel in position ensuring the overlap is even. Assemble the three levels with the roof on top, mark and fix hooks and eyes to hold the levels together.

4 Screw bracing battens to the upright post. Position the martin house so it is diagonal to the post. Nail each bracing batten to a corner of the house.

2-inch overhang

COMPLETED
MARTIN HOUSE

Cut at 45° angle

18in

14¹/₄in

BRACING
BATTENS

Nails

up to 10ft

4in x 4in

POST

20in

2¹/₄in

6in

SIDE PANEL

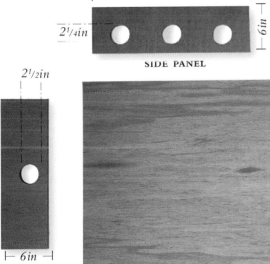

2¹/₂in

6in

SHELF PANEL

6in

19in

EXTERIOR
PANEL

Nails, and
hooks and eyes
– 3 sets for
3 levels

6in

20in

SIDE PANEL

OPEN-ENDED BOX

THIS BOX is used successfully for great horned owls, and other large owls that nest and roost in cavities. Made from ½-inch plywood for the roof and base, and ¾-inch lumber for the sides, end, and batten, it is attached at an angle to a branch to imitate the cavity that forms in the stump of a branch. Spread a thick layer of sawdust or peat in the bottom of the box to absorb the nestlings' feces. Screech-owls and other smaller birds may also be attracted to this box. This type of nestbox requires protection from raccoons and other nest predators *(see page 55)*.

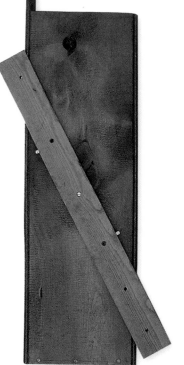

COMPLETED BOX

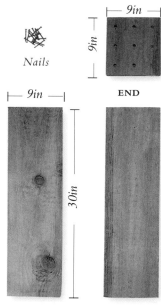

|← 10½in →|

30in

BASE

Nails

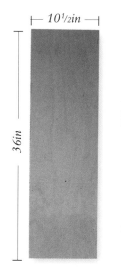

|← 9in →|

9in

END

|← 9in →|

30in

SIDES

|← 10½in →|

36in

ROOF

|← 2¾in →|

27½in

BATTEN

BOX PLACEMENT

Nail the box to the side of a tree branch, about 10 – 30ft up, so that the box is at an angle of more than 45°. The projecting roof over the opening helps keep the box dry.

ASSEMBLY

Drill several small drainage holes in the end. Drill three holes in the batten to attach it to the box, and one at each end to fix it to the tree. Hold the batten in position on one of the box sides, mark the three holes on the side, and make pilot holes in these positions with an awl. Nail the sides to the end, then nail the base and the roof to these. Finally, attach the batten to the side of the box with screws, making sure that these do not penetrate the side into the interior of the box.

Eastern screech-owls
These fledglings, although nocturnal, can also see clearly in daylight.

BIRD SHELF

A LARGE VARIETY of birds, including robins, barn swallows, phoebes, and great horned owls, will nest on suitable platforms when faced with a scarcity of natural nest sites. These can be made from scraps of cheap lumber, or ½-inch plywood, and are simple to construct.

Mirror plate | Nails 1½in | Long nails | Screws ½in

ROOF — 5¼in, 6in

SIDE — 4⅛in, 6¼in

BACK — 4in, 6¼in

SIDE — 5¼in, 6¼in, 100°, 2in

BASE — 4in, 4in

FRONT — 4in, 1¼in

RETAINING WALL
The front retaining wall should be tall enough to keep the nest secure and private.

COMPLETED SHELF

ASSEMBLY
The back and front are nailed to the base, before attaching the sides. Fasten the roof so that it overhangs the front. Finally, screw the mirror plate to the back. Mount it in the chosen position with a strong, weatherproof bracket.

BOWL NEST

C LIFF SWALLOWS and cave swallows usually use traditional nesting sites, but you can entice them to the eaves or gutter of your house by placing artificial nests there. These are easily made from fast-drying cement or plaster-of-paris, molded over a 5-inch-diameter rubber ball.

REFINING THE MOLD
Using a flat knife, keep smoothing the drying material. After removing from the rubber mold, file the edges to fit the wooden support accurately.

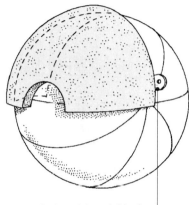

Set brass right-angled brackets into the material

CONSTRUCTION
Draw the outline of the nest on the ball, using chalk. The entrance hole should have a 2½-inch diameter and a 1-inch depth mark. Apply the wet molding material over the ball, approximately ⅜-inch thick, and implant a weatherproof bracket in each side. When the bowl is firm enough to be removed from the ball easily, screw the brackets to the wooden support. The cliff swallow nest is now ready.

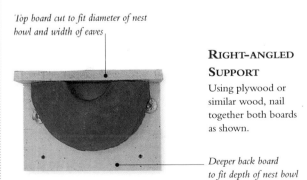

Top board cut to fit diameter of nest bowl and width of eaves

COMPLETED BOWL NEST
front view

RIGHT-ANGLED SUPPORT
Using plywood or similar wood, nail together both boards as shown.

Deeper back board to fit depth of nest bowl

MOURNING DOVE CONES

NAMED FOR their sad cooing, mourning doves have adapted well to suburban areas. They nest at almost any time of the year since, like all members of the pigeon family, they feed their young "pigeon's milk," a protein-rich secretion from the crop. Mourning doves usually build a thin and flimsy stick nest in the crotch of a tree or shrub, but strong winds and heavy rain can often destroy many nests. Nestling survival can be improved by building cone-shaped nests from 1/4- to 3/8-inch-thick hardware cloth. These easy-to-build nesting structures should be tied to forked branches 6 to 16 feet high in trees with moderate shade. Nest sites for doves should have an excellent view of the ground and a clear flight path to and from the nest. Since they sometimes nest in loose colonies, several cones can be placed in the same tree. California valley residents placed nest cones in February, March, and April, before most doves establish their nesting territories, and discovered that the nesting cones were well used. Clean old nests from the wire cone each spring.

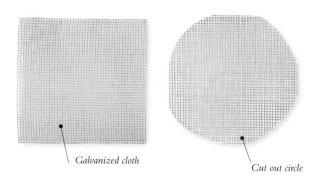

Galvanized cloth

Cut out circle

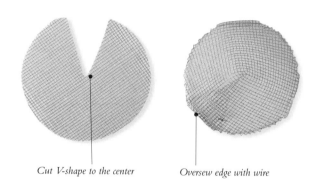

Cut V-shape to the center

Oversew edge with wire

CONSTRUCTING THE CONE

Cut one 12-inch square of the galvanized hardware cloth. Trim into a circle, make a cut into the center of the circle, then cut a notch to create a 'V' shape. Overlap the edges into a cone shape. Join the edges with a strand of thin wire as if sewing.

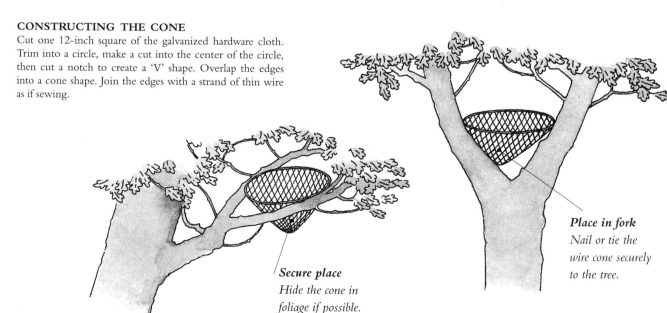

Secure place
Hide the cone in foliage if possible.

Place in fork
Nail or tie the wire cone securely to the tree.

NEST PREDATORS

FREE-ROAMING cats and raccoons are the worst threat to nesting and feeding birds, although snakes, squirrels, and mice are also a problem. A raccoon's keen sense of smell, quick mind, and climbing skills (it has long, dexterous, strong legs) permit it to find and raid bird nests in even the highest trees. As a defense, deepen the entrance

Gray squirrel
As well as stealing food from feeders, squirrels will seize any opportunity to feed on the nourishing birds' eggs.

Peek show *A screen of 2-inch wire netting over the entrance hole will keep raccoons and other predators out of a nestbox but will let the birds into their home.*

hole by mounting a block of wood 1 1/4 inches thick over the entrance to the nestbox. This may prevent raccoons from reaching deep into nestboxes – adult raccoons have 10 – 11-inch-long front legs.

Other ideas include applying a thick layer of grease to the mounting pole for a length of one foot down from the nestbox. Alternatively, try strapping a 3-feet-wide galvanized metal collar around the tree trunk or mounting pole. Paint metal guards brown to improve the look. Where tree canopies adjoin, however, it is impossible to prevent raccoons from climbing down to attack young birds in nestboxes.

Chapter Four

SUPPLEMENTAL FEEDING

Sweet food
An adult male hooded oriole visits a sugar feeder in a suburban backyard for sustenance.

Feeding time
A black-headed grosbeak eats from a feed mixture at a well-placed platform feeder in a backyard.

TO PUT feeding into perspective, consider that even regular visitors at feeders will not feed exclusively on human handouts. Most birds are quick to use whatever foods they can find in their environment, and when they are away from the backyard feeders, they will be busy foraging in the wild for various weeds, seeds, fruits, and insects. The question is, what effect does a frequent supply of food have on migration patterns, survival, and the population growth of each species? This chapter offers practical advice on feeding backyard visitors throughout the year, and detailed plans for the assembly and siting of suitable feeders. Once in place, feeders will bring hours of enjoyment to the keen backyard birdwatcher.

Seed dispenser
Hanging seed dispensers are useful for many birds, including the house finch.

FEEDING THROUGH THE SEASONS

SURVIVING THE first year of life is a major accomplishment for most birds. In many species, it is normal for 80 percent to die. This heavy toll comes from a variety of causes, but one is the failure to find food. Supplemental feeding can make a difference to young birds.

SPRING

Spring is an important season for feeding birds because most of the natural foods have been consumed over the winter. Late snows can bury the remaining food, creating starvation conditions. Ample food and water supplies are attractive to birds because of the energy cost of migration. Resident birds that are already familiar with the feeders may help attract migrants. Crushed eggshells or even finely crushed oyster shells are extremely good supplements to feed at this season, since the calcium requirements for female birds are high just prior to egg laying.

Take your pick *A male western tanager enjoys eating peanut butter from the crevices of a pinecone.*

SUMMER

This is the season when natural food is most abundant. Insect populations are at their highest and tree, shrub, and vine fruits are plentiful. But it is also the period of greatest food requirements, since parent birds must provide food for themselves and their young. The rapid growth rate of young birds requires a diet high in protein.

You can attract a surprising variety of birds that usually eat insects, such as tanagers, thrushes, and warblers, with a mixture of one part peanut butter, one part vegetable shortening, four parts cornmeal, and one part flour. Place the mixture in hanging food logs or suet feeders. In summer, fruit- and nectar-eating birds may be attracted by overripe citrus fruits and bananas, cut open to display the interiors, and placed on feeding tables. Summer is also the season to lure hummingbirds, orioles, and other nectar-feeding species *(see page 30).*

Bird table *A mixture of seeds on a flat feeding table serves many species, including the rose-breasted grosbeak, during fall and winter months when a bird's supply of natural food is scarce.*

FALL

Although natural foods are abundant in the fall, this is also a season of great food demand, since bird populations are at their highest levels from the crop of new fledglings. Migrants need to put on enough fat for the long journeys ahead. Oil-rich sunflower and niger seeds are eaten by birds that need to build up these fat reserves. Late summer and early fall are also the seasons when thousands of tiny flight and body feathers are replaced, and this requires large amounts of food.

By feeding birds in early fall, you can attract fall migrants. In the northeast, for example, feeding may entice the white-throated sparrow and rufous-sided towhee, short-distance migrants, to winter in your yard rather than farther south.

Searching for food *In deepest winter, birds such as this male northern cardinal have to search endlessly for natural food patches. To him, a feeder offers easy sustenance.*

Fruit snack *Fresh fruit hung or placed on top of a feeding table offers a sustaining snack for this male Bullock's oriole. Winter is a good time to entice fruit-eating birds.*

Also, many species have a postbreeding dispersal in which both adults and young scatter from their breeding areas. Frequently, this results in northward movements. Southern seed-eating birds are likely to stay for winter where they find food supplies, acting as pioneers to expand the species' range. If you wait until the first snow covers your feeders, you will miss these interesting additions to your backyard bird list.

WINTER

Natural food supplies decline drastically from the onset of the first frost until the burst of spring growth. This is when supplemental feeding is of the greatest value to all birds.

Make seed and suet supplies available at dawn and dusk. These are the two major periods in the day for foraging. Beef kidney suet provides a rich supply of fat and is eaten by 80 North American species, including many insect-eating birds such as woodpeckers, chickadees, titmice, and orioles. Feed it to birds whole, or melt and resolidify it for a more workable form. Increase the variety of birds that will feed on suet by adding other ingredients such as cornmeal, bacon fat, and

peanut butter until the mix is the consistency of bread dough. Offer suet mixtures in cupcake baking tins, or pressed into pinecones. Raisins, grapes, and cherries attract robins, mockingbirds, and waxwings, which do not usually visit feeders. Finally, remember to supply fresh water.

At the feeder *This female black-headed grosbeak enjoys a backyard sugar feeder while occasionally looking out for predators that may be lurking nearby in the undergrowth.*

STOCKING A FEEDING STATION

VARIETY OF food is clearly an important aspect to consider when stocking a feeder. Since each species has a definite food preference, offer a wide choice of foods that are high in fat and protein at a variety of feeders. This will reduce the competition that occurs when you have just one feeder.

SEED AND GRAIN MIXTURES

Seeds are the preferred foods of feeder birds, both because they contain concentrated nourishment and they are often available for extended periods when other foods may be difficult to find. Commercial seed mixtures are an uneconomical way to feed birds. Mixes that contain sunflower seeds are often wasted because birds preferring sunflower seeds pick through the other seeds and drop them to the ground where they rot. It is a good idea to place sunflower seeds in a separate, large container.

Provide millet and cracked corn on the ground for sparrows, doves, and quail; and place sunflower seeds, mixed grain, fresh fruit, such as apples and bananas, and dried fruit, such as currants and raisins, at tabletop level for cardinals, grosbeaks, and finches. Place feeders on tree trunks or hang them from the lower tree limbs for woodpeckers and chickadees.

REGULAR FOOD SUPPLY

One of rules for operating a feeding station is "Once you start, keep the food coming." Although most birds do not depend on feeder food, some birds do become dependent on a feeding area in winter and will starve to death if the new food supply disappears. Once you stop, it may be difficult to attract birds later if they are feeding elsewhere in the neighborhood.

A convenient perch for birds waiting to feed. Birds will fly to a feeder when a space becomes available

Roof provides cover for the seed

Birds choose from a variety of grains, seeds, peanuts, and beef suet

Smooth metal disk around the pole prevents predators reaching the birds

Multilevel feeding station *Build a multilevel structure with a strong support post incorporating a convenience perch, a covered platform for seed and grain mixtures, and a slippery metal or plastic baffle to protect feeding birds from predators.*

SITING YOUR FEEDER

WHEN SELECTING locations for the feeders, choose sites that are easily visible from your house and, if possible, facing south. This will keep strong northern winds from blowing grain out of the feeders and will provide a warmer, more protected area for birds to congregate. The speed with which the feeder is discovered and visited by birds depends not only on its location and visibility, but also on the kinds of birds in your neighborhood.

FEEDER VISITORS

The variety of birds that come to backyard feeders also depends on latitude. Farther north, far fewer species nest and winter in the region. However, birds that do winter over in northern habitats are quick to visit well stocked feeders. Even small feeders placed outside the windows of multistory apartment buildings may attract sparrows and a few migrating goldfinches.

If you have chickadees in your neighborhood, they will probably be the first to discover new birdfeeders, since these inquisitive birds are constantly searching for food. They are usually joined by a variety of birds such as nuthatches, titmice, and some woodpeckers, forming a small, mixed winter flock. Chickadees also remember feeder locations for up to eight months or more.

SAFE LOCATIONS

Feeders should be constructed on 5- to 6-feet-high poles and sited at least 10 feet away from a convenient "jump-off" point. This point could be a strategically placed shed or greenhouse roof, a clothesline post, or an overhanging branch.

Try to locate feeders near trees or shrubs since this will provide the birds with a refuge from predatory birds. However, dense undergrowth is

Feeder protector *A cage surrounds a hanging feeder, with holes that allow small birds to enter and feed, while excluding squirrels.*

dangerous since cats lurk there ready to pounce. Household pets are not the only threat to feeding birds. Other suburban wildlife, such as raccoons, skunks, opossums, and squirrels, are also attracted to feeders. The latter are persistent, athletic, and chew the feeders as well as eating all the food.

DISCOURAGING PREDATORS

Baffles, or squirrel guards, can be attached to the post supporting a feeder, creating a barrier against squirrels. A baffle can be purchased, or you can construct one from galvanized iron or aluminum sheets. A hanging feeder can be protected by a flat or dome-shaped baffle attached above the feeder. All surfaces should be slippery so that predators lose their grip.

HOPPER FEEDER

THIS TYPE OF feeder helps keep food sources dry. You can also use just the base of the feeder, shown here as an open platform. Use ½-inch plywood for the tray, ¾-inch square softwood for the edges and uprights, and ⅜-inch plywood for the roof. The gaps in the edges on the base allow water to drain from the feeder. Simply screw four cup hooks through the four corners of the roof into the gables, thread a weatherproof chain through the hooks on the roof and attach the unit to a freestanding post, or suspend the feeder from a tree branch or a strong line hung between two objects.

Wood that has been treated with a nontoxic preservative is best, and apply a nontoxic stain to camouflage the feeder. To avoid rusting, use galvanized nails and brass or coated screws.

A roof will keep the food dry and provide a place to hang a seed hopper

COMPLETED PLATFORM

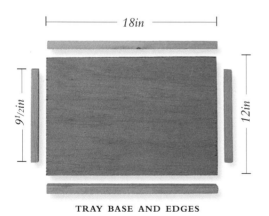

18in

9½in

12in

TRAY BASE AND EDGES

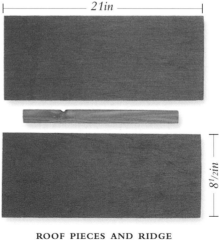

21in

12in

8½in

ROOF PIECES AND RIDGE
The ridge is a V-shape, and one side of each roof piece is beveled

13in

UPRIGHTS
Each upright is 13in long with an angle at either end to fit the slope of the roof

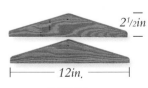

2½in

12in.

GABLES
Center is 2½in high

ASSEMBLY

Study the layout of the pieces before you start work on the project. Cut pieces to size. Screw the uprights to the inside corners of the tray. Make sure that the uprights slope outward slightly. Fix the gables to the outer sides of the uprights, and attach the roof ridge between them. Attach the roof pieces, ensuring that each of the beveled edges meets at the ridge.

Chain and cuphooks

Screws 1¼in

Nails 1¼in

OPEN PLATFORM FEEDER

THERE ARE many types of birdfeeder suitable for all types of locations and tastes. Feeders will encourage birds to leave the longer grass and the cover of the shrubbery.

Non-migratory birds are, in general, more likely to benefit from supplemental feeding than mobile species. A simple open platform is not as

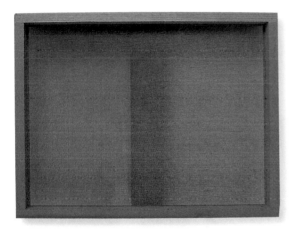

A mesh platform *This aids the rain drain away faster allowing the feed to dry more quickly, thus minimizing chances of mold growth.*

common these days, but for the beginner, it is the simplest and cheapest type of feeder. Filled with kitchen scraps or cheaper food, it will attract nearby birds. A platform feeder can be made at home with a few tools and materials.

Use either a fine mesh screen or a sheet of plywood slotted between lumber frames mounted on a metal pole at least 4 feet high. Your feeder is likely to attract a few species, and competition on an open platform will often lead to friction between voracious feeders. Until you have a

regular number of bird visitors, view feeding birds from a distance. Sometimes, small children, in their enthusiasm, can frighten away even the tamer birds. A trust has to be built up and in the end, those who wait and watch quietly will eventually be rewarded.

COMBATING DISEASE

Crowded conditions at large feeders increase the likelihood of spreading diseases, especially when uneaten food and droppings are allowed to accumulate. A common disease problem at feeders is a mold that spreads rapidly on wet grain. This affects the lungs and sometimes the windpipes of feeder birds. Keep a watchful eye for birds that gasp or wheeze while attempting to feed, because this is one of the early symptoms of this eventual killer. Cleanliness is one way to combat such disasters.

CLEANING REGULARLY

All sodden grain should be removed and the platform should be scrubbed down with a good germ destroying cleanser on a weekly basis. Rinse it thoroughly, thus removing all traces of the cleaning agent, before putting it back in its place in the backyard.

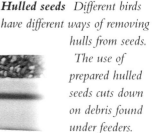

Hulled seeds *Different birds have different ways of removing hulls from seeds. The use of prepared hulled seeds cuts down on debris found under feeders.*

Chapter Five

WATER IN THE GARDEN

I N VERY DRY habitats, water is even more attractive to some visiting birds than food. Water may also be scarce in northwestern and northeastern states, especially during the summer. It is inaccessible for most of the northern winter, locked away in ice and snow. Birds can obtain much of the water they require in their food, but all species need it both for drinking and bathing throughout the year. Providing clean water in the correct backyard habitat and at the right time of year is difficult, but persevere because an area of open water, no matter how small, is one of the most useful tools for attracting birds to the backyard. In this chapter, there is practical advice on building a small pond, as well as a list of plants that are ideal for landscaping a garden pond.

Waterside plant
Arrowhead (Sagittaria sagittifolia) is ideal for planting at the edge of a pond. It has edible tubers that attract birds.

The natural look
A well-designed garden pond is attractive to some birds both as a nesting site and as a food source.

Floating beauty
The waterlily Nymphaea 'American Star' makes an attractive addition to a pond.

BATHS FOR BIRDS

A PREDATOR-SAFE birdbath that offers open water throughout the year will help attract birds that seldom visit feeders, such as warblers and vireos. All birds, ranging in size from eagles to chickadees, bathe in water at any time of the year.

Birdbaths are generally sold with raised pedestals or stands, but it seems that many species prefer baths at ground level, the normal location for natural rain puddles. However, a pedestal birdbath does provide necessary protection from cats.

You can make a birdbath from a household item such as a trash can lid. Place the lid close to the ground, or on a stack of cement blocks. Birdbaths require a gentle incline of no more than two to three inches and the trash can lid is an ideal

Safe height A birdbath on a pedestal is easier for birds to find, especially in areas that have heavy snow.

shape. Avoid plastic lids since they have slippery sides, and birds will find it difficult to gain a foothold. A shallow ceramic pot saucer is another possibility. Change the water every few days and scrub off any algae, which thrive in bird-fertilized water.

The location of a birdbath determines which birds it will attract. Bold species, such as robins and jays, visit birdbaths in open areas or near shrubs, but warblers, wood thrushes, and other birds that like shade are more likely to use those placed in protected spots.

Do not put additives in the water to lower the freezing point. Keep the birdbath free of ice during northern winters with a submersible thermostat-controlled heater designed for outdoor birdbaths.

Small circle All birds need to bathe to maintain their plumage. A birdbath with a diameter of 12 inches should be large enough for a group of birds such as these wrentits to congregate in comfort.

Saucer baths Glazed saucers of many different sizes, dotted around the yard, offer more birds the chance to bathe.

WATER DRIPS

THE BACKYARD birdbath can be made much more appealing to birds by the creation of a rippling motion on the water's surface. This attracts the attention of birds flying by the garden that might otherwise overlook the water source.

Dripping water is especially attractive to warblers, which are drawn by the sound and motion of the drip meeting the surface of the still water. Fast-flowing, powerful sprays can startle and disperse birds.

The most effective way to provide dripping water is by the installation of an adaptor especially designed for bird use, called the water drip. This system includes a special Y-valve that is attached to an exterior water tap. The water flows into a hose attached to a hook-shaped metal pipe that then trickles water into the birdbath at a preset rate.

The fountain mist is another device designed for birds. This brings water from the exterior tap to a fountain spray that is placed in the center of the birdbath. The height of the spray can vary.

A simpler method is to hang a plastic bucket with a hole punched in its bottom over a birdbath. Start with a small nail hole, and keep enlarging it until a regular pattern of water drips from the bucket. About 20 to 30 drops per second is ideal. Cover the bucket to reduce evaporation and prevent clogging.

Water drip *Water is particularly important for seed- and fruit-eating birds.*

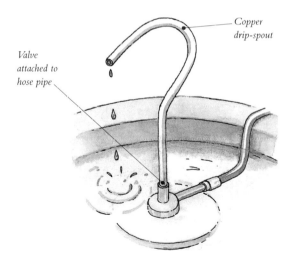

Valve attached to hose pipe

Copper drip-spout

Waterspout *This acts as a lure to passing birds, and is useful during migration. The sound and movement of the water bring a variety of birds into the backyard.*

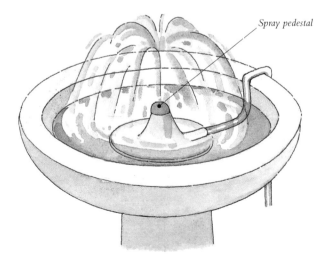

Spray pedestal

Spray effect *The fountain mist system produces a fine spray or mist, especially popular with many hummingbirds, which like to fly through the mist to clean their tiny feathers.*

BACKYARD PONDS

ALTHOUGH MOST birds can get the water they need mainly from their food, all birds enjoy an occasional dip; it is vital for keeping their plumage in good order. A pond designed for birds, if space permits, will attract many species and more visual interest to a bird-feeding area, especially if it is landscaped with ferns or other marginal aquatic plants. Ponds are particularly useful in arid or hot climate zones where water sources are scarce for most of the year.

Fresh supply Water quenches a bird's thirst, cools its body temperature, and cleans its feathers. A small pond is of benefit to many species all year. Keep the water fresh by changing it frequently.

CLEAN LOCATION

Make sure you place the pond far enough away from bird feeders so that it is not a repository for seed hulls and dropped grain. Choose a site within easy reach of the garden hose, since cleaning a water source is important for the birds and other occasional wildlife visitors.

SAFE DEPTH

The shape of the pond does not affect its attractiveness to birds *(see page 66),* but the pitch of its slope is very important. Ideally, the pond should grade gently from 1/2 inch of water to no more than 4 inches at the deepest point. This slope allows birds to wade in safely. If you have inherited a garden pond with deeper sides, adapt it to attract birds by half-submerging small boulders and stones around its edge. Plant a few bird-attracting plants in and around these.

Ponds measuring several square feet wide, and containing both shallow and deep water, will attract not only smaller birds, such as warblers,

Bathing spot An in-ground backyard pond should have a shallow slope and rocks placed in deeper water to serve as convenient perches.

Water hose *A leaking hose will attract many birds to a backyard, including this western tanager. Birds do not sweat, but pant to keep cool. This behavior evaporates moisture from their mouths and lungs, so water is always welcome.*

but also larger birds, such as robins and jays. Tree swallows and purple martins are attracted to larger-sized ponds, and they may decide to take up residence nearby – swallows in trees and dense shrubs; purple martins in a multilevel house mounted on a pole near trees *(see page 48)* – since they prefer to build their nests close to water.

CHOOSING A POND

To decide upon the best shape, size, and material for a pond, consider the size and style of your backyard. Even in a small area, it is possible to build a small pond, as long as it is in proportion to the rest of the backyard. Then decide upon the construction method. This may be dictated by your budget.

Flexible liners are ideal because they allow you to design virtually any shape and size of pond. They are good for creating a natural

look, since the edge is hidden by landscaping. They are also an excellent choice for larger backyard ponds that require rigidity.

Concrete ponds are stronger and long-lasting. They are, however, difficult to construct and will take more time to complete.

Preformed ponds, contoured from fiberglass or plastic, are made in many shapes and sizes. They are hard-wearing and weather-resistant. Some plant nurseries also stock preformed pools and a selection of water pumps.

Pond plants *Common cattail and meadowsweet grow around this well-established pond.*

MAKING A POND

YOU CAN design and build a pond in just one weekend. Most of the new backyard ponds are now constructed using a strong yet flexible lining sheet of synthetic rubber or plastic, which provides a thick waterproof barrier between the soil and the water. Flexible liners are available in a wide range of sizes and can be cut to fit the shape of any pond. Before buying the liner,

Small pond *A shallow depth of water is sufficient for a few birds to splash in and drink from, as these orioles and tanagers demonstrate.*

depth, by the maximum length plus twice its depth. Add one foot to both width and length to allow for a 6-inch flap at each edge to prevent leakage. For example, a pool measuring 6 x 8 feet and 2 feet deep would require a liner measuring 11 x 13 feet. It is very important that you take accurate measurements at this preliminary stage.

decide on the site and size of the pond. Mark out the desired shape with string and pegs in order to make it easier to check the final placement of the flexible liner.

Butyl rubber is arguably the best pond-lining material. Much stronger than either polyethylene or PVC, it has a life expectancy of about 40 – 50 years but is expensive. Pliable and tough enough to resist tearing or deterioration caused by ultra-violet light, it is also resistant to bacterial growth and temperature extremes. The recommended thickness of a butyl liner is 1/4 inch.

PVC liners are reasonably strong and tear-resistant. Some are guaranteed for ten years. After several years of exposure to sunlight they may harden and eventually crack.

Polyethylene is the cheapest lining material, but it is easily torn, and cracks with constant exposure to sunlight.

MEASURING THE LINER

To calculate the size of the required liner, first determine the maximum length, width, and depth of the pond. The liner should measure the maximum width of the pond plus twice its

DESIGN AND CONSTRUCTION

A length of rope is useful for laying out the desired shape of the pond (see opposite). Adjust the rope on the ground until you are pleased with the shape and it suits the surrounding area. Then use a shovel to dig the hole to a depth of 9 inches, making the pond sides slope inward at an angle of 20° from the vertical. The slope prevents the sides from caving in, makes it easier to install the liner, and ensures that if the pond freezes in winter, the ice can expand upward without causing any damage to the liner.

If planning to plant marginal aquatics, cut a shelf about 9 inches wide to provide adequate space for planting, and then continue digging at a slight angle until the correct depth – normally about 20 – 24 inches – is reached. If including edging stones, remove 2 inches of soil to a width of 12 inches all around the pond. This will provide the basis for a marshy, shallow shoreline for small birds and provide a source of mud for barn swallows and phoebes. The pond and aquatic plants may also attract insect-eating birds into your backyard that might otherwise have flown on to more appealing habitat.

INSTALLING A FLEXIBLE LINER

1 Shaping *Mark out the proposed shape of the pond using string and wooden pegs or a hose, and then start to excavate the hole. Create planting shelves along the edge where required.*

2 Leveling *Use a board and spirit level to check that the hole is level. Remove all tree roots and sharp stones that might otherwise puncture the liner when it is installed.*

3 Lining *Spread fiberglass insulation or heavy-duty landscape cloth over the base and sides to act as a cushion for the flexible liner. Trim the material level with the top of the hole.*

4 Filling *Drape the liner evenly across the hole and weight all edges. Slowly fill the pond with water, tugging at the liner edges to eliminate creases. Trim off any excess, leaving a 6-in overlap.*

5 Edging *Make an edging around the rim of the pond with paving stones or slabs, bedded on mortar, or with sod. Check that they are level and then press them into place.*

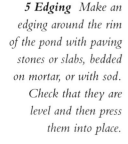

6 Finishing *The edging stones should overhang the pool by about 2in so that the liner cannot be seen. Do not drop mortar into the water or the pond will have to be emptied and refilled.*

AQUATIC PLANTS

WATERFOWL AND marsh birds, such as coots, rails, and gallinules, are intimately tied to various mixtures of emergent, floating, and submerged vegetation.

Most of the plants in this group are prolific seed-producers, an adaptation that increases a plant's chances for its seed to find just the right new environment. The birds benefit by eating the seed, and sometimes spread it to new locations. They also feed on underground tubers, stems, rootstocks, and leaves of marsh and aquatic plants.

Other groups of aquatics to consider for a backyard pond include 42 species of paspalum, and wetland species of polygonum (known as smartweeds, or knotweeds). Lady's thumb and pink knotweed are good examples of this type of plant. Spike rushes, duckweeds, wild celery, and wigeon grass are also attractive to both waterfowl and landbirds.

In addition to providing food for water birds, aquatic plants also offer cover for smaller animals which either feed on the plants or hide among the vegetation. Frogs, water insects, and fish could not survive in your backyard wetland without plants.

To attract herons and kingfishers to your backyard pond, stock it with small fish. The type of fish you select will vary depending on your locality. For the northern latitudes, stock blunt-nosed minnows *(Hyborhyncus notatus)*. Topminnows *(Fundulus spp.)* thrive in warmer waters. These fish are prodigious breeders and will also help control mosquito populations.

BULRUSH
Schoenoplectus lacustris

Bulrushes are important wetland plants for water and marsh birds. The tall perennial native plant provides nesting cover for the marsh wren, blackbirds, bitterns, coots, and grebes. The seeds are a food source for at least 24 kinds of waterfowl. Zones 6 – 9.

CORDGRASS
Spartina pectinata 'Aureo marginata'

Known as variegated prairie cord grass, this is a herbaceous, spreading grass with arching, long yellow-striped leaves. The seeds are an important food for seaside and sharp-tailed sparrows. Zones 5 – 9.

SEDGE
Carex flacca

There are at least 500 species of Carex sedges in North America that attract 53 species of waterfowl, shorebirds, and songbirds, which feed on their abundant seeds. The seeds are favored by tree and swamp sparrows. Zones 6 – 9.

TUFTED SEDGE
Carex elata 'Aurea'

An evergreen perennial sedge with golden yellow leaves. Many sedges grow in dense clumps, thus creating a habitat that provides excellent nesting cover for waterfowl and many other ground-nesting birds, including the sora. Zones 6 – 9.

WATERLILY
Nymphaea 'Rose Arey'

In summer, its reddish green leaves feature star-shaped, semidouble, deep rose-pink flowers 4 – 6 inches across. These pale with age, and have a strong aniseed fragrance. Seeds and rootstocks are eaten by the wood duck and blue-winged teal. Zones 8 – 10.

COMMON BUTTONBUSH
Cephalanthus occidentalis

Prefers wet soils where it forms dense stands. White flower clusters appear in June through to September, when brown, nutlike seeds develop. The seeds are eaten by many waterfowl and at least 10 species use it for cover and as a nesting site. Zone 4.

WATERLILY
Nymphaea 'Attraction'

In summer, this deciduous waterlily bears cup-shaped, semidouble garnet red flowers, flecked with white, measuring 6 inches across. The seeds are eaten by ducks, especially the redhead, canvasback, wood duck, and shoveler. Zones 5 – 10.

WATERLILY
Nymphaea 'Virginia'

A deciduous, perennial water plant with floating leaves. Its purplish green leaves reveal star-shaped, semidouble white flowers, measuring 4 – 6 inches across, in summer. Leaves provide good cover for fish. Moorhens and gallinules walk over the leaves. Zones 5 – 10.

ARROWHEAD
Sagittaria sagittifolia

Also known as duck potato. The seeds and tuberous roots are consumed by ducks, including the canvasback, black duck, and ring-necked duck. They are also eaten by at least another 10 species of dabbling and diving ducks. Zone 3.

C h a p t e r   S i x

REGIONAL GUIDE TO PLANTS AND BIRDS

Lookout bird
Adult cedar waxwings eat mostly fruit and berries, and are especially attracted by red berries.

Attractive blossom
A male hooded oriole rests on a branch of white Banksia rose blossom.

RELATIVELY LITTLE is known about the feeding habits of birds, and this is especially so with many insect-eating species such as flycatchers and warblers. There is even a question about whether purple martins do in fact favor a meal of mosquitoes, since there is little actual documentation of their dietary habits. What scant detailed information researchers do have about the attraction of certain birds to the colorful fruits and flowers of various native plants has been gleaned from the observations of sharp-eyed birdwatchers.

Following are lists of plants that are known to provide food and cover for many bird species. The listings give each plant's bird-attracting qualities to assist you in making decisions.

Seed-eater
The house finch's normal diet consists mainly of weed seeds.

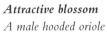

HOW TO USE THIS CHAPTER

THIS PART of the book is divided into the five regions of the United States of America and Canada – according to the map opposite. For each region, there is a landscape design for the ideal bird garden, followed by information on the most common birds sighted in the region, and recommended bird-attracting plants.

KEY TO THE REGIONS

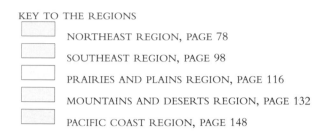

NORTHEAST REGION, PAGE 78

SOUTHEAST REGION, PAGE 98

PRAIRIES AND PLAINS REGION, PAGE 116

MOUNTAINS AND DESERTS REGION, PAGE 132

PACIFIC COAST REGION, PAGE 148

GUIDE TO EACH REGIONAL SECTION

Map
Shows whole area covered by region

Illustration
A landscape design using ideal bird-attracting plants

Bird interest
Birds sighted in gardens at different times of the year

KEY TO BIRD SYMBOLS

RESIDENT THROUGHOUT THE YEAR

WINTER VISITOR

MIGRATES THROUGH IN SPRING AND FALL

SUMMER RESIDENT (NESTING)

Garden landscape design

For each region, there is a garden planting plan that uses a selection of native plants. Birds attracted by these plants are also shown.

Identification
Each bird's size and plumage is shown in detail

Attraction
Plant detail shows the flower or fruit that attracts birds

Plant reference
List organized by plant type, for example, evergreen and deciduous trees and shrubs, and groundcovers

Common birds of each region
For each bird entry, latin and common name, nest and song details, food preferences, and plants to which it is attracted are listed.

Recommended plants
A selection of the best bird-attracting plants for each region, with full cultivation details and climate zones.

Other good plants
A list of other plants that are suitable for the region, with full cultivation details and climate zones.

THE CLIMATE OF NORTH AMERICA

WITHIN EACH REGION, plant hardiness zones suggest the northern distribution or limit of a plant's growth. The zone system used here follows the plant hardiness zones established by the U.S. National Arboretum, the Agricultural Service, the U.S. Department of Agriculture, and the American Horticultural Society. The zones are based on many years of weather data used to chart average annual low temperatures. To identify appropriate plants for your property, find your plant hardiness zone on the map. When you read through the recommended plants and other good choices listings, check that the zone given for the plant is either the same or lower (farther north) than your own climate zone. Remember that these zones are only estimates and that microclimate differences can account for as much as a one- or even a two-zone difference, even though the microclimates may be only a few miles or merely feet apart from each other.

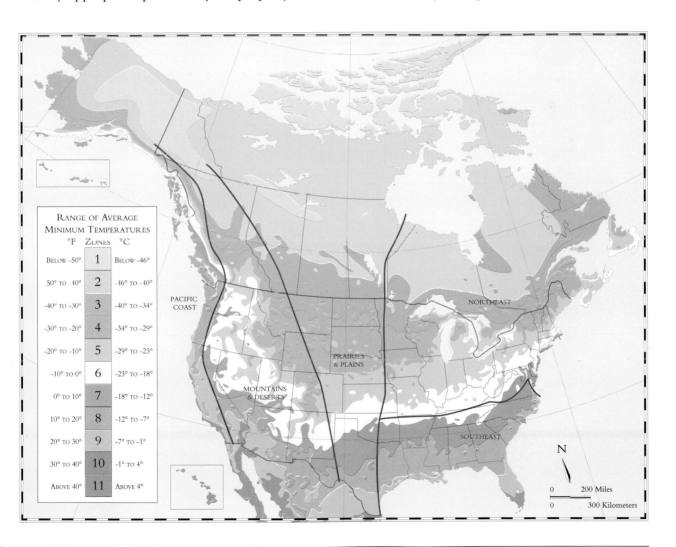

RANGE OF AVERAGE
MINIMUM TEMPERATURES

°F	ZONES	°C
BELOW -50°	1	BELOW -46°
50° TO -40°	2	-46° TO -40°
-40° TO -30°	3	-40° TO -34°
-30° TO -20°	4	-34° TO -29°
-20° TO -10°	5	-29° TO -23°
-10° TO 0°	6	-23° TO -18°
0° TO 10°	7	-18° TO -12°
10° TO 20°	8	-12° TO -7°
20° TO 30°	9	-7° TO -1°
30° TO 40°	10	-1° TO 4°
ABOVE 40°	11	ABOVE 4°

PACIFIC COAST

NORTHEAST

PRAIRIES & PLAINS

MOUNTAINS & DESERTS

SOUTHEAST

N

0   200 Miles
0   300 Kilometers

NORTHEAST REGION

THE IDEAL garden design in this vast region includes native plants that provide cover and nest sites, and bear fruit throughout the year. The area's range of climate zones (2 – 7) offers many good choices.

Dogwood
Cornus spp.

This can be grown as a bushy tree or large shrub and has showy flowers in spring, and red and orange leaves in fall. Best in a sunny or dry climate. *(See page 89.)*

American highbush cranberry
Viburnum trilobum

This hardy shrub is useful for borders and hedges. The fruit persists through winter, thus offering food to the brown thrasher, cedar waxwing, and 29 other species. *(See page 87.)*

SIZE
7"

CEDAR WAXWING
BOMBYCILLA CEDRORUM

Waxwings feed on the berries of pyracantha and cotoneaster shrubs, and the mountainash tree. They fly in tight groups of up to 20 birds.

SIZE
10"

AMERICAN ROBIN
TURDUS MIGRATORIUS

A member of the thrush family, this bird forages for earthworms on lawns and in leaf-litter at the edges of flower beds.

Flower garden
Plant a border of colorful annuals and perennials inside the low shrub layer. Annuals such as marigold, zinnia, and sunflower have abundant seeds; perennials such as foxglove, phlox, and columbine provide important nectar for hummingbirds.

Composting leaves
Create a border 3 feet wide and allow leaves to fall and make leaf litter in front of the small shrub layer. Ground-feeding birds such as sparrows, catbirds, towhees, and thrashers will dig through the leaves to extract earthworms and millipedes.

White oak
Quercus alba

A magnificent tree, this oak can grow to 100 feet. It develops a massive canopy spread. Although it is not for a small garden, it attracts 28 bird species because of its annual acorn crop. *(See page 87.)*

PURPLE FINCH

CARPODACUS PURPUREUS

This bird's diet consists mainly of seeds, yet in spring it eats buds, and it enjoys the berries of cotoneaster in the fall. It is a frequent visitor to backyard feeders during winter.

Small shrubs
Low-growing mounds of shrubs provide further variety and depth to a border. Plant clumps of small shrubs about 4 feet apart, selecting fruiting shrubs such as pyracanthas, cotoneasters, hollies, and viburnums. Blue jays, Baltimore orioles, purple finches, and northern bobwhites also feed from these shrubs.

Rough grass
This provides cover for feeding birds, especially from airborn predators such as hawks. If the area is also littered with leaves, it is even more useful, especially to robins.

GARDEN FOR COVER AND COLOR

Resident and migrant birds will visit this Northeast region garden. The focal point is the large white oak tree, which provides both cover and food. The smaller evergreen and deciduous trees and shrubs are planted at the edges of the backyard. The flower gardens add color to the scheme.

Groundcover
Creeping mats of bunchberry, bearberry, and wild strawberry can fill in the floor of the bird-attracting border. These plants grow no more than 12 inches high.

Tended lawn
A small central patch of mown grass is useful for viewing birds that feed and nest in the shrubs and trees, but it is not a good food source for visiting birds.

COMMON BIRDS

UNUSUAL VISITORS often appear in backyards of the Northeast region during the migratory periods of spring and fall. Then, 100 or more species may be discovered in a bird-landscaped garden. Southbound songbirds concentrate at coastal points such as Cape May, New Jersey, where they fatten up on bayberries, holly berries, and the fruits of other native plants before flying over Chesapeake Bay. These birds are continuing a habit that spans thousands of generations, resting at traditional places and wintering in the same tropical areas as their ancestors.

In contrast, some of the resident birds, such as blue-gray gnatcatchers, woodpeckers, cardinals, and chickadees, remain on their territories throughout the year, feeding on the multitude of insects and fruits that they find on foliage near their nesting places. The range of some of these birds is vast, so there is ample opportunity to attract them to your backyard.

SIZE
6¹/₂ – 7"

EASTERN PHOEBE
Sayornis phoebe

NEST *A cup-shaped structure of mud mixed with grass, approximately 4¹/₂ inches in diameter, lined with hair and fine grasses, and covered with thick moss. Often nests in rafters of barns and sheds, or under the eaves and sills of houses.*
SONG *Like its name, fee-bee, repeated, with the second note usually alternating higher or lower.*
ATTRACTED TO *the fruit of hackberry, serviceberry, and juneberry plants. Sumacs provide both food and shelter.*

SIZE
6¹/₂ – 7"

DOWNY WOODPECKER
Picoides pubescens

NEST *A cavity excavated in dead trees, using the wood chips to line the bottom of the nest. The entrance hole is only just over 1 inch wide, as a defense against predators.*
SONG *Short, flat pils and unusual horselike whinnying calls.*
ATTRACTED TO *the fruit of serviceberry and wild strawberry plants, and to dogwood, mountainashes, and Virginia creeper. Also eats beetles, spiders, and snails.*

RUBY-THROATED HUMMINGBIRD
Archilochus colubris

SIZE
3 – 3³/4"

NEST *Walnut-sized and constructed of soft plant material, it is attached to a branch with spider's silk or the web of a tent caterpillar's nest. Usually placed between 5 and 20 feet above the ground and, covered with a green-gray lichen, it is well camouflaged.*

SONG *A soft tchew call but, when agitated, it makes a series of high-pitched squeals.*

ATTRACTED TO *the nectar of columbine, trumpet vine, scarlet lobella, and bee balm plants.*

BLACK-CAPPED CHICKADEE
Parus atricapillus

SIZE
4³/4 – 5¹/2"

NEST *A cavity dug out of a rotted tree or an old woodpecker hole, lined with soft plant fibers, hairs, mosses, and feathers. Placed up to 10 feet above the ground.*

SONG *A chicka-dee-dee-dee call keeps the flock together. Males whistle a territorial fee-bee.*

ATTRACTED TO *the fruit of serviceberry, bayberry, winterberry, and viburnum shrubs, plus pines and birches.*

BLUE JAY
Cyanocitta cristata

SIZE
11 – 12"

NEST *Built in the crotch of a tree, between 7 and 8 inches across. Lined inside with fine rootlets, and covered with a mixture of moss, grasses, string, wool, paper, and rags. Usually found 10 to 15 feet up.*

SONG *A loud jay-jay or jeer-jeer. Alarm call is a bell-like tulliull.*

ATTRACTED TO *the fruit of blueberry, holly, and red mulberry shrubs, varieties of sumac, wild cherry, and wild grapes, and sunflower seeds.*

BLUE-GRAY GNATCATCHER
Polioptila caerulea

NEST *A cup-shaped structure made of plant material held together with spider's webs and covered with lichen. Usually located between 20 and 70 feet above the ground.*

SONG *A very high-pitched sound, like zee-u-zee-u, which is heard constantly as it searches for food in trees and dense thickets.*

ATTRACTED TO *oaks for food and shelter. The bird gleans insects and spiders from leaves and the outer twigs. Sometimes eats suet.*

SIZE
4¹/2 – 5"

RED-BREASTED NUTHATCH
Sitta canadensis

NEST *A tree cavity, or old woodpecker's hole, lined with plant materials, built 5 to 40 feet above the ground. Nuthatches smear pine pitch around the entrance hole to protect the nest from predators.*

SIZE 4¹/2 – 4³/4"

SONG *Most common calls are: it it it, a high-pitched ank ank ank, and wa-wa-wa-wa.*

ATTRACTED TO *the seeds of pine, spruce, and fir trees.*

PILEATED WOODPECKER
Dryocopus pileatus

NEST *An excavated cavity in dead trees situated close to water in shady areas, from 15 to 85 feet above the ground.*

SONG *The regular yucka yucka yucka call is replaced with a slow, irregular cuk cry when the bird is attempting to attract a mate.*

ATTRACTED TO *the fruit of serviceberry, blackberry, wild strawberry, elderberry, hackberry, and red mulberry shrubs. It also searches in the foliage for insects.*

SIZE 17 – 19¹/2"

ROSE-BREASTED GROSBEAK
Pheucticus ludovicianus

SIZE
7 – 8¹/₂"

NEST *Built in thickets and trees, and is made of loosely woven twigs and stems, and lined with grasses, rootlets, and hair. Usually located between 5 and 20 feet above the ground.*
SONG *The courtship song of the male is a long, liquid carol. The female's song is similar, but softer and shorter. The male even sings on the nest.*
ATTRACTED TO *the delicious blossom of the cherry tree, pecking out the developing seeds. It is also attracted to maple, dogwood, and hawthorn trees for food and shelter. This species is known as the "potato-bug bird" from its habit of eating potato beetles. Other insect pests, caterpillars, moths, and grasshoppers make up about half of its diet. It searches for these in Virginia creeper, elderberry, and mulberry shrubs, and in the leaves and fruit of wild grapevines.*

COMMON YELLOWTHROAT
Geothlypis trichas

SIZE
4¹/₂ – 5¹/₂"

NEST *Constructed of grasses, dead ferns, and grapevine bark, with a lining of soft plant fiber or hair. Usually located close to the ground, attached to reeds, briars, and strong grasses.*
SONG *A loud, clear witchity witchity, witchity, or witch-a-wee-o, witch-a-wee-o.*
ATTRACTED TO *insects.*

SCARLET TANAGER
Piranga olivacea

NEST *A shallow, saucer-shaped structure, lined with fine grasses or pine needles. Found on large tree limbs, 4 to 75 feet above the ground.*
SONG *The territorial song is querit, queer, queery, querit, queer.*
ATTRACTED TO *oak trees for the many insects that constitute over 80 percent of the bird's diet. It also eats a variety of wild fruits.*

SIZE
6¹/₂ – 7¹/₂"

AMERICAN TREE SPARROW
Spizella arborea

SIZE
6 – 6¹/₂"

NEST *Cup-shaped, made of grasses, plant stems, bark, and mosses. Has an unusual lining of feathers, lemur fur, and dog-hair. Usually found in trees and shrubs south of the tundra, between 1 and 5 feet above the ground.*
SONG *A very light and musical sound like teedle-eet, teedle-eet.*
ATTRACTED TO *the seeds of perennial wild native grasses such as bluestems and beardgrasses.*

DARK-EYED JUNCO
Junco hyemalis

NEST *Grasses, rootlets, moss, bark, and twigs are used to build a deep cup-shaped depression concealed under tree roots.*
SONG *A simple trill, or a twittering warblerlike call of short faint notes.*
ATTRACTED TO *the seeds of grass and weeds. The seeds of conifers are eaten by this ground-foraging bird. Seed-bearing annuals such as cosmos and zinnias also provide food in the backyard.*

SIZE
6 – 6¹/₂"

RED-WINGED BLACKBIRD
Agelaius phoeniceus

SIZE
7½ – 9½"

NEST *A cup-shaped structure, loosely woven of grasses and sedges, in cattails, reeds, and shrubs often in marshes and over water.*
SONG *The male sings a repeated, gurgling onk-la-reeee, or o-ka-leeee, ending in a trill. The common call is a loud chack sound, given when flying in flocks.*
ATTRACTED TO *the seeds of marsh grasses and open pastureland. This species especially likes to eat seeds from any of the 150 species of annual and perennial sunflowers.*

COMMON GRACKLE
Quiscalus quiscula

SIZE
11 – 13"

NEST *A compact mass of twigs, reeds, and grasses, lined with a mixture of natural and manmade materials. Grackles often nest in loose colonies wherever possible. Usually built in a coniferous tree or shrub.*
SONG *The male mating call is koguba-le, and the common call is a loud chuck; the song is squeaky like a rusty hinge.*
ATTRACTED TO *seeds, acorns, and fruit. Often eats grain.*

AMERICAN GOLDFINCH
Carduelis tristis

SIZE
5 – 5½"

NEST *Woven of plant fibers, and lined with thistle or milkweed down. Built in hedges, brushy areas, or hardwood trees. Usually found a few feet above the ground.*
SONG *The common call is per-chick-o-ree, repeated twice. In flight, the call is see-me, see-me.*
ATTRACTED TO *a wide variety of weed seeds that are consumed in vast quantities. Seeds of lettuce and thistles are favorites. A small quantity of aphids and caterpillars are eaten.*

BALTIMORE ORIOLE
Icterus galbula

NEST *A woven pouch of plant fibers, string, and hair, lined with fine grasses and suspended from large deciduous trees, from about 25 to 30 feet up.*
SONG *A long flutelike varied whistle. Its alarm call is a rolling chatter.*
ATTRACTED TO *wild fruits, garden peas, and flower nectar, but its main diet is insects, found in the foliage of shade trees. In winter, orioles may visit feeders stocked with oranges and apples.*

SIZE
7 – 8"

PINE SISKIN
Carduelis pinus

SIZE
4½ – 5"

NEST *A saucer-shape, made of twigs, rootlets, and grasses, lined with fine rootlets, moss, fur, and feathers. It rests on a horizontal limb, far away from the trunk of the tree.*
SONG *The calls include a long swee, a harsh buzzing zzzzzz, and a tit-ti-tit given in flight.*
ATTRACTED TO *pine and alder seeds. It also eats other tree seeds, weed seeds, and insects, hanging upside down when foraging and eating.*

RECOMMENDED PLANTS

THE SELECTION of plants for this region should be based on the plant's winter hardiness since severe winters in this region may devastate the more fragile plants. Use the plant hardiness and climate zones given at the end of each entry as a guide. These zones are estimates only; variations in micro-climates can account for as much as a one- or two-zone difference.

The length of each season varies throughout the region, so the plant's fruiting periods are listed by season rather than by month. Choose a mixture of flowering and fruiting periods so that the birds have fruit from summer through to winter, when they most need food.

Most of the plants listed here are North American natives, although a few exotic (those not native to North America) have been included. These are not known to be invasive, and are particularly attractive to native birds.

Some of the plants in the illustrated listings in the Southeast region are also suitable for planting in parts of this region, and vice versa, making the choices for the gardener keen to attract birds extremely wide-ranging.

TREES

AMERICAN MOUNTAINASH
Sorbus americana

A moderate-sized deciduous tree with light blue-green leaves, divided into 11 – 17 narrow oval leaflets, that turn a brilliant orange-red in fall. Its showy white spring flowers and clusters of bright red pome fruits make this ideal for city backyards as well as larger properties. Likes full sun. Prefers moist soil. Height: 40 feet. Fully hardy. Zones 3 – 8.

Attracts *some 14 species, including the cedar waxwing, brown thrasher, eastern bluebird, gray catbird, and evening and pine grosbeaks that eat the fruit.*

DOWNY SERVICEBERRY
Amelanchier arborea

A genus of small, deciduous, spring-flowering trees and shrubs, grown for their profuse flowers and foliage. This is one of the most common and widely distributed members of this important native group. It produces white flowers from early spring to midsummer, when small purple pome fruits appear. It is an excellent choice for shady yards. Likes sun/semishade. Prefers well-drained, but not dry, soil. Height: 20 – 40 feet. Hardy. Zone 3.

Attracts *at least 19 species that eat the fruit of serviceberry plants, including the hairy woodpecker, wood thrush, ruffed grouse, red-eyed vireo, and rose-breasted grosbeak.*

EASTERN REDCEDAR
Juniperus virginiana

A slow-growing, hardy, native tree that thrives naturally as far south as Georgia and west to Minnesota and Texas. The fruit ripens in early fall and persists through winter. Only the female plant produces the blue berrylike cones, so plant several trees to improve the chances of a good fruit crop. Likes sun/partial shade. Prefers limestone-derived soils, but it will grow in a variety of sites and thrives in poor, eroded soils. Height: to 50 feet. Hardy. Zones 3 – 9.

FLOWERING CRAB APPLE
Malus magdeburgensis

Highly decorative, small, deciduous spring-flowering tree with shallow cup-shaped flowers and fruits. Most of the 80 cultivars are hybrids created by crossing several exotic species. For attracting the greatest variety of birds, it is best to select trees that have small fruits, and produce fruit through winter. Likes full sun/tolerates semishade. Prefers any but waterlogged soil. Height: 8 – 50 feet. Fully hardy. Zones 5 – 8.

FLOWERING DOGWOOD
Cornus florida

One of the most widely distributed wildlife trees in the eastern United States. An attractive deciduous tree with white flower clusters, it has brilliant red fruits that appear in late summer and most are eaten by late fall. Fall foliage varies from russet to deep red. The exotic kousa dogwood is disease-resistant, but its fruit is not favored by birds. Likes full sun/partial shade. Height: 3 – 10 feet. Fully hardy. Zones 5 – 8.

Attracts *at least 54 species that are known to eat the fruit, including the cedar waxwing, northern mockingbird, brown thrasher, and gray catbird. Also a nest site for songbirds.*

Attracts *a great variety of birds, including the northern flicker and white-throated sparrow, which like to eat the small fruits, because they are most readily plucked and swallowed.*

Attracts *36 species that eat the dogwood's fruit, including six species of thrush, the northern flicker, pileated woodpecker, summer tanager, evening grosbeak, and pine grosbeak.*

HAWTHORN
Crataegus flabellata

These poplar-leafed, round-topped deciduous trees make up a widespread group of similar species. They are grown for their clustered, five-petaled, occasionally double, pink and white flowers in spring and summer, small red or orange pome ornamental fruits, and their fall color. Excellent choice for backyards and property borders. Their dense forked br anches provide choice nesting places for the robin, cardinal, blue jay, and many other birds. Likes full sun but are suitable for almost all situations. Prefers rich, well-drained soil. Height: 15 – 35 feet. Fully hardy. Zone 5.

RED MULBERRY
Morus rubra

Few trees are as attractive to songbirds as this deciduous species, grown for its foliage and edible red fruits. The inconspicuous green male and female flowers usually grow on different trees. Although pollen is spread by wind, a male and female tree may be necessary for a good fruit crop. Red mulberry is a good choice for a central backyard bird tree. Likes full sun. Prefers fertile, well-drained soil. Height: 25 – 40 feet. Fully hardy. Zone 6.

SUGAR MAPLE
Acer saccharum

A deciduous, spreading tree with an oval crown. Its 5-lobed, bright green leaves turn brilliant scarlet in fall. The sugar maple produces small but attractive flowers that are followed by 2-winged fruit. These attributes make it an attractive choice for larger properties. Its sap is processed into maple syrup. It is intolerant of city conditions. Likes woods with areas of sun/semi-shade. Prefers fertile, well-drained soil. Height: 70 feet. Fully to frost hardy. Zones 4 – 8.

Attracts *at least 18 species, especially the cedar waxwing, which readily consume the fruit. Shown above are the rounded red fruits of the single seed hawthorn tree.*

Attracts *at least 44 species that eat this fruit when there is a good crop, including yellow-billed and black-billed cuckoos, and scarlet and summer tanagers.*

Attracts *the American robin and the white-eyed vireo which nest in the sugar maple's branches. The oriole, wren, and warbler eat insects from the foliage.*

SHRUBS

WHITE OAK
Quercus alba

A large, deciduous, spreading tree grown for its foliage. This species is best on larger properties. Produces insignificant flowers from late spring to early fall, followed by rounded, small brown fruits (acorns). Unlike most oaks, the white oak produces an annual acorn crop. The acorns are a very important food for both mammals and birds. Likes full sun. Prefers moist, well-drained soil. Height: to 100 feet, with a trunk 4 feet in diameter. Fully to frost hardy. Zone 5.

Attracts *the northern flicker, red-headed woodpecker, blue jay, and other birds that eat the tree's acorns. Shown here is the staminate flower of the white oak.*

SHRUBS

AMERICAN CRANBERRYBUSH
Viburnum trilobum

Also known as American highbush cranberry, this deciduous shrub has dark green foliage, which turns red in fall, and brilliant red fruits that often last from fall through winter, to be eaten by spring migrants. Fruiting is most prolific when several plants of different clones are planted together. Likes sun/semishade. Prefers deep, fertile soil. Height: 8 feet. Fully to frost hardy. Zone 2.

Attracts *at least seven species that eat the fruit of this shrub, including the spruce and ruffed grouse, wild turkey, brown thrasher, cedar waxwing, and eastern bluebird.*

AMERICAN ELDERBERRY
Sambucas canadensis

A deciduous shrub that forms dense thickets. It has large white flower clusters from early to late summer and its tiny dark-purple fruits ripen from midsummer to early fall. Likes sun. Prefers fertile, moist soil. Height: young plants grow only a few inches in the first year, but individual canes may grow as tall as 15 feet in subsequent years. Fully hardy. Zones 4 – 9.

Attracts *at least 33 species to its colorful fruit including the red-bellied and red-headed woodpecker, eastern bluebird, and cardinal. The robin often eats the fruit before it is ripe.*

BRAMBLES
Rubus spp.

This is the collective name for blackberries, raspberries, dewberries, and thimbleberries, a group of deciduous, evergreen and semievergreen shrubs. Brambles vary greatly in height and form spiny dense tangles. All produce fruit that is readily consumed by birds. Brambles also provide dense cover and excellent nest sites safe from predators. For maximum fruiting and branching they should be pruned. Plant at the edge of a small property. Likes sun. Prefers fertile, well-drained soil. Height: to 10 feet. Fully to frost hardy. Zones 4 – 9.

COMMON SPICEBUSH
Lindera benzoin

A deciduous, tall, and bushy shrub with fragrant green leaves that turn yellow in fall. Tiny, greenish-yellow flowers appear before the leaves throughout spring, followed by red berries on the female plants from midsummer to midfall. It is propagated by cuttings in summer or by seed in fall. Likes full sun/partial shade. Prefers moist, fertile soil. Height: 15 feet, and spreads from 2 – 8 feet. Fully hardy. Zone 5.

HIGHBUSH BLUEBERRY
Vaccinium corymbosum

A native, dense, deciduous shrub that occurs along the Atlantic coast from eastern Maine to northern Florida. Ideal for creating a hedge. It fruits when 8 – 10 years old, although under ideal conditions, some plants fruit when 3 years old. It is a favorite nest site for the gray catbird. Likes full sun/tolerates partial shade. Prefers acid, well-drained, or wet soil. Height: 6 – 15 feet. Hardy. Zones 4 – 8.

Attracts *at least 49 species that eat the fruit, including the wild turkey, blue jay, gray catbird, veery, cedar waxwing, yellow-breasted chat, and orioles.*

Attracts *migrants as well as resident birds, such as the northern bobwhite and northern flicker, to its fruit which is high in fats and therefore an important food source.*

Attracts *the American robin, eastern bluebird, orchard oriole, and at least 34 other species, whose preferred food is the sweet blue-black fruit of the highbush blueberry.*

NANNYBERRY
Viburnum lentago

Also known as the sheepberry, this vigorous, deciduous, upright shrub has oval, glossy, dark green leaves that turn red and purple in fall. It produces flattened heads of small, fragrant, star-shaped, white flowers in spring, and then egg-shaped, red fruits that ripen to black in summer. Likes full sun/partial shade. Prefers deep, rich, moist soil. Height: 10 feet, making it the largest viburnum. Fully to frost hardy. Zones 3 – 8.

NORTHERN BAYBERRY
Myrica pensylvanica

A deciduous, aromatic shrub found in coastal and sandy inland areas. The northern bayberry is adaptable. It flowers in late spring through mid summer, and produces small gray, waxy berries consistently throughout the winter. Some species, such as the red-winged blackbird, commonly use it for nesting. Likes full sun/partial shade. Prefers sandy, dry soil, but will tolerate moist soil. Height: 3 – 8 feet. Hardy. Zone 2.

PAGODA DOGWOOD
Cornus alternifolia

Also known as alternate-leaved dogwood because of its arrangement of leaves alternating along the stem. An attractive tree or shrub, it is grown for its flowers, foliage, or brightly colored winter stems. Leaves turn red in fall. Likes semishade/tolerates full sun. Prefers moist, well-drained soil. Height: pagoda dogwood can sometimes grow into a graceful tree as high as 30 feet, with wide, arching branches. Zones 2 – 8.

Attracts at least five species that use the dense foliage for cover. The gray catbird, American robin, eastern bluebird, and cedar waxwing are a few of the birds that eat its colorful fruit.

Attracts at least 25 species, including the yellow-rumped warbler, red-bellied woodpecker, and tree swallow that consume the bayberry's fruit. An important food for migratory birds.

Attracts at least 34 species with its fruit, including the downy woodpecker, brown thrasher, wood thrush, eastern bluebird, and cedar waxwing.

RED-OSIER DOGWOOD
Cornus stonifera

This low, deciduous shrub is shown in its 'Flaviramea' form. Small, star-shaped white flowers appear in late spring and early summer, followed by spherical white fruits in summer. Most of these are consumed by birds by early fall. Likes full sun. It adapts to a variety of soils, but is useful in moist sites to reduce soil erosion. Height: grows to a maximum of only 4 – 8 feet, with a spread of 10 feet or more. Fully hardy. Zones 2 – 8.

STAGHORN SUMAC
Rhus typhina

A deciduous, spreading, suckering, open shrub with minute, greenish-white flowers from mid- to late summer. Leaves are brilliant orange in fall, with clusters of spherical, deep red fruits only on female plants. Here, it is beginning to show its fall color. A fragrant sumac may be preferable in some gardens because of its shorter stature. Likes sun. Prefers well-drained soil. Height: 15 feet. Fully hardy. Zones 4 – 9.

WILD ROSE
Rosa virginiana

Wild roses are a diverse group of low-growing and sun-loving shrubs that are perfect for planting as a hedge on property borders and as clumps. Their dense thorny branches often provide important cover and nest sites for thicket birds such as the northern cardinal and the brown thrasher. The fruit period is in summer/early fall. Likes sun. Prefers dry/moist soil. Height: 4 – 6 feet. Hardy. Zones 4 – 9.

Attracts at least 18 species that eat the fruit, including the wild turkey and gray catbird. It is an important shrub for songbirds since it provides dense cover during the summer.

Attracts some ground-nesting birds which shelter under the broad leaves. At least 21 species eat the fruit of this winter-persistent plant, including the red-eyed vireo and American robin.

Attracts at least 20 species which enjoy the scarlet rose hips that appear in late summer. Above is a close-up of the flower of the native rose, Rosa rugosa.

GROUNDCOVERS

BEARBERRY
Arctostaphylos uva-ursi

An evergreen, low-growing shrub with arching, intertwining stems clothed in small, oval bright green leaves. Bears urn-shaped pinkish-white flowers in summer, followed by scarlet berries which are persistent through the winter. Provides shelter from strong winds. Likes full sun. Prefers well-drained, acid soil. Height: to 12 inches. Fully hardy to frost tender. Zones 2 – 8.

Attracts the fox sparrow and grouse, which eat the pea-sized red berries. Also known as kinnikinnick. Native Americans smoked the dried leaves as tobacco.

COWBERRY
Vaccinium vitis-idaea

A vigorous, evergreen prostrate shrub, with underground runners that make it ideal groundcover. Also known as ligonberry and mountain cranberry. Forms hummocks of oval, leathery leaves. Has bell-shaped, white to pink flowers in nodding racemes from early summer to fall, and produces bright red fruits in fall and winter. Likes sun/semi-shade. Prefers moist but well-drained, peaty or sandy, acid soil. Height: $^3/4$ – 10 inches when in flower. Fully hardy. Zones 2 – 5.

Attracts the white-throated sparrow which eat the red fruit. Mountain cranberry makes good groundcover in small areas. The edible red fruits make wonderful preserves and syrups.

CROWBERRY
Empetrum nigrum

The genus name of this low, evergreen shrub means "upon rock," a reference to crowberry's preferred rocky and alpine habitat. It is found throughout the subarctic in exposed habitats where few plants can grow. It has a pungent fragrance. Its elliptic, sharp-tipped leaves are $^1/4$ inch long, and similar to conifer needles. The purplish black drupes appear in late summer, lasting until early winter. Likes sun. Prefers moist or moderately dry soil. Height: 3 – 4 inches. Hardy. Zone 4.

Attracts at least 40 different birds which come to eat the berries, including the pine grosbeak, brown thrasher, catbird, and towhee. It is an important source of winter food.

OTHER GOOD PLANTS

EVERGREEN TREES

Abies balsamea
BALSAM FIR
A favorite nesting site for the robin and mourning dove, this native tree does not flourish in large cities. Its seeds are eaten by at least 13 species, including the evening grosbeak, purple finch, and pine grosbeak. *Height:* 40 – 60ft; likes sun/shade. Prefers moist soil. The fruit appears in late spring through early summer. *Fruit type:* CONE. ZONE 4.

Picea glauca
WHITE SPRUCE
This native tree provides important nesting and winter cover, and at least 19 species eat the seeds. It is the preferred food of the evening grosbeak, red-breasted nuthatch, and crossbills. *Height:* 80 – 100ft; likes sun/shade. Prefers moist/drained soil. The fruit appears in early fall. *Fruit type:* CONE. ZONE 3.

Picea pungens
COLORADO SPRUCE
See Mountains and Deserts region illus. listing, p.138.

Picea rubens
RED SPRUCE
Native. *Height:* 60 – 70ft; likes sun/shade. Prefers drained soil. The fruit appears in early fall. *Fruit type:* CONE. ZONE 2.

Pinus resinosa
RED PINE
At least 48 species eat the seeds of this native pine. Heavy seed crops occur every 3 to 7 years. It is very hardy and will grow even in poor soil. *Height:* to 80ft; likes sun/half sun. Prefers dry/drained soil. The fruit appears in late summer through fall. *Fruit type:* CONE. ZONE 3.

Pinus rigida
PITCH PINE
This is the best native pine tree to plant in poor, sandy, or even gravelly locations. Its seed attracts many birds. *Height:* 40 – 60ft; likes sun. Prefers dry/moist soil. The fruit appears in late fall. *Fruit type:* CONE. ZONE 5.

Thuja occidentalis
EASTERN ARBORVITAE
A native shrub that forms dense hedges; used as a nest site by the common grackle, robin, and house finch. The seeds are a preferred food for the pine siskin. *Height:* 20 – 40ft; likes sun/half sun. Prefers moist soil. The fruit appears in early fall. *Fruit type:* cone. ZONE 3.

Tsuga canadensis
EASTERN HEMLOCK
This native tree, which is intolerant of air pollution, is the preferred nest site for the robin, blue jay, and wood thrush, as well as an important food tree for chickadees. It forms hedges when trimmed. *Height:* 50 – 80ft; likes a variety of light but is very shade tolerant. Prefers moist/drained soil. The fruit appears in early fall. *Fruit type:* cone. ZONE 3.

LARGE DECIDUOUS TREES

Acer negundo
BOXELDER
This native tree is a preferred winter food of the evening grosbeak and purple finch. Used in shelterbelt plantings, it is very hardy and grows fast, but is short lived. *Height:* 50 – 75ft; likes sun/shade. Prefers moist soil but tolerates poor soil. The fruit appears in late summer through fall. *Fruit type:* brown samara. ZONE 3.

Acer rubrum
RED MAPLE
This very hardy native tree may live for 150 years and its foliage turns a spectacular red in fall. *Height:* 50 – 70ft; likes sun/half sun. Prefers moist soil. The fruit appears in early summer. *Fruit type:* red samara. ZONE 3.

Acer saccharinum
SILVER MAPLE
This city-tolerant native tree is fast growing but relatively short-lived. Its buds are favored by the evening grosbeak. *Height:* 60 – 100ft; likes sun/half sun. Prefers moist/dry soil. The fruit appears in early summer. *Fruit type:* green or red samara. ZONE 3.

Betula alleghaniensis
YELLOW BIRCH
This native tree produces good seed crops every 1 to 2 years. Its seeds are eaten by at least 12 species, including the goldfinch, junco, pine siskin, and chickadees.

Height: 60 – 70ft; likes sun/half sun. Prefers cool/moist/drained soil. The fruit appears in late summer through fall. *Fruit type:* samara. ZONE 4.

Betula lenta
SWEET BIRCH
Native. *Height:* 50 – 60ft; likes sun/shade. Prefers moist/fertile/rocky soil. The fruit appears in late summer through late fall. *Fruit type:* samara. ZONE 4.

Betula papyrifera
PAPER BIRCH
Native. *Height:* 50 – 80ft; likes sun/half sun. Prefers moist/drained soil. The fruit appears in late summer through early fall. *Fruit type:* samara. ZONE 2.

Carya glabra
PIGNUT HICKORY
Native. *Height:* 50 – 70ft; likes sun/shade. Prefers drained soil. The fruit appears in fall. *Fruit type:* nut. ZONE 5.

Carya ovata
SHAGBARK HICKORY
See Southeast region illus. listing, p.107.

Carya tomentosa
MOCKERNUT HICKORY
Native. *Height:* 40 – 50ft; likes sun/shade. Prefers drained soil. The fruit appears in fall. *Fruit type:* nut. ZONE 5.

Celtis occidentalis
COMMON HACKBERRY
See Prairies & Plains region illus. listing, p. 123.

Diospyros virginiana
COMMON PERSIMMON
See Southeast region illus. listing, p.105.

Fagus grandifolia
AMERICAN BEECH
The nut crop of this native tree provides excellent food for many birds and mammals; at least 25 species eat its fruit, including the northern bobwhite and cedar waxwing. It presents an imposing appearance with its spreading crown. *Height:* 40 – 70ft; likes sun/shade. Prefers moist loam soil. The fruit appears in early fall. *Fruit type:* cone. ZONE 4.

Fraxinus americana
WHITE ASH
The winged seed of this native tree is a preferred food of the evening grosbeak and purple finch. It is disease-resistant. *Height:* 70 – 100ft; likes sun/half sun. Prefers dry/moist soil. The fruit appears in early to late fall. *Fruit type:* samara. ZONE 4.

Fraxinus pennsylvanica
GREEN ASH
This native tree is tolerant of city conditions, and is therefore a good landscaping plant to include in a backyard. Its seeds are a preferred food of the wood duck, bobwhite, evening and pine grosbeak, and purple finch. *Height:* 30 – 50ft; likes sun/half sun. Prefers moist/dry/drained soil. The fruit appears in early fall. *Fruit type:* samara. ZONE 2.

Juglans cinerea
BUTTERNUT
The nuts of this fast-growing native tree are a favorite of the Carolina wren, red-bellied woodpecker, chickadees, and nuthatches. *Height:* 40 – 60ft; likes sun. Prefers moist/dry/drained soil. The fruit appears in early to late fall. *Fruit type:* nut. ZONE 3.

Juglans nigra
BLACK WALNUT
This excellent native specimen tree should be isolated because it has roots that release toxic material that may kill some plants. It has edible nuts that are eaten by many birds and mammals. *Height:* 70 – 120ft; likes sun/half sun. Prefers well-drained soil. The fruit appears in early to late fall. *Fruit type:* nut. ZONE 5.

Larix laricina
AMERICAN LARCH
This native tree is an important seed source for crossbills and the purple finch, and is often used for nesting. *Height:* 40 – 80ft; likes sun. Prefers moist soil. The fruit appears in late summer through early fall. *Fruit type:* nut. ZONE 2.

Liquidambar styraciflua
AMERICAN SWEETGUM
See Southeast region illus. listing, p.104.

Liriodendron tulipifera
TULIPTREE
An ornamental native, also known as the tulip or yellow poplar, it is a hardy street tree. Its flower nectar attracts the ruby-throated hummingbird. *Height:* 60 – 160ft; likes sun. Prefers moist/drained soil. The fruit appears in fall. *Fruit type:* samara. ZONE 6.

Populus balsamifera
BALSAM POPLAR
The buds of this hardy native tree are a favorite food of the ruffed grouse. *Height:* 60 – 80ft; likes sun. Prefers dry/drained soil. The fruit appears in early summer. *Fruit type:* capsule. ZONE 2.

Populus deltoides
EASTERN COTTONWOOD
Woodpeckers excavate the softwood of this native tree for nest sites. This tree grows best on flood plains and riverbanks. *Height:* 80 – 100ft; likes sun/half sun. Prefers moist soil. The fruit appears in spring through early summer. *Fruit type:* capsule. ZONE 2.

Populus tremuloides
QUAKING ASPEN
The buds and catkins of this native tree are a preferred food of the ruffed grouse, and its buds are readily eaten by the evening grosbeak and purple finch. Its buds and catkins are also eaten by at least 8 other species. *Height:* 40 – 60ft; likes sun/half sun. Prefers dry/moist soil. The fruit appears in late spring through early summer. *Fruit type:* capsule. ZONE 1.

Prunus serotina
BLACK CHERRY
See Southeast region illus. listing, p.104.

Quercus coccinea
SCARLET OAK
This native tree with a biennial acorn crop is the preferred food of the common grackle, blue jay, and turkey. It is also popular as an ornamental tree due to its red color in fall. *Height:* 70 – 80ft; likes sun/half sun. Prefers dry/sandy soil. The fruit appears in fall. *Fruit type:* acorn. ZONE 4.

Quercus macrocarpa
BUR OAK
This native tree tolerates city conditions and poor soils. It is a favorite food of the wood duck. *Height:* 80 – 150ft; likes sun. Prefers dry/drained soil. The fruit appears in fall. *Fruit type:* acorn. ZONE 4.

Quercus palustris
PIN OAK
This native is useful as an ornamental tree in backyards and along streets and is popular for its unusually broad crown. At least 29 species eat its acorn crop. *Height:* 60 – 75ft; likes sun/half sun. Prefers moist soil. The fruit appears throughout fall. *Fruit type:* acorn. ZONE 5.

Quercus rubra
NORTHERN RED OAK
A native tree that tolerates city conditions; its acorns are eaten by many birds. It is also an excellent shade tree. There are often 3 to 5 years between acorn crops. *Height:* 60 – 80ft; likes sun/half sun. Prefers

moist/rich/drained soil. The fruit appears throughout fall. *Fruit type:* acorn. ZONE 4.

Quercus velutina
BLACK OAK
This popular native shade tree may live for 200 years. It has acorn crops about every third year, providing the preferred food of the turkey, bobwhite, blue jay, and rufous-sided towhee. *Height:* 80 – 150ft; likes sun/half sun. Prefers rich/moist/drained soil. The fruit appears in early to late fall. *Fruit type:* acorn. ZONE 4.

Sassafras albidum
SASSAFRAS
See Southeast region illus. listing, p.106.

SMALL DECIDUOUS TREES

Carpinus caroliniana
AMERICAN HORNBEAM
This native tree, also known as musclewood because of its attractive trunk, has seeds that are a preferred food of the ruffed grouse. *Height:* 20 – 40ft; likes sun/shade. Prefers dry/moist soil. The fruit appears in late summer through fall. *Fruit type:* brown nutlet. ZONE 5.

Crataegus crus-galli
COCKSPUR HAWTHORN
See Prairies & Plains region illus. listing, p.122.

Malus pumila
COMMON APPLE
This native tree is used as a nest site by the eastern bluebird, red-eyed vireo, great crested flycatcher, and robin, and its fruits are eaten by many birds. It has fragrant spring blossoms that are eaten by the cedar waxwing. *Height:* 20 – 30ft; likes sun. Prefers clay-loam, but can grow in a variety of soils. The fruit appears in fall. *Fruit type:* green-red pome. ZONE 4.

Ostrya virginiana
AMERICAN HOP HORNBEAM
This native is a useful understory tree with its tolerance to shade. Its fruits are highly preferred by the ruffed grouse. *Height:* 20 – 45ft; likes sun/half sun. Prefers dry/drained soil. The fruit appears in late summer through fall. *Fruit type:* brown nutlet. ZONE 5.

Prunus pennsylvanica
WILD RED CHERRY
This native tree grows best in disturbed or waste places and is best planted in clumps away from walks and patios. It provides

very valuable wildlife food; the eastern bluebird is attracted to its edible fruits. *Height:* 10 – 30ft; likes sun. Prefers dry soil. The fruit appears in summer through early fall. *Fruit type:* red drupe. ZONE 2.

Prunus virginiana
CHOKECHERRY
See Prairies and Plains region illus. listing, p.124.

Sorbus aucuparia
EUROPEAN MOUNTAINASH
There are many cultivated varieties of this readily available and useful exotic tree, which is similar to American mountainash. *Height:* 30 – 45ft; likes sun. Prefers dry/moist/drained soil. The fruit appears in fall. *Fruit type:* yellow-scarlet pome. ZONE 2.

Sorbus decora
NORTHERN MOUNTAINASH
The most northern of our native species, this mountainash sometimes grows as a shrub. *Height:* to 15ft; likes sun. Prefers dry/moist/drained soil. The fruit appears in early fall through winter. *Fruit type:* orange pome. ZONE 2.

EVERGREEN SHRUBS

Gaylussacia brachycera
BOX HUCKLEBERRY
More than 50 species, including the northern flicker, blue jay, and red-headed woodpecker, are known to eat the fruit of native huckleberries. These low shrubs are frequently used as nest sites. *Height:* to 2ft; likes sun. Prefers dry/acid/drained soil. The fruit appears throughout summer. *Fruit type:* black berry. ZONE 6.

Ilex glabra
INKBERRY
Also known as gallberry or evergreen winterberry, it is an especially good plant for attracting birds. The plants are monoecious, so both male and female plants must be planted in clumps to successfully produce fruit. *Height:* 6 – 10ft; likes sun but tolerates shade. Prefers acid soil. The fruit appears in fall through spring. *Fruit type:* black berry. ZONE 4.

Juniperus chinensis
CHINESE JUNIPER
Many cultivated varieties of this exotic species are available. The fruits appear only on female plants. *Height:* 2 – 12ft; likes sun/half sun. Prefers dry/moist/drained soil. The fruit persists through fall. *Fruit type:* blue-green berry. ZONE 4.

Cultivars of Chinese juniper:
'Hetzii' juniper
This exotic shrub is notable for its rapid growth, and it spreads to 12 – 15ft, with blue-green foliage. *Height:* 10 – 12ft; likes sun/half sun. Prefers dry/moist/drained soil. The fruit persists. *Fruit type:* blue-green berry. ZONE 5.

'Pfitzerana' juniper
This exotic shrub has a vase-shaped form with spreading branches. *Height* to 6ft; likes sun. Prefers dry/moist/drained soil. The fruit persists. *Fruit type:* blue-green berry. ZONE 5.

'Sargentii' juniper
This exotic shrub spreads to over 6ft wide. *Height:* to 2ft; likes sun. Prefers dry/moist/drained soil. The fruit persists. *Fruit type:* blue-green berry. ZONE 5.

Juniperus communis
COMMON JUNIPER
See Southeast region illus. listing, p.112.

Taxus canadensis
CANADIAN YEW
This tree is a most useful native to use as cover and as a nest site. It produces sparse fruit, with 7 species known to eat the fruit. *Height:* to 3ft; likes shade. Prefers moist/drained/rich humus soil. The fruit appears in summer through early fall. *Fruit type:* red drupelike. ZONE 3.

TALL DECIDUOUS SHRUBS

Alnus rugosa
SPECKLED ALDER
This native shrub is a useful naturalizer for ponds and stream borders. It reproduces quickly in full sun. The seeds are an important food for the American goldfinch, pine siskin, and redpolls. *Height:* 15 – 25ft; likes sun. Prefers moist/swampy soil. The fruit appears in late summer through fall. *Fruit type:* cone. ZONE 5.

Alnus serrulata
HAZEL ALDER
Native. *Height:* 6 – 12ft; likes sun. Prefers moist/swampy soil. The fruit appears in late summer through fall. *Fruit type:* cone. ZONE 5.

Aronia arbutifolia
RED CHOKECHERRY
This native shrub is notable for its brilliant fall foliage. Its fruits are eaten by at least 12 species, and are a preferred food of the cedar waxwing and brown thrasher. The berries persist into the winter. *Height:* to 10ft; likes sun/half sun. Prefers moist/dry soil. The fruit appears in late summer through late fall. *Fruit type:* black berry. ZONE 6.

Aronia melanocarpa
BLACK CHOKECHERRY
Black chokecherry is equal in beauty to its relative the red chokecherry (see above), but grows taller. A valuable planting for borders where it will not compete with neighbors for space. *Height:* to 10ft; likes sun/half sun. Prefers moist/dry soil. The fruit appears in late summer through late fall. *Fruit type:* black berry. ZONE 5.

Cephalanthus occidentalis
COMMON BUTTONBUSH
See Aquatic Plants listing, p.73.

Corylus americana
AMERICAN HAZEL
This native shrub provides good cover, and its nuts are preferred by the blue jay and hairy woodpecker. *Height:* to 10ft; likes sun. Prefers dry/moist soil. The fruit appears in summer through fall. *Fruit type:* brown nut. ZONE 5.

Crataegus uniflora
ONE-FLOWER HAWTHORN
This shrubby native species provides nest sites for birds such as the willow flycatcher, and at least 36 species eat hawthorn fruit. *Height:* 3 – 8ft; likes sun/half sun. Prefers dry/sandy soil. The fruit appears in fall. *Fruit type:* yellow/red pome. ZONE 5.

Ilex laevigata
SMOOTH WINTERBERRY
This native shrub produces attractive fruits in fall that persist in winter. Many birds are attracted by its berries, including the mockingbird, catbird, brown thrasher, and hermit thrush. *Height:* 10 – 20ft; likes sun/shade. Prefers dry/moist soil. The fruit appears in early fall through winter. *Fruit type:* red berry. ZONE 5.

Ilex verticillata
COMMON WINTERBERRY
See Southeast region illus. listing, p.109.

Lonicera morrowii
MORROW HONEYSUCKLE
This is an ornamental exotic, with flowers, foliage, and fruit. At least 20 species eat honeysuckle fruits; flowers are a favorite source of nectar for the ruby-throated hummingbird. It makes an excellent vegetation screen, and provides abundant food and cover. *Height:* 6 – 8ft; likes sun. Prefers dry/moist/drained soil. The fruit appears early to late summer. *Fruit type:* red/yellow berry. ZONE 5.

Lonicera standishii
STANDISH HONEYSUCKLE
This is ideal for planting as a screen, and provides abundant food and cover for at least 20 species. It has attractive flowers, foliage, and fruit. *Height:* 5 – 6ft; likes sun/partial sun. Prefers sandy soil. The fruit appears early summer. *Fruit type:* red berry. ZONE 5.

Malus sargentii
SARGENT CRABAPPLE
See Prairies and Plains region illus. listing, p.124.

Malus sieboldii
TORINGO CRABAPPLE
This exotic shrub has white flowers and winter-persistent fruits, and sometimes grows as a small tree. *Height:* 5 – 8ft; likes sun. Prefers well-drained soil. The fruit appears in fall through late winter. *Fruit type:* red-yellow pome. ZONE 5.

Pyracantha coccinea
SCARLET FIRETHORN
Its fall foliage makes this one of the most attractive exotic ornamental evergreens for the southern part of this region, and it is useful along walls and as formal hedges. At least 17 species eat its berries. *Height:* 8 – 15ft; likes sun/partial shade. Prefers drained soil. The fruit appears in late summer. *Fruit type:* red-orange berry. ZONE 7.

Rhamnus cathartica
COMMON BUCKTHORN
An excellent background or hedge shrub that tolerates city conditions. Its fruits are eaten by at least 15 species. *Height:* 10 – 20ft; likes sun/shade. Prefers dry/moist/peaty soil. The fruit appears in summer through fall. *Fruit type:* black drupe. ZONE 2.

Rhamnus frangula
GLOSSY BUCKTHORN
This native shrub makes an excellent contribution to city gardens when used as a hedging or background plant. The fruits are popular with 15 species, including the mockingbird and brown thrasher. *Height:* 8 – 12ft; likes shade/partial sun. Prefers dry/moist/peaty soil. The fruit appears in summer through fall. *Fruit type:* black drupe. ZONE 2.

Rhus copallina
SHINING SUMAC
Native. *Height:* 4 – 10ft; likes sun. Prefers dry/rocky soil. The fruit appears in fall. *Fruit type:* red drupe. ZONE 5.

Rhus glabra
SMOOTH SUMAC
At least 31 species are known to eat the fruits of this native sumac, especially the catbird, wood thrush, eastern bluebird, and starling. Sumac fruits remain on the branches into late winter and thus serve as "emergency" food. *Height:* 10 – 15ft; likes sun. Prefers a variety of soil and also tolerates poor soils. The fruit appears in late summer through fall. *Fruit type:* red drupe. ZONE 2.

Rosa carolina
PASTURE ROSE
Native. *Height:* 5 – 7ft; likes sun. Prefers dry soil. The fruit appears in summer through early fall and persists. *Fruit type:* scarlet hip. ZONE 5.

Rosa palustris
SWAMP ROSE
Dense thickets of this native shrub provide excellent nest sites. The rose hips are eaten by at least 20 species, and are a preferred food of the mockingbird, Swainson's thrush, and cedar waxwing. *Height:* to 8ft; likes sun. Prefers damp soil. The fruit appears in late summer through early fall. *Fruit type:* scarlet hip. ZONE 5.

Salix discolor
PUSSY WILLOW
The buds of this native shrub are eaten by the ruffed grouse, and it is a favorite nest site for goldfinch. *Height:* 10 – 20ft; likes sun. Prefers low/moist soil. The fruit appears in early spring through late spring. *Fruit type:* capsule. ZONE 2.

Sambucus pubens
AMERICAN RED ELDER
At least 23 species eat the abundant fruit of this native shrub. It is a preferred food of the red-bellied woodpecker, robin, veery, and rose-breasted grosbeak. European *S. racemosa* is similar. *Height:* 2 – 12ft; likes sun. Prefers dry/rocky/drained soil. The fruit appears in early summer through early fall. *Fruit type:* red berry. ZONE 5.

Viburnum acerifolium
MAPLELEAF VIBURNUM
A native shrub that is highly tolerant of different soil and light conditions. At least 10 species are known to eat its fruit, including the cedar waxwing and American robin. *Height:* 3 – 6ft; likes sun/shade. Prefers dry/drained soil. The fruit appears in summer and winter. *Fruit type:* purple drupe. ZONE 4.

Viburnum alnifolium
HOBBLEBUSH VIBURNUM
This native shrub is useful for understory planting in woodlands, and its ripe fruits are eaten by at least 6 species. *Height:* to 10ft; likes shade. Prefers moist soil. The fruit appears in summer through fall. *Fruit type:* purple drupe. ZONE 4.

Viburnum cassinoides
WITHEROD VIBURNUM
This attractive native shrub is tolerant of salty conditions, making it a good choice for coastal planting. It bears ornamental flowers and fruits that are readily eaten by at least 9 species. *Height:* 6 – 12ft; likes sun/shade. Prefers moist soil. The fruit appears in early fall through winter. *Fruit type:* blue-black drupe. ZONE 4.

Viburnum dentatum
ARROWWOOD VIBURNUM
See Southeast region illus. listing, p.108.

Viburnum prunifolium
BLACKHAW VIBURNUM
A native shrub with a lovely reddish fall color and attractive white flowers in spring. At least 8 species, including the cedar waxwing, eat its fruit. *Height:* 8 –15ft; likes sun/shade. Prefers dry/moist/drained soil. The fruit appears in fall and persists through winter. *Fruit type:* blue-black drupe. ZONE 3.

Viburnum recognitum
NORTHERN ARROWWOOD
This hardy shrub grows in clumps or thickets that provide good habitat cover for many animals. It is a popular landscape shrub since it transplants well, grows slowly, and requires little maintenance. Use it where dense foliage is desired, such as a border, hedge, or living wall. *Height:* 10 – 20ft; likes sun/partial shade. Prefers well-drained soil. The fruit appears in late summer. *Fruit type:* blue drupe. ZONE 2.

SMALL DECIDUOUS SHRUBS

Amelanchier bartramiana
BARTRAM SERVICEBERRY
This native shrub flowers and fruits later than other serviceberries. Its berries are a preferred food for the cedar waxwing and eastern bluebird; at least 40 northeast species eat the serviceberry fruit. *Height:* 2 – 4ft; likes sun/half sun. Prefers rich/peaty/variety soil. The fruit appears in early summer through early fall. *Fruit type:* purple-black pome. ZONE 3.

Amelanchier stolonifera
RUNNING SERVICEBERRY
This low, dense, native shrub grows in sand and gravel. As with other serviceberries, this is an important summer food for many songbirds. *Height:* 1 – 3ft; likes sun. Prefers dry/moist/drained soil. The fruit appears in summer. *Fruit type:* black pome. ZONE 5.

Berberis thunbergii
JAPANESE BARBERRY
An exotic, this small shrub is useful as a hedge planting. It is very ornamental in all seasons and not susceptible to black stem rust. A prolific fruiter, it has a variable palatability to birds. *Height:* to 5ft; likes sun/partial sun. Prefers dry/drained soil. The fruit appears in summer through winter. *Fruit type:* red berry. ZONE 5.

Cornus amomum
SILKY DOGWOOD
This medium-sized dogwood thrives in moist areas where it forms fine hedges. At least 18 species feed on its fruits, including the Swainson's thrush, purple finch, eastern bluebird, and gray catbird. *Height:* 4 – 10ft; likes sun/partial shade. Prefers moist/well-drained soil. The fruit appears in late summer. *Fruit type*: blue-white berry. ZONE 4.

Cotoneaster horizontalis
ROCKSPRAY COTONEASTER
See Southeast region illus. listing, p.108.

Gaylussacia baccata
BLACK HUCKLEBERRY
This attractive ornamental native with edible, sweet fruits forms a low shrub with a crown of up to 4ft. At least 24 species eat huckleberry fruit. *Height:* to 3ft; likes sun/half sun. Prefers dry/rocky/sandy soil. The fruit appears in summer through early fall. *Fruit type:* black berry. ZONE 2.

Gaylussacia dumosa
DWARF HUCKLEBERRY
This native shrub provides useful ground cover in wet meadows and boggy areas. *Height:* 1 – 2ft; likes sun. Prefers wet soil. The fruit appears in early summer through fall. *Fruit type:* black berry. ZONE 2.

Gaylussacia frondosa
DANGLEBERRY
An attractive native shrub, especially when used in borders and clumps. Its berries are eaten by the mourning dove, mockingbird, and scarlet tanager, among other species. *Height:* 3 – 6ft; likes sun. Prefers acid/well-drained soil. The fruit appears in early summer through early fall. *Fruit type:* dark blue berry. ZONE 5.

Hypericum prolificum
SHRUBBY ST.-JOHN'S-WORT
This shrub has attractive blooms and is good as a mixed border species. Its fruits are eaten by 5 species, including the ring-necked pheasant, bobwhite, and junco. *Height:* 1 – 4ft; likes half sun/shade. Prefers rocky/sandy soil. The fruit appears in late summer through winter. *Fruit type:* reddish brown achene. ZONE 5.

Lonicera canadensis
FLY HONEYSUCKLE
Native. *Height:* 3 – 5ft; likes shade. Prefers moist soil. The fruit appears in early summer. *Fruit type:* red berry. ZONE 4.

Lonicera oblongifolia
SWAMP FLY HONEYSUCKLE
This native shrub provides food and shelter for at least 20 species, including the catbird, robin, and goldfinch. *Height:* 2 – 5ft; likes sun/half sun. Prefers moist soil. The fruit appears in summer through early fall. *Fruit type:* red berry. ZONE 4.

Lonicera quinquelocularis
MISTLETOE HONEYSUCKLE
Exotic. *Height:* to 5ft; likes sun/half sun. Prefers moist soil. The fruit appears in summer through early winter. *Fruit type:* white translucent berry. ZONE 6.

Rhamnus alnifolius
ALDERLEAF BUCKTHORN
This highly ornamental native shrub has dark fruits and leaves, and its dense foliage makes it good in border plantings. At least 15 species eat the berries, including the mockingbird, pileated woodpecker, and

brown thrasher. *Height:* 2 – 3ft; likes shade. Prefers damp soil. The fruit appears in late summer through fall. *Fruit type:* black drupe. ZONE 2.

Ribes cynosbati
DOGBERRY
This native gooseberry, also known as dog bramble, does well in barren soil and thrives in garden soil. It provides a good nest site, and at least 16 species eat its berries. An excellent shrub for halting soil erosion in open pastures. *Height:* 3 – 4ft; likes sun/shade. Prefers dry/moist/poor/drained soil. The fruit appears in summer through early fall. *Fruit type:* purple berry. ZONE 5.

Rosa blanda
MEADOW ROSE
Native. *Height:* 1 – 4ft; likes sun/half sun. Prefers dry/moist/rocky soil. The fruit appears in summer through early fall. *Fruit type:* scarlet hip. ZONE 2.

Rosa rugosa
RUGOSA ROSE
Exotic. *Height:* to 6ft; likes sun/half sun. Prefers drained soil. The fruit appears in early summer through early fall. *Fruit type:* scarlet hip. ZONE 2.

Rubus allegheniensis
ALLEGHENY BLACKBERRY
Like other members of the raspberry genus, this native shrub provides a very important late-summer bird food; at least 40 species eat raspberry or blackberry fruit in the northeast. *Height:* 3 – 8ft; likes sun. Prefers drained soil. The fruit appears in summer through early fall. *Fruit type:* black drupelets. ZONE 4.

Rubus flagellaris
AMERICAN DEWBERRY
As with other members of the raspberry family, this native shrub provides both important summer food and nest sites. At least 49 northern species eat the fruit, and 12 species use the shrub to nest. *Height:* 1 – 2ft; likes full sun. Prefers dry/drained soil. The fruit appears in summer. *Fruit type:* black drupelets. ZONE 4.

Rubus occidentalis
BLACK RASPBERRY
Native. *Height:* 3 – 6ft; likes sun. Prefers neutral damp soil. The fruit appears in summer through fall. *Fruit type:* black drupelets. ZONE 4.

Spiraea alba
MEADOWSWEET
This native shrub forms thickets and is important to wildlife as cover and as a nest site. *Height:* 1 – 4ft; likes sun. Prefers natural damp soil. The fruit appears in summer through fall. *Fruit type:* inconspicuous. ZONE 5.

Symphoricarpos albus
COMMON SNOWBERRY
See Prairies and Plains region illus. listing, p.126.

Symphoricarpos orbiculatus
CORALBERRY
See Prairies and Plains region illus. listing, p.124.

Vaccinium angustifolium
LOWBUSH BLUEBERRY
See Prairies and Plains region illus. listing, p.127.

VINES

Campsis radicans
COMMON TRUMPET CREEPER
See Southeast region illus. listing, p.110.

Celastrus scandens
AMERICAN BITTERSWEET
A deciduous, ornamental vine with yellow fall color. Plant male and female plants nearby. At least 15 species eat its fruit. Likes sun. Prefers dry/drained soil. The fruit appears in late summer through early winter. *Fruit type:* red and yellow pod. ZONE: 2.

Menispermum canadense
COMMON MOONSEED
The ivylike foliage of this deciduous vine can climb up to 12ft. It also provides useful groundcover, but dies back in winter. At least 5 species are known to eat its fruit. Likes sun/shade/variety. Prefers moist/drained soil. The fruit appears in late summer through fall. *Fruit type:* black drupe. ZONE 4.

Parthenocissus quinquefolia
VIRGINIA CREEPER
See Southeast region listing, p.114.

Smilax glauca
SAWBRIER
This deciduous native vine offers excellent cover, food, and nest sites for at least 19 species. Its berries are a preferred food for the mockingbird, catbird, and Swainson's thrush. Likes sun/variety. Prefers swampy soil. The fruit appears in fall. *Fruit type:* blue-black berry. ZONE 6.

Smilax rotundifolia
COMMON GREENBRIER
This deciduous native vine is similar to the above, but has strong thorns. Its fruits survive through winter and at least 20 species eat it. Likes sun. Prefers moist/drained soil. The fruit appears in early fall. *Fruit type:* blue-black berry. ZONE 5.

Vitis aestivalis
SUMMER GRAPE
The grapes of this deciduous native vine attract many birds, especially the cardinal and catbird. At least 52 species eat grapes; they are a preferred food of 24 species. Many insect-eating birds, such as vireos, warblers, flycatchers, and cuckoos, nest among grapevines or use grape bark in their nests. Likes sun. Prefers dry soil. The fruit appears in fall. *Fruit type:* black berry. ZONE 5.

Vitis labrusca
FOX GRAPE
The same birds that eat the summer grape are attracted to this deciduous native vine. Likes sun/ shade/variety. Prefers moist/dry/drained soil. The fruit appears in late summer through fall. *Fruit type:* black-amber berry. ZONE 5.

Vitis novae-angliae
NEW ENGLAND GRAPE
The same birds that eat the summer grape are attracted to this deciduous native vine. Likes sun. Prefers fertile/drained soil. The fruit appears in early fall. *Fruit type:* black berry. ZONE 5.

Vitis riparia
RIVERBANK GRAPE
The same birds that eat the summer grape are attracted to this deciduous native. Likes sun. Prefers moist soil. The fruit appears in late summer through early fall. *Fruit type:* blue-black berry. ZONE 3.

Vitis vulpina
FROST GRAPE
Deciduous native. Likes sun. Prefers rich/drained soil. The fruit appears in fall. *Fruit type:* black berry. ZONE 6.

GROUNDCOVERS

Ajuga reptans
CARPET BUGLEWEED
See Southeast region illus. listing, p.111.

Cornus canadensis
BUNCHBERRY
See Mountains and Deserts region illus. listing, p.143.

Cotoneaster adpressus
CREEPING COTONEASTER
This deciduous exotic grows 1 – 2ft tall and up to 8ft across. Likes sun/half sun. Prefers moist soil. The fruit appears in late summer through fall. *Fruit type:* red pome. ZONE 5.

Fragaria chiloensis
BEACH STRAWBERRY
This native evergreen provides cover and food for at least 29 species. Likes sun/half sun. Prefers drained soil. The fruit appears in spring through summer. *Fruit type:* red berry. ZONE 5.

Fragaria virginiana
VIRGINIA STRAWBERRY
An evergreen native with smaller fruits than those of the strawberry plant listed above. Likes sun/half sun. Prefers drained soil. The fruit appears in spring through summer. *Fruit type:* red berry. ZONE 4.

Gaultheria procumbens
WINTERGREEN
See Southeast region illus. listing, p.111.

Juniperus horizontalis
CREEPING JUNIPER
See Prairies and Plains region illus. listing, p.127.

Cultivar of Creeping Juniper:
'Wiltoni' juniper
This native evergreen grows 3 – 6in tall and forms a dense mat 10ft wide. Likes sun. Prefers shallow soil. The fruit appears in late summer through winter. *Fruit type:* blue-green berry. ZONE 3.

Mitchella repens
PARTRIDGEBERRY
An attractive evergreen, it forms a dense creeping mat. Its berries are eaten by at least 8 birds. Likes shade. Prefers moist/acid soil. The fruit appears in early summer through late summer. *Fruit type:* red berry. ZONE 3.

Vaccinium uliginosum
BOG BILBERRY
An evergreen that is good for rock gardens and shallow soils. At least 87 species eat its fruit. Likes sun. Prefers dry/drained soil. The fruit appears in late summer through fall. *Fruit type:* blue berry. ZONE 2.

SOUTHEAST REGION

Tʜɪs ɪs ᴛʜᴇ ʀᴇɢɪᴏɴ to which many of the northern species migrate for the winter. An ideal garden plan includes native plants that produce seeds and berries for these birds during fall and winter.

Sugar hackberry
Celtis laevigata
A deciduous native tree that grows in drier areas. Its fruit, a favorite of the cedar waxwing, persists through winter.

SIZE
4¹/₂ – 5"

HOUSE WREN

TROGLODYTES AEDON

This bird's diet consists of spiders, wasps, caterpillars, crickets, and grasshoppers that it finds in the leaves of trees and shrubs such as the American beautybush.

Live oak
Quercus virginiana
A symbol of the South, its acorn crop is an important food for birds, and its branches provide good nesting sites.
(See page 113.)

American holly
Ilex opaca
The brilliant red fruits are produced only on female trees, so a male tree must be planted nearby.
(See page 110.)

SIZE
5"

WHITE-EYED VIREO

VIREO GRISEUS

Vireos visit gardens with shrubs, roses, and tangles of blackberries. They eat insects plucked from foliage near the ground, and berries of plants such as creeping juniper, in fall.

Yaupon holly
Ilex vomitoria
An excellent hedge providing nest sites and fruit for many birds.
(See page 110.)

Creeping juniper
Juniperus horizontalis
It forms a dense mat and its blue-green berries attract many species. (See page 127.)
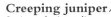

Stepping stones
Construct a stepping-stone path using old flagstones, or groups of bricks, that leads through both the shrubbery and flower borders.
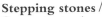

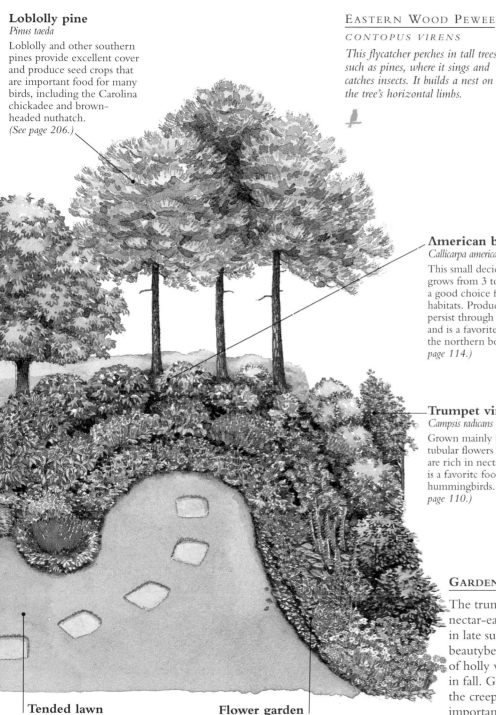

Loblolly pine
Pinus taeda

Loblolly and other southern pines provide excellent cover and produce seed crops that are important food for many birds, including the Carolina chickadee and brown-headed nuthatch. *(See page 206.)*

EASTERN WOOD PEWEE
CONTOPUS VIRENS

This flycatcher perches in tall trees such as pines, where it sings and catches insects. It builds a nest on the tree's horizontal limbs.

SIZE
6 – 6^1/$_2$"

American beautyberry
Callicarpa americana

This small deciduous shrub grows from 3 to 6 feet tall and is a good choice for light-shade habitats. Produces berries that persist through to midwinter and is a favorite winter food of the northern bobwhite. *(See page 114.)*

Trumpet vine
Campsis radicans

Grown mainly for its tubular flowers that are rich in nectar, this is a favorite food of hummingbirds. *(See page 110.)*

GARDEN FOR FALL FOOD

The trumpet vine will entice nectar-eating hummingbirds in late summer, and the beautyberry and the varieties of holly will produce berries in fall. Groundcover such as the creeping juniper plant is important for food in winter, and tall pines and an oak provide both seeds and nesting sites for resident birds.

Tended lawn
Birds that nest in shrubs and trees may venture onto lawn – especially if lured by a small fountain or pond, hanging feeders, and dust baths.

Flower garden
Colorful annuals planted inside the low shrub layer provide nectar for birds. California poppy and chrysanthemum are good choices.

COMMON BIRDS

BACKYARD GARDENERS in the Southeast have great opportunities for attracting a wide variety of birds since the area is the winter home for many Northeastern birds. For example, most eastern bluebirds, hermit thrushes, American robins, brown thrashers, rufous-sided towhees, northern flickers, tree swallows, and song sparrows make this short migration to the Southeast where they wait out the frigid winter months.

The region contains a variety of habitats ranging from the spruce-fir trees high in the Appalacians to the coastal shrubs and lush subtropical plants of south Florida. Fruit-eating birds have made this warmer area their winter home because fruiting trees and shrubs survive through winter. The white-breasted nuthatch haunts fruit orchards, joining birds such as kinglets to forage for food in winter.

SIZE
9 – 11"

NORTHERN MOCKINGBIRD
Mimus polyglottos

NEST *A coarse, bulky, loosely-woven, cup-shaped structure made of dead twigs and lined with grass and small roots. Built in the fork of a tree or shrub and usually located between 3 and 10 feet above the ground, but can be found as high as 50 feet.*
SONG *A vigorous song, mimicking other birds in phrases repeated between 3 and 6 times before changing to another. The mockingbird also imitates dog barks and hen cackles.*
ATTRACTED TO *the fruits of bayberry, elderberry, hackberry, mulberry, sumac, and serviceberry shrubs, and flowering dogwood, but it is mainly insectivorous in spring and summer.*

RED-BELLIED WOODPECKER
Melanerpes carolinus

NEST *An excavated hole, measuring 10 to 12 inches deep, in a dead or soft-wooded tree. Usually found between 5 and 40 feet above the ground.*
SONG *Frequently makes a churr sound that is repeated several times.*
ATTRACTED TO *pine seeds, acorns, and the fruits of shrubs, including bayberry, elderberry, and red mulberry shrubs, and flowering dogwood. It also eats insects.*

SIZE
9½ – 10½"

PURPLE MARTIN
Progne subis

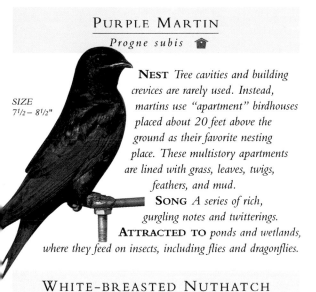

SIZE
7½ – 8½"

NEST *Tree cavities and building crevices are rarely used. Instead, martins use "apartment" birdhouses placed about 20 feet above the ground as their favorite nesting place. These multistory apartments are lined with grass, leaves, twigs, feathers, and mud.*
SONG *A series of rich, gurgling notes and twitterings.*
ATTRACTED TO *ponds and wetlands, where they feed on insects, including flies and dragonflies.*

TREE SWALLOW
Tachycineta bicolor

NEST *Usually found in tree cavities, particularly in old woodpecker holes in sycamore trees. It may nest in buildings and fence posts. The tree swallow will also make good use of birdhouses if they are fairly low to the ground and close to ponds, streams, or wet meadows.*
SONG *A twittering, liquid* klweet *or* cheet *sound.*
ATTRACTED TO *the berrylike succulent cones, called juniper berries, of the evergreen juniper, and to small waxy fruits of bayberry and wax myrtle shrubs.*

SIZE
5 – 6"

WHITE-BREASTED NUTHATCH
Sitta carolinensis

NEST *A natural cavity, or an old woodpecker hole, in native oak, chestnut, or maple trees is a favorite location for nuthatch nests. Sometimes, they will excavate a hole in a dead or dying tree limb. The cavity is lined with rootlets, grasses, and feathers.*
SONG *A hollow whistled* tew-tew-tew-tew *sound. A distinctive nasal* yank-yank *or soft* hit-hit *call is heard in spring.*
ATTRACTED TO *maple, oak, and pine trees for food and shelter. The birds like to eat acorns, beechnuts, and hickory nuts. The white-breasted nuthatch also eats sunflower seeds and cracked corn. If food is plentiful, the bird stores supplies in small crevices in the tree bark and, in winter, will feed from this hidden larder. It will also visit backyard feeders to eat beef suet.*

SIZE
5 – 6"

TUFTED TITMOUSE
Parus bicolor

NEST *The tufted titmouse prefers the inside of a natural tree cavity, or an empty woodpecker hole, lined with leaves, moss, bark, and hair, sometimes pulled from animal and human heads. Usually located between 2 and 90 feet above the ground.*
SONG *A loud, clear series of four to eight notes sounding like* peta-peta-peta-peta.
ATTRACTED TO *oak trees for their acorn crops. The fruits of bayberry, elderberry, hackberry, and serviceberry shrubs are also eaten. Caterpillars form half the bird's diet.*

SIZE
5 – 6"

BROWN-HEADED NUTHATCH
Sitta pusilla

NEST *Usually the brown-headed nuthatch excavates a hole in a tree, stump, or snag, but sometimes natural cavities located less than 10 feet above the ground are used by this species.*

SIZE
4 – 5"

SONG *Frequently a high and rapid* pit-pit-pit-pit *sound, unlike the sound made by other nuthatches.*
ATTRACTED TO *pine tree seeds and insects picked from the bark. At feeders, it eats chopped peanuts and suet.*

EASTERN BLUEBIRD
Sialia sialis

SIZE
6¹/₂ – 7¹/₂"

NEST *It likes old woodpecker holes and natural cavities in old trees or tree stumps. Artificial birdhouses, especially those placed in orchards, are also used for nesting. Usually located between 3 and 20 feet above the ground.*
SONG *A soft chu-wee, or a plaintive cheu-ery, cheu-ery.*
ATTRACTED TO *the fruits of elderberry, hackberry, serviceberry, and sumac shrubs, and to flowering dogwood, holly, and redcedar trees. It is also attracted to fox grape and Virginia creeper vines. Approximately 70 percent of its diet consists of insects, including caterpillars, beetles, ants, and spiders.*

CAROLINA WREN
Thryothorus ludovicianus

NEST *Tree cavities or openings in stone walls, overturned tree roots, or crevices in man-made structures. Often located less than 10 feet above the ground.*
SONG *A three-syllable, clear chant sounding like teakettle-teakettle-teakettle.*
ATTRACTED TO *leaf mulch, which it probes for spiders, beetles, crickets, and sowbugs. It also eats the fruit of native bayberry shrubs.*

SIZE
5¹/₂ – 6"

EASTERN SCREECH-OWL
Otus asio

NEST *Often uses abandoned flicker nests in sycamore, elm, and dead pine trees, but also readily accepts man-made nestboxes designed for kestrels and wood ducks. Usually located 5 to 30 feet above the ground.*
SONG *A quavering, whinnylike whistle, unusual for an owl.*
ATTRACTED TO *large insects, salamanders, mice, and frogs.*

SIZE
8 – 10"

CAROLINA CHICKADEE
Parus carolinensis

NEST *Usually an excavated cavity in a dead tree, or an old woodpecker hole, filled with plant down, moss, leaves, and feathers. Often located about 5 to 6 feet above the ground.*
SONG *A whistling fee-bee, the first note being higher.*
ATTRACTED TO *wild fruits and the seeds of conifers. In winter, chickadees visit feeders to eat sunflower seeds and suet.*

SIZE
4¹/₂ – 4³/₄"

YELLOW WARBLER
Dendroica petechia

NEST *A compact, well-formed cup constructed by the female in an upright tree, shrub fork, or crotch. It is composed of milkweed fibers, grasses, lichens, mosses, and fur. Found 3 to 8 feet above the ground.*
SONG *A lively and rapid rendering of sweet-sweet-sweet-I'm so sweet.*
ATTRACTED TO *trees and shrubs in search of caterpillars and other insects.*

SIZE
5"

YELLOW-RUMPED WARBLER
Dendroica coronata

SIZE
5 – 6"

NEST *A bulky and loose structure, built of rootlets, twigs, and grass, interwoven with hair from animals. Usually located on a horizontal branch of coniferous trees, close to the trunk, 5 to 50 feet above the ground.*
SONG *A trill, similar to that of a junco, but falling and rising in pitch at the end.*
ATTRACTED TO *the fruit of the bayberry shrub, hollies, and to insects in spring and summer. Grass and sunflower seeds are also eaten.*

SONG SPARROW
Melospiza melodia

NEST *A structure made of rough plant materials with a soft grass and hair lining. Usually well hidden under weeds and grasses, or in a low shrub, between 2 and 3 feet above the ground, but has been found as high as 12 feet.*
SONG *Several clear notes of sweet, sweet, sweet, continuing in a rapid and clear musical trill.*
ATTRACTED TO *seeds and fruits from blackberry, elderberry, and highbush blueberry shrubs.*

SIZE
5 – 6¾"

PAINTED BUNTING
Passerina ciris

NEST *A shallow cup made of dried grasses, weed stems, and leaves, with a soft lining of finer materials. Usually found 3 to 6 feet above the ground in bushes, vines, or small trees.*
SONG *A musical and bright sound like pew-eata, pew-eata j-eaty you too.*
ATTRACTED TO *the seeds of thistle, dandelion, goldenrod, and several grasses. The birds also visit feeders to eat sunflower seeds and white millet.*

SIZE
5½"

SUMMER TANAGER
Piranga rubra

NEST *A loosely built, shallow cup made of stalks, grasses, leaves, and bark on a horizontal limb, usually located 10 to 35 feet above the ground.*
SONG *Chattering and musical, robinlike, with phrases of pik-i tuk-i-tuk.*
ATTRACTED TO *the colorful fruits of the blackberry and red mulberry. Insects, beetles, wasps, spiders, and worms are also eaten by the summer tanager. It visits backyard feeders for peanut butter and cornmeal mixed with shortening.*

SIZE
7 – 8"

FIELD SPARROW
Spizella pusilla

NEST *A well-made cup of weed stems and grasses, lined with hair and other fine materials. Usually found on or near the ground, but sometimes found up to 4 feet above the ground in a tangle of vines.*
SONG *Begins slowly on clear, sweet notes which speed up and end in a trill.*
ATTRACTED TO *a wide variety of native weeds and grasses that produce seeds, insects, and food crumbs. Field sparrows also visit backyard feeders.*

SIZE
5"

RECOMMENDED PLANTS

DESPITE HAVING a milder climate, particularly in the winter, many of the bird-attracting plants suitable for the Southeast are the same as those recommended for the Northeast *(see page 112)*. However, since the extreme summer heat in this region can cause stress to some newly-planted specimens, it is important to water the plants regularly during the summer.

Planting conifers provides year-round cover to protect the birds from both winter chills and summer heat, and also creates nesting places during spring and summer.

Within the Southeast recommended plant section there are many evergreen trees and shrubs, including some varieties of magnolia, oak, and holly trees. These give the birds shelter throughout the year as well as providing food during the breeding season and when food would otherwise be in short supply.

One of the best aspects of this region is the wide variety of plant species that thrive in local conditions. However, always check the hardiness zones when making your selection. Even the Southeast has occasional frosts that can devastate valuable plantings.

TREES

AMERICAN HOLLY
Ilex opaca

The evergreen foliage makes it a useful cover tree for birds year-round. Its brilliant red drupe fruits are produced only on female trees. Since the flowers are pollinated by insects rather than wind, plant at least one male tree nearby. Likes partial shade. Prefers a variety of soils, ranging from rich to sandy. Height: to 50 feet. Hardy. Zone 6.

Attracts at least 12 species which eat the fruit, including the cedar waxwing eastern bluebird, and northern mockingbird. For maximum benefit, plant trees in clumps.

AMERICAN SWEETGUM
Liquidambar styraciflua

A fast-growing, stately, deciduous tree. Native to mid-Atlantic. Beautiful star-shaped foliage and ornamental seed capsules. Flowers in early spring and seeds from September through November. Likes full sun. Prefers moist, rich soil. Height: up to 120 feet; grows 1 – 2 feet each year. Hardy. Zone 6.

Attracts at least 21 species that consume the seeds. They include the red-winged blackbird, bobwhite, cardinal, mourning dove, and evening grosbeak.

BLACK CHERRY
Prunus serotina

A rapidly maturing native deciduous tree. Spikes of fragrant white flowers appear in late spring, followed by small red cherries that turn black in fall. Bears fruit every 3 – 4 years, from early summer through to mid fall. Glossy, dark green leaves become yellow in fall. Likes sun. Tolerates a variety of soils from rich and moist to light and sandy. Height: to 50 feet; it may live for over 150 years. Hardy. Zones: 4 – 8.

BLACK TUPELO
Nyssa sylvatica

A deciduous, broadly conical tree that is also commonly known as sour gum. Notable for its oval, glossy, dark to medium green leaves that turn brilliant yellow, orange, and red in fall. Branches are usually heavy with small, dark blue drupes by late summer or mid fall. Excellent tree for backyards or for landscaping pond banks. Occurs from Maine to Missouri and south to Texas and Florida. Likes sun. Prefers moist soil. Height: 60 feet. Hardy. Zone 5.

COMMON PERSIMMON
Diospyros virginiana

A deciduous, broadly spreading tree that is also known as possumwood. Usually found in old fields and on roadsides. Produces bell-shaped flowers in midsummer. First produces its yellow fruit when it is about 6 feet tall. The fleshy berries ripen to yellowish red or orange-red from early through late fall. Occurs from southern Connecticut south to Florida and west to Texas and Kansas. Likes full sun. Prefers dry, light soil but will tolerate moist soil. Height: 30 – 50 feet. Hardy. Zone 5.

Attracts at least 47 species that eat the fruit, including the red-headed woodpecker, northern flicker, northern mockingbird, rose-breasted grosbeak, and white-throated sparrow.

Attracts many species to its delicious dark blue fruit, including the wood thrush, northern flicker, rose-breasted grosbeak, cedar waxwing, and scarlet tanager.

Attracts the mockingbird, gray catbird, cedar waxwing, American robin, northern bobwhite, eastern bluebird, eastern phoebe, and many other species that eat this fruit.

LAUREL OAK
Quercus laurifolia

A deciduous, broadly conical tree. Narrow, glossy, bright green leaves persist through fall and winter, giving the tree a semievergreen appearance. Produces insignificant flowers from late spring to early summer, followed by egg-shaped to rounded, brownish fruits (acorns). It is a frequent nest site for hawks and many other birds. May be affected, though not usually seriously, by oak wilt. Likes sun or partial shade. Prefers deep, well-drained soil. Height: 60 – 70 feet. Fully to frost hardy. Zone 8.

LOBLOLLY PINE
Pinus taeda

A fast-growing evergreen pine that thrives on a variety of soils from poorly drained coastal plains to better-drained hill country. It produces abundant seed crops that are an important food source for many birds of the southeast pinelands. An excellent choice to provide cover for birds on larger properties. Likes a sunny position. Prefers moist soil. Height: to 100 feet. Hardy. Zone 8.

RED BUCKEYE
Aesculus pavia

A native deciduous horse chestnut that can be grown as a small tree or a very large shrub. It has a round-headed form and is an enthusiastic bloomer. In summer, 3 – 6-inch panicles of deep red flowers appear among lustrous, dark green leaves which have five narrow, oval leaflets. The fruits that follow may have spiny outer casings. Likes sun or partial shade. Prefers loamy, well-drained soil. Height: 20 feet. Fully to frost hardy. Zones 6 – 9.

Attracts *many species, including bobwhite, brown thrasher, wood duck, common grackle, blue jay, and red-headed woodpecker, which eat the acorns of the laurel oak.*

Attracts *the rufous-sided towhee, which rakes with its feet on the ground to reveal seeds and insects; it also attracts the brown-headed nuthatch.*

Attracts *many hummingbird species with the vivid coral red of its panicle. As many as 30 birds have been sighted around one tree in a feeding frenzy.*

SASSAFRASS
Sassafras albidum

A deciduous, upright tree that may develop a spreading habit. It has aromatic, glossy, dark green leaves that vary in shape from oval to deeply lobed and turn yellow or red in fall. It produces inconspicuous, yellowish green flowers in spring. Egg-shaped, deep blue drupe appear in late summer or fall. Likes sun or partial shade. Prefers deep, fertile, well-drained, acid soil. Height: 50 feet. Fully hardy. Zones 5 – 8.

SHAGBARK HICKORY
Carya ovata

A deciduous, broadly columnar tree, grown for its stately habit, divided leaves, fall color, and edible nuts. It is found on dry hillsides in mixed forests and is ideal for planting on larger properties. This slow-growing tree does not produce large fruit crops until it is 40 years old, but it is a long-term investment for birds since it may live to be 300 years old. Likes an open, sunny habitat, but will also grow in partial shade. Prefers deep, fertile soil. Height: 100 feet. Hardy. Zone 5.

SUGAR HACKBERRY
Celtis laevigata

This deciduous, native tree usually grows in moist woodlands, but it will also grow in drier areas, and thus makes an excellent choice for a backyard bird-attracting tree. Fruits ripen in late summer and stay on the tree through winter. Sugar hackberry produces the most fruit when 30 – 70 years old. Occurs from Virginia and southern Indiana, south to eastern Texas and central Florida. Likes sun. Prefers fertile, well-drained soil. Height: to 100 feet. Hardy. Zone 7.

Attracts at least 22 species that eat its delicious blue fruit. It is the preferred food of the pileated woodpecker, eastern kingbird, gray catbird, and eastern bluebird.

Attracts the carolina chickadee, pine warbler, white-breasted nuthatch, and rufous-sided towhee, which pick at the tree's nut scraps after they have been opened and discarded by squirrels.

Attracts the cedar waxwing, yellow-bellied sapsucker, northern mockingbird, and at least 23 other species that prefer to eat the small, orange-to-black fruits.

SHRUBS

ARROWWOOD VIBURNUM
Viburnum dentatum

This deciduous shrub provides excellent cover and nesting sites for birds. It forms dense thickets, tolerates city pollution, and is useful for planting at pond edges. Produces blue drupes from late summer through late fall. Fruit is most prolific when several plants of different clones are planted together. Likes sun/partial shade. Prefers deep, moist, fertile soil. Height: to 15 feet. Fully hardy. Zone 2.

ROCKSPRAY COTONEASTER
Cotoneaster horizontalis

A semievergreen, stiff-branched, spreading shrub. Excellent in rock gardens or as groundcover. Its small, rounded, dark green leaves turn bright orange-red in late fall. Bears pinkish white flowers from late spring to early summer, followed by red fruits. Likes sun or partial shade. Prefers well-drained soil, making it particularly useful for dry sites. Will not tolerate water-logged soil. Height: 2 – 3 feet, spreading to 15 feet. Fully to frost hardy. Zone 6.

INKBERRY
Ilex glabra

An evergreen, dense, upright shrub. Small, oblong to oval, dark green leaves are smooth-edged or may have slight teeth near the tips. Produces black fruits (berries) in fall, following insignificant flowers borne in spring. Slow-growing and spreading. Hollies do not transplant well, but respond well to hard pruning and pollarding, which should be carried out in late spring. Likes sun or partial shade. Prefers well-drained soil, but will tolerate dry, sandy soil. Thrives on acid soil. Height: 8 feet. Fully hardy. Zones 5 – 9.

Attracts *many birds, including the eastern bluebird, red-eyed vireo, northern flicker, and rose-breasted grosbeak, which all eat the fruit.*

Attracts *many species, including the rufous-sided towhee, American robin, brown thrasher, gray catbird, and northern mockingbird, that all eat the fruit.*

Attracts *at least 15 species that eat the berries of this shrub, including the northern mockingbird, hermit thrush, and northern bobwhite. The berries follow the white flowers.*

POSSUM HAW
Ilex decidua

This small deciduous tree produces its inconspicuous white flowers in late spring and early summer, followed by orange or red berries in fall. The fruit persist through winter, making it an important food source for birds. Plant in clumps, borders, or hedges. Likes sun and partial shade. Prefers acid, well-drained soil, but will tolerate alkaline, dry, or moist soil. Height: 10 – 20 feet. Hardy. Zone 6.

WEIGELA
Weigela florida 'Variegata'

A deciduous, bushy, dense shrub. Carries a profusion of funnel-shaped deep rose flowers in late spring and early summer. Inside, the flowers are paler, fading to almost white. Green leaves are broadly edged with creamy white. Likes sun. Prefers fertile, well-drained but moist soil. Height: 8 feet. Fully hardy. Zones 5 – 9.

WINTERBERRY
Ilex verticillata

A large, spreading, deciduous shrub. Young branches are purplish green. Produces oval or lance-shaped, saw-toothed, bright green leaves. In late summer through fall it bears a profusion of attractive, long-lasting red berries that persist on bare branches during winter months. Likes sun and partial shade. Prefers wet, rich, slightly acid soil. Height: 10 feet, spreading to 8 feet. Fully hardy. Zones 4 – 9.

Attracts many species, including the eastern bluebird, robin, cedar waxwing, purple finch, and red-bellied woodpecker. It is a good source of winter food for these birds.

Attracts the ruby-throated hummingbird that feeds on the nectar of the deep red flowers. Shown above is the flower of the 'Bristol Ruby' variety.

Attracts many birds, including the mockingbird, catbird, brown thrasher, and hermit thrush, to its red berries, which persist through winter and are therefore an important food source.

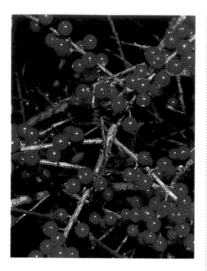

YAUPON HOLLY
Ilex vomitoria

This holly makes an excellent wildlife hedge, providing abundant nest sites and fruit. The plentiful red drupe fruits ripen by mid fall, and stay on the branches through winter. As with most hollies, fruits usually appear only on female plants, but occasionally both male and female flowers grow on the same shrub. Occurs from West Virginia south to the Gulf Coast and northern Florida. Likes full sun and partial shade. Prefers well-drained, moist, sandy soil. Height: to 25 feet. Hardy. Zone 7.

Attracts the gray catbird, northern mockingbird, northern bobwhite, brown thrasher, and many other songbirds which like to eat the fruit of the yaupon holly.

VINES

TRUMPET HONEYSUCKLE
Lonicera sempervirens

A native, semievergreen climbing vine with oval leaves. Has salmon-red to orange, trumpet-shaped flowers. Produces red berries in late summer through fall. Found as far west as Texas. Likes sun. Prefers moist, well-drained soil. Will not tolerate wet soil. Height: may grow to 20 feet, or without support, serves as a good groundcover, (covering 12 feet or more in width). Frost hardy. Zone 4.

Attracts hummingbirds, which feed on nectar from the tubular flowers, and songbirds, which eat the small red berries. Often grows in woods, old fields, and thickets.

TRUMPET VINE
Campsis radicans

A native, deciduous, dense-foliaged vine that clings tenaciously to a trellis or stone wall. Leaves of 7 – 11 oval, toothed leaflets are downy beneath. Has small clusters of tube-shaped orange flowers that are several inches deep. Flowers in the summer through fall. It is native from Connecticut south to Florida and west to Iowa and Texas. Thrives on south-facing sides of buildings in the northern part of its range. Likes sun. Prefers well-drained, fertile soil. Height: to 30 feet Hardy. Zone 5.

Attracts many hummingbirds, including the rufous and Anna's hummingbird, which come to the decorative, tube-shaped orange, scarlet, or yellow flowers.

GROUNDCOVERS

CARPET BUGLE
Ajuga reptans

This evergreen perennial spreads freely by runners, and has small rosettes of glossy, deep bronze-purple leaves. Short spikes of blue flowers appear in spring. Likes sun/partial shade. Tolerates any soil, but grows more vigorously in moist conditions. Height: 6 inches, spreading to 3 feet. Fully hardy. Zone 4.

COMMON JUNIPER
Juniperus communis

An evergreen, dense, matlike, spreading shrub, with needlelike leaves. Has high wildlife value because it provides both protected nesting sites and edible fruits. In fall, it produces pea-sized, dark blue fruits that take 2 years to mature and may persist on the shrub for 3 years. Also known as dwarf pasture, or ground juniper. Above is the variety 'Depressa'. Likes full sun. Prefers sterile soil. Height: 1 – 4 feet, spreads to 10 feet. Fully hardy. Zone 2.

WINTERGREEN CHECKERBERRY
Gaultheria procumbens

This small, creeping, evergreen shrub is also known as checkerberry or teaberry. The leaves, when crushed, are aromatic, smelling of wintergreen oil. Small white flowers appear in midsummer, and edible red berries may persist from fall into spring. Likes sun. Prefers acid, well-drained soil. Height: the leathery leaves may reach 2 inches in length, but the plant rarely grows higher than 6 inches. Half- to fully hardy. Zone 4.

Attracts many songbird species, and ruby-throated, Anna's, black-chinned, and rufous hummingbirds. It makes a lovely ornamental groundcover.

Attracts the eastern bluebird, cedar waxwing, American robin, pine and evening grosbeaks, and purple finch, which all eat the ripe berries. Bobwhite use it for cover.

Attracts the ring-necked pheasant, bobwhite, and at least 8 other species that eat the red berries. Plant wintergreens 1 foot apart to provide groundcover in cool, damp areas.

OTHER GOOD PLANTS

EVERGREEN TREES

Ilex cassine
DAHOON
This native tree provides many birds with a good food source through the winter. *Height:* to 40ft; likes sun/shade. Prefers moist/drained soil. The fruit appears in fall through winter. *Fruit type:* red/yellow berry. ZONE 7B.

Juniperus virginiana
EASTERN REDCEDAR
See Northeast region illus. listing, p.85.

Magnolia grandiflora
SOUTHERN MAGNOLIA
At least 19 species eat the fruit of this native tree, including the catbird, fish crow, northern flicker, eastern kingbird, and mockingbird. *Height:* to 50ft; likes sun. Prefers moist/drained soil. The fruit appears in summer through fall. *Fruit type:* rose drupe. ZONES 7 – 10.

Persea borbonia
REDBAY
This native tree grows in swamps and along streams, and provides a choice food of the eastern bluebird, robin, and bobwhite. *Height:* to 70ft; likes sun. Prefers moist soil. The fruit appears in late summer through fall. *Fruit type:* blue or purple drupe. ZONE 8.

Pinus clausa
SAND PINE
This native tree occurs in coastal Florida, and is a nest site of the scrub jay. *Height:* to 60ft; likes sun. Prefers sandy/infertile soil. The fruit is persistent. *Fruit type:* cone. ZONE 9.

Pinus echinata
SHORTLEAF PINE
Many species eat the seed of this tree and also use it as a nest site. *Height:* to 100ft; likes sun. Prefers sandy/loam soil. The fruit appears in fall. *Fruit type:* cone. ZONE 6.

Pinus elliottii
SLASH PINE
This native is one of the most rapid-growing, early-maturing eastern trees. *Height:* to 100ft; likes sun. Prefers sandy/moist soil. The fruit appears in fall. *Fruit type:* conc. ZONE 8.

Pinus palustris
LONGLEAF PINE
This native tree grows very well near the sea. It is often used as a nest site and is a choice food for the cardinal, brown-headed nuthatch, and tufted titmouse. *Height:* to 125ft; likes sun. Prefers sandy soil. The fruit appears in fall. *Fruit type:* cone. ZONE 7.

Pinus virginiana
VIRGINIA PINE
This native tree is often used as a nest site. Its seeds are a choice food for the bobwhite, cardinal, Carolina chickadee, brown-headed nuthatch, and song sparrow. *Height:* to 40ft; likes sun. Prefers dry/drained soil. The fruit appears in fall. *Fruit type:* cone. ZONE 5.

Sabal palmetto
CABBAGE PALMETTO
This branchless tree grows in prairies, marshes, pinelands, and disturbed soils. It produces clusters of small black fruits that are frequently eaten by many species, including the northern bobwhite, cardinal, and eastern phoebe. *Height:* to 80ft; likes sun. Prefers sandy soil. The fruit appears in late fall. *Fruit type:* black drupe. ZONE 9A.

Serenoa repens
SAW PALMETTO
This hardy Florida native is the only native palm with branching habit. Its trunk often grows horizontal and creeping. It requires little maintenance, and will thrive in poor soils. The leaves are attractive fan-shaped blades, ranging from 2 – 3ft in diameter. The round, egg-shaped fruit provides food for many species. *Height:* to 23ft; likes sun. Prefers sandy soil. The fruit appears in late fall through winter. *Fruit type:* bluish-black drupe. ZONE 9.

Tsuga canadensis
EASTERN HEMLOCK
See Northeast region listing, p.92.

Vaccinium arboreum
FARKLEBERRY
The fruits of this native tree are eaten by many birds, and are especially favored by the mockingbird. *Height:* to 20ft; likes sun/shade. Prefers dry/drained soil. The fruit appears in early fall. *Fruit type:* black berry. ZONE 6.

Viburnum rufidulum
RUSTY BLACKHAW
This semievergreen native tree is the preferred food of the eastern bluebird and cedar waxwing. *Height:* 16 - 18ft; likes sun. Prefers sandy/loam soil. The fruit appears in summer through fall. *Fruit type:* blue-black drupe. ZONE 6.

TALL DECIDUOUS TREES

Acer rubrum
RED MAPLE
See Northeast region listing, p.92.

Acer saccharum
SUGAR MAPLE
See Northeast region illus. listing, p.86.

Betula nigra
RIVER BIRCH
A native tree that has an open form. It is resistant to drought and does well where other plants cannot grow. Its flowers are catkins that appear mid spring. Its tan seeds are the favorite food of the pine siskin and redpolls, and the fox and tree sparrow. *Height:* 50 – 75ft; likes sun/partial shade. The fruit appears in early summer. *Fruit type:* seed. ZONE 5.

Carya aquatica
BITTER PECAN
This native tree, also known as water hickory, provides food for the wood duck and mallard. *Height:* to 100ft; likes sun. Prefers moist soil. The fruit appears in fall. *Fruit type:* nut. ZONE 7.

Carya illinoinensis
PECAN
This native is the largest of all the hickories. It provides a favorite food of the wood duck, and its nuts are eaten by at least 9 other species. *Height:* to 150ft; likes sun. Prefers dry/moist/drained soil. The fruit appears in early fall. *Fruit type:* nut. ZONE 6.

Celtis occidentalis
COMMON HACKBERRY
See Prairies and Plains region illus. listing, p.123.

Crataegus brachyacantha
BLUEBERRY HAWTHORN
This native tree is frequently used as a nest site. At least 36 species eat the fruit of hawthorns. *Height:* to 40ft; likes sun/half sun. Prefers sandy/loam soil. The fruit appears in summer through fall. *Fruit type:* bright blue/black pome. ZONE 8.

Morus rubra
RED MULBERRY
See Northeast region illus. listing, p.86.

Quercus coccinea
SCARLET OAK
See Northeast region listing, p.93.

Quercus falcata
SPANISH RED OAK
This native tree is a frequent nest site for hawks and other species, and is a choice food for the northern bobwhite, common grackle, brown thrasher, and red-headed woodpecker. *Height:* to 80ft; likes sun/half sun. Prefers dry/sandy/clay soil. The fruit appears in fall. *Fruit type:* acorn. ZONE 7.

Quercus marilandica
BLACKJACK OAK
Many of the birds listed above are attracted to this native tree. *Height:* to 30ft; likes sun/half sun. Prefers dry/sandy/sterile soil. The fruit appears in fall. *Fruit type:* acorn. ZONE 6.

Quercus michauxii
SWAMP CHESTNUT OAK
A native tree that attracts many birds that eat its fruit and nest in its branches. *Height:* 60 – 80ft; likes sun/half sun. Prefers moist soil. The fruit appears in fall. *Fruit type:* acorn. ZONE 6.

Quercus nigra
WATER OAK
Native. *Height:* 60 – 70ft; likes sun/half sun. Prefers moist soil. The fruit appears in fall. *Fruit type:* acorn. ZONE 6.

Quercus palustris
PIN OAK
See Northeast region listing, p.93.

Quercus phellos
WILLOW OAK
Native. *Height:* 60 – 80ft; likes sun/half sun. Prefers drained soil. The fruit appears in fall. *Fruit type:* acorn. ZONE 6.

Quercus prinus
CHESTNUT OAK
Native. *Height:* 60 – 80ft; likes sun/half sun. Prefers dry/sandy/gravelly soil. The fruit appears in fall. *Fruit type:* acorn. ZONE 6.

Quercus rubra
NORTHERN RED OAK
See Northeast region listing, p.93.

Quercus stellata
POST OAK
Native. *Height:* 40 – 50ft; likes sun/half

sun. Prefers dry/sterile soil. The fruit appears in fall. *Fruit type:* acorn. ZONE 5.

Quercus velutina
BLACK OAK
See Northeast region listing, p.93.

Quercus virginiana
LIVE OAK
This symbol of the south is a very important tree for wildlife. Its nutritious nuts are an excellent food source for many bird species and mammals. It is salt-tolerant, and makes an ideal choice for coastal properties. It has dark green leaves. *Height:* to 50ft; likes sun/partial shade. Prefers sandy soil. The fruit appears in early fall. *Fruit type:* acorn. ZONE 8.

Taxodium distichum
COMMON BALDCYPRESS
This native tree has a conical habit, with needles that occur in a spiral in spring and drop from the branches by mid-fall. Purplish brown cones appear in early October. It is a frequently used nest tree for the red-shouldered hawk, egrets, and small land birds. Height: 75 – 100ft; likes sun/partial shade. Prefers a variety of soil. The fruit appears in mid fall. Fruit type: cone. ZONE 5.

SMALL DECIDUOUS TREES

Chionanthus retusus
CHINESE FRINGETREE
The datelike seeds of this exotic tree are eaten by many species. *Height:* 20 – 25ft; likes sun/shade. Prefers rich/acid soil. The fruit appears in fall. *Fruit type:* dark blue drupe. ZONE 6.

Chionanthus virginicus
WHITE FRINGETREE
This native tree tolerates city conditions. Its fruit is eaten by many species, particularly, in more rural areas, the pileated woodpecker. *Height:* 20 – 25ft; likes sun/half sun. Prefers moist/drained soil. The fruit appears in fall. *Fruit type:* dark blue drupe. ZONE 5.

Cornus alternifolia
PAGODA DOGWOOD
See Northeast region illus. listing, p.89.

Cornus florida
FLOWERING DOGWOOD
See Northeast region illus. listing, p.85.

Crataegus marshallii
PARSLEY HAWTHORN
The thorny thickets of this native tree provide good cover for birds. *Height:* 5 – 25ft; likes sun. Prefers swampy soil. The fruit appears in late summer through winter. *Fruit type:* bright red pome. ZONE 6.

Crataegus phaenopyrum
WASHINGTON HAWTHORN
A native tree that has flat-topped white flower clusters that appear in early summer, followed by orange-red fruits that persist over winter until the following spring. The fruits are eaten by the cedar waxwing, California thrasher, northern mockingbird, and many other species. *Height:* 20 – 35ft; Likes full sun; prefers dry soil, but does well in a variety of soils. The fruit appears in early fall. *Fruit type:* pome. ZONE 5.

Malus spp.
FLOWERING CRABAPPLE
See Northeast region illus. listing, p.85.

Myrica cerifera
WAX MYRTLE
See Pacific Coast region illus. listing, p.160.

Ostrya virginia
AMERICAN HOP HORNBEAM
See Northeast region listing, p.93.

Prunus americana
AMERICAN PLUM
See Prairies and Plains region illus. listing, p.122.

Prunus angustifolia
CHICKASAW PLUM
A native tree with fleshy purple fruit that is eaten by the American robin and northern mockingbird. *Height:* to 15ft; likes partial sun. Prefers moist and well-drained soil. The fruit appears in summer. *Fruit type:* yellow-red drupe. ZONE 6.

Quercus chapmanii
CHAPMAN OAK
This native tree covers wide areas with its shrubby growth, giving much shelter and food to many birds. It has an annual acorn crop. *Height:* to 25ft; likes sun. Prefers well-drained soil. The fruit matures in the first season. *Fruit type:* acorn. ZONE 9.

Quercus incana
BLUEJACK OAK
This native tree is a very plentiful acorn producer, providing a choice food of the northern bobwhite and rufous-sided

towhee. *Height:* to 20ft; likes sun/half sun. Prefers dry/sandy soil. The fruit appears in fall. *Fruit type:* acorn. ZONE 8.

Rhamnus caroliniana
CAROLINA BUCKTHORN
The berries of this native tree are eaten by many songbirds, especially the catbird. *Height:* 25 – 35ft; likes sun/shade. Prefers moist/drained soil. The fruit appears in fall. *Fruit type:* red/black drupe. ZONE 6.

Sorbus americana
AMERICAN MOUNTAINASH
See Northeast region illus. listing, p.84.

Sorbus aucuparia
EUROPEAN MOUNTAINASH
See Northeast region listing, p.94.

Viburnum nudum
POSSUM HAW VIBURNUM
This deciduous native tree provides good protection for many species in areas with heavy rainfall. *Height:* to 20ft; likes sun. Prefers swampy/sandy/acid soil. The fruit appears in fall. *Fruit type:* pink to blue drupe. ZONE 7.

EVERGREEN SHRUBS

Cotoneaster dammeri
BEARBERRY COTONEASTER
An exotic. *Height:* to 1ft; likes sun/half sun. Prefers drained soil. The fruit appears in fall through winter. *Fruit type:* red pome. ZONE 6.

Cotoneaster franchettii
FRANCHET COTONEASTER
See Prairies and Plains region illus. listing, p.125.

Gaylussacia brachycera
BOX HUCKLEBERRY
See Northeast region listing, p.94.

Ilex coriacea
LARGE GALLBERRY
Native. *Height:* to 8ft; likes varied light. Prefers sandy/acid soil. The fruit appears in fall. *Fruit type:* black berry. ZONE 7.

Ilex myrtifolia
MYRTLE DAHOON
Native. *Height:* to 23ft; likes varied light. Prefers sandy/acid soil. The fruit appears in fall through winter. *Fruit type:* red/orange berry. ZONE 7B.

Juniperus chinensis
CHINESE JUNIPER
See Northeast region listing, p.94.

Juniperus conferta
SHORE JUNIPER
This exotic shrub is very tolerant of salt, and provides good ground shelter. Plant male and female plants for fruit. *Height:* to 1ft; likes sun/half sun. Prefers moist/drained soil. The fruit appears in late spring through summer. *Fruit type:* blue berry. ZONE 6.

Prunus caroliniana
CAROLINA CHERRY LAUREL
This native shrub is a choice food of the bluebird, mockingbird, robin, and cedar waxwing. *Height:* to 18ft; likes varied light. Prefers varied soil. The fruit is persistent. *Fruit type:* black berry. ZONE 7.

Quercus minima
DWARF LIVE OAK
The acorns of this native shrub are a favorite food of the wild turkey. *Height:* to 3ft; likes varied light. Prefers sandy/clay soil. The fruit appears in late summer. *Fruit type:* acorn. ZONE 10.

Sabal minor
DWARF PALMETTO
This native shrub provides good songbird food, and is an excellent nest site for ground-nesting birds, such as the ovenbird and northern bobwhite. *Height:* to 8ft; likes sun. Prefers varied soil. The fruit appears all year round. *Fruit type:* black berry. ZONES 8 – 9.

Taxus canadensis
CANADIAN YEW
See Northeast region listing, p.94.

Vaccinium myrsinites
GROUND BLUEBERRY
This native shrub is among the most important summer and early fall food sources for the ruffed grouse. *Height:* to 3ft; likes sun. Prefers drained/sandy soil. The fruit appears in late spring. *Fruit type:* purple/black berry. ZONE 7.

Viburnum obovatum
WALTER'S VIBURNUM
This is a fast-growing native tree with a broad, spreading crown. In spring, the showy, whitish flowers emerge followed, in summer, by red/black fruit. Many species eat the fruit, including the cedar waxwing and northern flicker. *Height:* to 9ft; likes sun/partial shade. Prefers fertile soil. The fruit appears in late fall

through early spring. *Fruit type:* red/black berry. ZONE 9B.

DECIDUOUS SHRUBS

Alnus rugosa
SPECKLED ALDER
See Northeast region listing, p.94.

Amelanchier arborea
SERVICEBERRY
See Northeast region illus. listing, p.84.

Aralia spinosa
DEVIL'S WALKINGSTICK
A native shrub with an open growth form. White flowers appear from mid summer, followed by black fruits. It provides a nest site for the cardinal and smooth-billed ani. The fruits are eaten by the white-throated sparrow, and Swainson's and wood thrushes. *Height:* 35 – 50ft; likes sun/partial shade. Prefers a variety of soils. The fruit appears in late summer. *Fruit type:* black berry. ZONE 5.

Callicarpa americana
AMERICAN BEAUTYBERRY
This native deciduous shrub is an excellent choice for light-shade habitats. Small bluish flowers appear in leaf axils from early spring to early summer. At least 12 species consume the fruit, which are especially favored by the northern bobwhite during the winter. *Height:* 3 – 6ft; likes sun/partial shade. Prefers well-drained soil. The fruit appears in late summer. *Fruit type:* pink-purple berries. ZONE 6

Cephalanthus occidentalis
COMMON BUTTONBUSH
See Aquatic Plants listing, p.73.

Cornus amomum
SILKY DOGWOOD
See Northeast region listing, p. 96.

Cornus stolonifera
RED-OSIER DOGWOOD
See Northeast region illus. listing, p.90.

Euonymus alata
WINGED BURNING BUSH
This exotic deciduous shrub has bright red foliage in fall that makes it an attractive addition to a garden bed. It provides an excellent food source for the eastern bluebird, mockingbird, fox sparrow, and yellow-rumped warbler. *Height:* 8 – 15ft; likes sun/half sun. Prefers

moist/drained soil. The fruit appears in late summer. *Fruit type:* purple capsule. ZONE 4.

Gaylussacia dumosa
DWARF HUCKLEBERRY
See Northeast region listing, p.95.

Gaylussacia frondosa
BLACK DANGLEBERRY
See Northeast region listing, p.95.

Lindera benzoin
SPICEBUSH
See Northeast region illus. listing, p.88.

Lonicera fragrantissima
WINTER HONEYSUCKLE
This exotic deciduous shrub provides an excellent nesting site for many birds. It is very fragrant, as its name suggests, and it is the preferred food of the catbird and mockingbird. *Height:* 6 – 8ft; likes sun. Prefers drained soil. The fruit appears in fall through winter. *Fruit type:* red berry. ZONE 6.

Myrica pensylvanica
NORTHERN BAYBERRY
See Northeast region illus. listing, p.89.

Pyracantha coccinea
SCARLET FIRETHORN
See Northeast region listing, p.95.

Rhus glabra
SMOOTH SUMAC
See Northeast region listing, p.95.

Rhus typhina
STAGHORN SUMAC
See Northeast region illus. listing, p.90.

Rosa carolina
PASTURE ROSE
See Northeast region listing, p.95.

Rosa palustris
SWAMP ROSE
See Northeast region listing, p.95.

Rosa rugosa
RUGOSA ROSE
See Northeast region listing, p.96.

Rubus spp.
BLACKBERRIES
See Northeast region illus. listing, p.88.

Sambucus canadensis
AMERICAN ELDER
See Northeast region illus. listing, p.87.

Symphoricarpos orbiculatus
CORALBERRY
See Prairies and Plains region illus. listing, p.124.

Vaccinium corymbosum
HIGHBUSH BLUEBERRY
See Northeast region illus. listing, p.88.

Vaccinium stamineum
COMMON DEERBERRY
This native shrub provides important food for the ruffed grouse, bobwhite, and other ground-feeding birds *Height:* 6ft; likes sun/shade. Prefers dry/drained soil. The fruit appears in late summer. *Fruit type:* green/purple berry. ZONE 5.

Viburnum acerifolium
MAPLELEAF VIBURNUM
See Northeast region listing, p.95.

Viburnum alnifolium
HOBBLEBUSH VIBURNUM
See Northeast region listing, p.95.

VINES

Berchemia scandens
ALABAMA SUPPLEJACK
This deciduous native vine climbs from 15 – 20ft. At least 14 species eat its fruit. Likes sun. Prefers moist/rich soil. The fruit appears in summer through fall. *Fruit type:* blue/black drupe. ZONE 6.

Cocculus carolinus
CAROLINA MOONSEED
The pea-sized fruit of this native often persists through winter. Only the female plant bears fruit, which is eaten by the brown thrasher, mockingbird, and eastern phoebe. This vine is deciduous to semievergreen. Likes sun. Prefers moist/dry/drained soil. The fruit appears in late summer. *Fruit type:* red drupe. ZONE 7.

Parthenocissus quinquefolia
VIRGINIA CREEPER
This native deciduous vine produces small berries that are a favorite food of at least 35 species including thrushes, woodpeckers, vireos, and warblers. It will climb the tallest trees, trellis, and walls, but be careful of its tendency to smother small shrubs. Turns a brilliant crimson color in fall. Likes sun/shade. Hardy. Prefers moist/drained soil. The fruit appears in late summer and lasts through winter. *Fruit type:* berry. ZONE 4.

Smilax glauca
SAWBRIER
See Northeast region listing, p.96.

Smilax laurifolia
LAUREL GREENBRIER
This native evergreen vine provides excellent cover, food, and nest sites for many birds, including the northern flicker, pileated woodpecker, ruffed grouse, and red-bellied woodpecker. Likes sun/half sun. Prefers moist soil. The fruit appears in late summer and persists. *Fruit type:* black berry. ZONE 7.

Vitis aestivalis
SUMMER GRAPE
See Northeast region listing, p.96.

Vitis cinerea
SWEET WINTER GRAPE
These native deciduous grapevines that overtop other plants provide nest sites for birds such as the cardinal, catbird, and brown thrasher, which also use grape bark in their nests. Likes sun/shade. Prefers moist/drained soil. The fruit appears in fall. *Fruit type:* black/purple berry. ZONE 5.

Vitis labrusca
FOX GRAPE
See Northeast region listing, p.97.

Vitis vulpina
FROST GRAPE
See Northeast region listing, p.97.

GROUNDCOVERS

Arctostaphylos uva-ursi
BEARBERRY
See Northeast region illus. listing, p.91.

Cornus canadensis
BUNCHBERRY
See Mountains and Deserts region illus. listing, p.143.

Cotoneaster adpressa
CREEPING COTONEASTER
See Northeast region listing, p.97.

Fragaria chiloensis
BEACH STRAWBERRY
See Northeast region listing, p.97.

Fragaria virginiana
WILD STRAWBERRY
See Northeast region listing, p.97.

Juniperus horizontalis
CREEPING JUNIPER
See Prairies and Plains region illus. listing, p.127.

Prairies and Plains Region

THE EXTREMES of heat and cold in summer and winter in this region can make it inhospitable to birds. The ideal garden should include trees and shrubs that provide shelter, and bear fruit in fall and winter.

SIZE
6 – 7½"

Blue Grosbeak

GUIRACA CAERULEA

A member of the cardinal family, this bird forages for insects, weed seeds, and wild fruit. It will nest in young orchard trees.

SIZE
5¼"

Chipping Sparrow

SPIZELLA PASSERINA

This bird is a common yard species. It often feeds on lawns, and nests in evergreens and shrubs near houses. Its diet consists of seeds and insects.

Colorado spruce
Picea pungens
This evergreen provides excellent nesting sites, and many birds eat its seeds, including the pine siskin. *(See page 188.)*

Ponderosa pine
Pinus ponderosa
A huge tree that develops a trunk diameter of 5 – 8ft, this pine is good to use in a windbreak on larger properties. *(See page 123.)*

Ninebark
Physocarpus opulifolius
A deciduous shrub grown for its foliage and its white or pale pink flowers. *(See page 159.)*

Gray dogwood
Cornus racemosa
A thicket-forming shrub with white fruit on scarlet stems, it is a favorite of many birds, including the eastern kingbird. *(See page 123.)*

Water
A landscaped pond will become a breeding ground for insects, and thus attract insect-eating birds that might not otherwise visit the garden throughout the year.

SIZE
8"

Bur oak
Quercus macrocarpa

This grand native oak usually bears acorns in fall and tolerates city conditions, making it a good choice for the larger backyard. *(See page 93.)*

EASTERN KINGBIRD
TYRANNUS TYRANNUS

Kingbirds mostly feed on flying insects, catching them in midair, and they have a fondness for bees. They also pluck berries and seeds from trees and shrubs such as the gray dogwood.

Coralberry
Symphoricarpos obiculatos

The fruit of this deciduous, bushy shrub persists through winter. Its deep purplish red berries are a favorite of the American robin and the blue grosbeak. *(See page 124.)*

Eastern redcedar
Juniperus virginiana

At least 54 species are known to eat redcedar fruit, including the cedar waxwing, gray catbird, northern mockingbird, sparrows and grosbeaks. *(See page 85.)*

FOOD AND SHELTER GARDEN

Resident and migrating birds will be attracted by the plants in this plan. Spruce, pine, and oak trees provide constant food and nest sites, and shrubs such as coralberry provide juicy berries. The small pond is a good source of both water and insects.

Cockspur hawthorn
Crataegus crus-galli

This native, small, deciduous tree is a prolific fruiter, and is a favorite of many birds, especially the cedar waxwing and sparrows. *(See page 122.)*

COMMON BIRDS

THE NORTHERN part of this region is noted for its howling winds, long winters, deep snows, and subzero temperatures. These icy conditions force most birds southward, where they find insects and seeds to eat. Most summer residents, such as orchard orioles and great crested flycatchers, migrate to Central America, while others, such as dickcissels and bobolinks, winter farther south in the tropical climates of Argentina and Venezuela.

This land was once dominated by native prairie grasses, but it is now planted with crops of wheat, oats, corn, and milo. These crops help feed short-distance migrants, such as the yellow-headed blackbird, Brewer's blackbird, Harris' sparrow, and lark sparrow, that stay within the United States throughout the year. The gardener who lives on the northern plains or the prairies region south to Kansas can help birds survive the rigors of winter by planting windbreaks and shrubs along property borders to provide year-round cover.

SIZE
13 – 14"

NORTHERN FLICKER
Colaptes auratus 🦅🏠

NEST *Excavated in a live or dead tree, usually located between 2 and 6 feet above the ground. Found also in birdhouses, fence posts, and utility holes. Entrance hole is 3 inches across, but the cavity size varies.*
SONG *The call is a loud and rapidly repeated wick-wicka-wick, and a single kee-yer.*
ATTRACTED TO *the fruits of elderberry and blueberry shrubs and dogwood trees, and the seeds of clover and grasses. Wild strawberries are another favorite source of food.*

LARK BUNTING
Calamospiza melanocorys ✿🦅🏠

NEST *A loosely constructed cup of grasses, and rootlets placed on the ground, usually in a slight depression. Often lined with plant down.*
SONG *A rich combination of trills with clear and harsh notes.*
ATTRACTED TO *the seeds of weeds, including pigweed, knotweed, dandelion, Russian thistle, and verbena. The main diet is of insects, including grasshoppers, weevils, and beetles.*

SIZE
5½ – 7½"

GRAY CATBIRD
Dumetella carolinensis

SIZE
8½ – 9¼"

NEST *A bulky structure of twigs and coarse plant materials, with a deep inner cup of rootlets. Located 3 to 10 feet high in dense thickets.*

SONG *A catlike mewing. Also a chattery, disjointed song similar to the mockingbird and thrasher, but without phrase repetition.*

ATTRACTED TO *blackberries, highbush blueberries, mulberries, spicebushes, sumacs, and many other wild fruits; also eats ants, beetles, and caterpillars.*

INDIGO BUNTING
Passerina cyanea

NEST *Usually found low to the ground in dense cover. It is a compact and well-woven cup of dried grasses, bark strips, twigs, and weed stems anchored to a bush, sapling, or blackberry tangle.*

SIZE
5¼ – 5¾"

SONG *High-pitched and strident couplets, each on a different pitch, that descend and weaken at the end.*

ATTRACTED TO *the seeds of goldenrod, aster, thistle, dandelion, and grasses. It sometimes eats white proso millet at backyard feeders.*

BREWER'S BLACKBIRD
Euphagus cyanocephalus

NEST *Usually made of interlaced twigs and coarse grass reinforced with mud or dried cow dung. Often lined with rootlets and fine grass. The nest is found on the ground in thick vegetation, but is also located in tall conifers, sometimes as high as 150 feet above the ground.*

SONG *Trills, squeaks, and whistled notes. Sometimes, a creaky-sounding ksheeik.*

ATTRACTED TO *the seeds of sunflower plants, wild cherry trees, and grasses (for nesting). It also eats insects, waste grain, and weed seeds.*

SIZE
8 – 9½"

YELLOW-BREASTED CHAT
Icteria virens

NEST *The female builds a large cup of dead leaves, grass, and bark, concealed in dense shrubs. Usually found between 2 and 6 feet above the ground. Several pairs may nest in a loose colony.*

SONG *An unusual procession of clear but distorted whistles, scolds, mews, and cackles.*

SIZE
7 – 7½"

ATTRACTED TO *the fruit of blackberry raspberry, strawberry, and elderberry shrubs.*

EVENING GROSBEAK
Coccothraustes vespertinus

NEST *A frail shallow cup of rootlets and twigs, built by the female and well hidden in the foliage of a conifer tree, about 20 to 60 feet above the ground.*

SONG *A brief musical warble and the call is peeear. The evening grosbeak gives a variety of chip notes almost constantly.*

SIZE
7½ – 8½"

ATTRACTED TO *the fruits of dogwood and wild cherry trees, and to the maple tree and sunflower plant for their seeds.*

MOURNING DOVE
Zanaida macroura

NEST *A loose stick platform, with little or no lining. It is so thin that the eggs can be seen through it. Arranged in the crotch or the branch of a tree, sometimes even in low vines. Usually found between 5 and 25 feet above the ground.*

SIZE
11 – 13"

SONG *A mournful coo-ing, oo-awoo-woo-cwoo.*

ATTRACTED TO *weed seeds as their principal food source, including yellow woodsorrel and foxtail grasses. Mourning doves also eat spilled grains, pine nuts, and pokeberries.*

YELLOW-HEADED BLACKBIRD
Xanthocephalus xanthocephalus

NEST *The female builds the nest from strands of aquatic vegetation, woven around upright marsh plants. These form a basket usually located between 6 inches and 3 feet above the water. Nests are often found in colonial groups.*
SONG *Like rusty hinges; a raspy, cacophonous jumble of sounds.*
ATTRACTED TO *oats, corn, and other grains, plus the seeds of bristlegrass and ragweed. It also eats beetles, grasshoppers, caterpillers, and other insects found in the marshland.*

SIZE
9 – 11"

AMERICAN KESTREL
Falco sparvarius

SIZE
9 – 12"

NEST *This bird does not build its own nest, but uses old woodpecker holes and any other cavities it finds empty, including niches on buildings or a natural tree cavity.*
SONG *A quick, high-pitched klee-klee-klee.*
ATTRACTED TO *dead snags, which often contain nest holes left by flickers and woodpeckers. It eats grasshoppers, mice, and reptiles.*

BROWN THRASHER
Toxostoma rufum

NEST *A loose construction of twigs, dry leaves, vines, and grass stems, occasionally found on the ground but usually in a low shrub or tree up to 10 feet above the ground.*
SONG *Similar to the mockingbird and catbird. A musical succession of bold and abrupt phrases sung in pairs. Sometimes mimics other birds.*
ATTRACTED TO *the fruit of common blackberry, blueberry, elderberry, viburnum, and serviceberry shrubs, wild strawberry plants, and the fox grape vine.*

SIZE
10½ – 12"

GREAT CRESTED FLYCATCHER
Myiarchus crinitus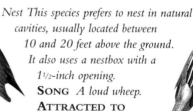

Nest *This species prefers to nest in natural cavities, usually located between 10 and 20 feet above the ground. It also uses a nestbox with a 1½-inch opening.*
SONG *A loud wheep.*
ATTRACTED TO *insects mostly, and mulberries, cherries, wild grapes, and sassafras.*

SIZE
8 – 9"

BARN SWALLOW
Hirundo rustica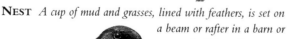

SIZE
6 – 7½"

NEST *A cup of mud and grasses, lined with feathers, is set on a beam or rafter in a barn or an outbuilding. Barn swallows also like to nest under bridges. Their nests are usually built in small colonies.*
SONG *A pleasing quiet twittering. The call is a repeated swit-swit-swit.*
ATTRACTED TO *foliage of trees and shrubs in search of insects.*

WHITE-THROATED SPARROW
Zonotrichia albicollis

NEST *A cup-shaped structure of grasses, pine needles, and twigs, lined with rootlets, grasses, and deer hair. Frequently located on the ground in a hummock under a low shrub.*
SONG *A whistle of old Sam Peabody-Peabody-Peabody.*
ATTRACTED TO *the seeds of ragweed, smartweed, bristlegrass, oats, corn, grapes, and strawberries. Also eats cracked corn and millets at feeders, and insects found under leaves.*

SIZE
6½ – 7"

ORCHARD ORIOLE
Icterus spurius

NEST *A woven basket of grasses suspended from a horizontal fork in a branch of a tree or shrub. Usually located about 10 and 20 feet above the ground, and often in colonies.*
SONG *A quick robinlike burst of varied notes and whistles, ending on a downward slur.*
ATTRACTED TO *the fruit of the red mulberry shrub, but its main diet is of insects, including ants and crickets.*

SIZE
6 – 7¼"

DICKCISSEL
Spiza americana

SIZE
6 – 7"

NEST *A bulky cup of weed stems, leaves, and grasses, lined with very fine grass, hair, and rootlets. Usually built between 2 and 14 feet above the ground, in a tree, hedge, or grass clump.*
SONG *Repeats its name in a staccato fashion, singing a cheery dick-dick dick-cissel.*
ATTRACTED TO *weed seeds of bristlegrass and ragweed. It mainly feeds on the ground, eating spiders and insects.*

AMERICAN CROW
Corvus brachyrhynchos

NEST *A bulky bowl of sticks and vines, lined with leaves and moss, usually hidden in the bark of a tree. Generally located between 25 and 75 feet above the ground; sometimes on the ground.*
SONG *A loud, repeated caw-caw-caw.*
ATTRACTED TO *the fruit of many shrubs and to the seeds of grain. It will eat anything edible, including insects, eggs, nestlings, and small reptiles.*

SIZE
17 – 21"

BROWN-HEADED COWBIRD
Molothrus ater

NEST *The female lays her eggs in nests of other birds, usually laying one egg in each nest, but she may lay 10 – 12 eggs in a season, each in a different nest. Host birds, such as warblers and sparrows, incubate the eggs for 11 – 12 days, and then feed the cowbird chicks at the expense of their own chicks.*
SONG *A high-pitched whistle. Also a glug-glu-glee.*
ATTRACTED TO *corn, wheat, oats, buckwheat, and the seeds of weeds such as ragweed, panic grass, and dandelion. It eats the fruit of common blackberry and huckleberry shrubs, and the cedar berry. This species also eats many insects, such as caterpillars, flies, beetles, and ants.*

SIZE
7 – 8"

LARK SPARROW
Chondestes grammacus

NEST *A good-sized structure made of grasses and plant stems. Usually found on the ground in a shallow depression under a tree or shady plant. Sometimes located in a shrub.*
SONG *A series of liquid trills, buzzes, and churrs introduced by two clear notes.*
ATTRACTED TO *the seeds of many varieties of brittlegrass, panicgrass, ragweed, sunflower, and wheat. About half of its diet consists of insects.*

SIZE
5½ – 6½"

RECOMMENDED PLANTS

THIS REGION stretches from northern Canada to the Mexican border. The eastern half of this area was once covered by vast, tall grass prairies, while short grass plains extended to the base of the Rocky Mountains and south into Texas.

These days, the prairies are croplands and the plains support cattle-ranching. Only small remnants remain of these once magnificent native grassland communities, and the birds which used to call these native habitats home are severely diminished.

In the north, select hardy plants that can combat the wind and cold. Planting conifers on the northwest side of the house offers protection from the bone-chilling winds that usually originate from that side. On the south side, plant deciduous trees such as oaks and maples. These will keep the house cool during the heat of the summer, and in the winter, when they have dropped their leaves, will allow the warming effect of sunlight to reach windows on the south-face of the house.

More plant choices are available in the south of the area, but the plants must be able to tolerate extreme heat and arid conditions.

TREES

AMERICAN PLUM
Prunus americana

This is a small, deciduous tree. It produces flat-topped white flower clusters in late spring, and bears red drupes in summer through fall. Very attractive backyard addition. Likes sun/partial shade. Prefers moist, well-drained soil. Height: 20 – 35 feet, spreading as broad as it is tall. Fully hardy. Zone 6.

Attracts *many species to the fruit, including the bobwhite, robin, ring-necked pheasant, and red-headed woodpecker. The American plum is occasionally used as a nest site.*

COCKSPUR HAWTHORN
Crataegus crus-galli

A deciduous, flat-topped tree that makes an ideal landscape form, with its rounded top, attractive white flowers, and colorful yellow-orange foliage. Has shoots armed with long, curved thorns and oval, glossy, dark green leaves that turn bright crimson in fall. Begins blooming in early spring through summer, producing clusters of white to red flowers. The red to green pomes mature from late summer through mid winter. Likes full sun. Prefers well-drained or rocky soil. Height: to 30 feet. Hardy. Zone 5.

Attracts *more than 20 species to the fruit. It is a favorite of the cedar waxwing, fox sparrow, and ruffed grouse. Eight species use this tree for cover or nesting habitat.*

COMMON HACKBERRY
Celtis occidentalis

A native, deciduous, spreading tree that grows on rocky hillsides, open pastures, and moist stream banks. Oval, sharply toothed, bright green leaves turn yellow in fall, when they are accompanied by purple drupe fruits. These may survive through winter if they are not consumed by birds. Drought-resistant. Likes sun. Prefers alkaline soil, but is adaptable. Height: 30 – 50 feet. Fully hardy. Zones 2 – 9.

GRAY DOGWOOD
Cornus racemosa

A common, thicket-forming shrub that turns a beautiful magenta in early through mid fall. Abundant clusters of white fruit sit on scarlet stems set against the dark reddish foliage. Gray dogwood grows well on a variety of sites, giving it great potential as a wonderful addition to backyard planting. Likes full sun/partial shade. Prefers fertile, well-drained soil. Height: rarely over 9 feet. Hardy. Zone 5.

PONDEROSA PINE
Pinus ponderosa

A huge, upright conifer, native to the west. Usually grows in large single-species stands, but can be planted in shelterbelts to provide cover year-round for birds and to serve as an effective windbreak. First produces seed when about 20 years old. Good seed crops occur every 2 to 5 years. Likes sun/partial shade. Tolerates many types of soil. Height: to 150 feet, with trunk diameter of 5 – 8 feet. Hardy. Zones 5 – 8.

Attracts *at least 24 species which consume the fruit. It is especially favored by the northern flicker, northern mockingbird, Swainson's thrush, and cardinal.*

Attracts *at least 17 species that are known to eagerly consume the delicious fruit, including the northern flicker, downy woodpecker, cardinal, and eastern bluebird.*

Attracts *many birds, including the band-tailed pigeon and Lewis' woodpecker, for which these tiny, abundant seeds (12,000 to a pound) are an important food source.*

SHRUBS

SARGENT CRABAPPLE
Malus sargentii

A deciduous, small tree or shrub. Oval, dark green leaves are sometimes lobed. Profusion of white flowers in late spring, followed by long-lasting, deep red fruit. For luring greatest variety of birds, it is best to select trees that have small fruits, since these are most readily plucked and swallowed. Likes full sun/tolerates partial shade. Prefers a variety of soils. Height: 6 – 14 feet. Fully hardy. Zones 4 – 8.

COMMON CHOKECHERRY
Prunus virginiana

A deciduous shrub or small tree, with dense spikes of small, star-shaped white flowers from mid- to late spring, followed by dark purple-red fruit. Wilted leaves of all cherries are poisonous to livestock. Likes full sun. Thrives in a variety of soils. Height: 6 – 30 feet. Hardy. Zones 3 – 8.

CORALBERRY
Symphoricarpos orbiculatus

This deciduous, bushy, dense shrub has white or pink flowers in late summer and early fall, followed by round, deep purplish red berries. Fruit persists through winter. Oval leaves are dark green. Plant it along property borders to form dense hedges or as isolated clumps. This sturdy shrub clings to steep slopes which makes it an ideal planting to slow soil erosion. Likes full sun/partial shade. Thrives in a variety of soils, from dry and rocky to moist and rich. Height: 2 – 5 feet. Fully hardy. Zones 3 – 9.

Attracts *a great variety of birds, including the cedar waxwing, robin, mockingbird, gray catbird, and evening grosbeak, that eat the small fruit.*

Attracts *at least 43 species in this region that readily consume the tart-tasting fruit. It is favored by the eastern bluebird, ruffed and sharp-tailed grouse, and prairie-chickens.*

Attracts *hummingbirds that visit the bell-shaped flowers. At least 14 other species eat the colorful fruit, including the evening grosbeak, pine grosbeak, and American robin.*

FRANCHET COTONEASTER
Cotoneaster franchettii

An evergreen or semievergreen arching shrub grown for its foliage, flowers, and fruit. Provides good ground shelter for birds. Leaves are gray-green, and white beneath. Produces small, 5-petaled, pink-tinged, white flowers in early summer, then a profusion of oblong, bright orange-red fruits in fall. Fireblight is a common problem. Likes sun/partial shade. Prefers well-drained soil, and is particularly useful for dry sites. Height: 10 feet, and spreads to 10 feet. Fully hardy. Zones 7 – 9.

DESERT WILLOW
Chilopsis linearis

This fast-growing shrub (up to 3 feet in a season) is deciduous from midsummer through winter. It has long, narrow leaves 2 – 5 inches long. Produces rose or pink-purple trumpet-like flowers in mid- to late spring. Likes full sun. Height: 6 – 25 feet, spreading about as wide as tall. Hardy. Zone 6.

FLOWERING CURRANT
Ribes sanguineum

A deciduous, upright shrub grown for its edible fruit and flowers. It is easily grown in a variety of backyard situations. 'Pulborough Scarlet' bears tubular, deep red flowers in spring, sometimes followed by spherical, black fruit (currants), with a white bloom. Has aromatic, dark green leaves, with 3 – 5 lobes. Likes full sun. Prefers fertile, well-drained soil. Height: 6 feet, and can spread as broad as it is high. Fully hardy. Zones 6 – 8.

Attracts *a variety of birds, including the brown thrasher, gray catbird, American robin, and cedar waxwing, that consume the red fruit.*

Attracts *southwestern hummingbirds, including the black-chinned and broad-tailed, to the nectar-filled, trumpetlike flowers.*

Attracts *the rufous hummingbird as well as other hummingbirds that obtain nectar from the flowers. The fruit is eaten by the northern flicker and Townsend's solitaire, among other species.*

OCOTILLO
Fouquieria splendens

This native, evergreen shrub is sometimes grown as a hedge. Produces clusters of red-orange flowers in the spring through summer. The trunk is heavily furrowed and covered with stout thorns. Likes full sun. Prefers well-drained soil. Height: 10 – 15 feet. Hardy. Zone 8.

SNOWBERRY
Symphoricarpos albus

This deciduous, thicket-forming shrub grows on rocky hillsides, and other sites that are too difficult for most shrubs. Berries ripen in late summer through early fall, and persist through winter. Good bird planting for hedges and property borders. Likes full sun/partial shade. Prefers well-drained, fertile soil. Height: 6 feet in good soil, but usually much smaller. Hardy. Zones 4 – 7.

THREE-LEAF SUMAC
Rhus trilobata

A deciduous, drought-resistant, deep-rooted shrub that makes an excellent shelterbelt planting. Deep green leaves, each with 3 oval leaflets, turn orange or reddish purple in fall. Tiny yellow flowers are borne in spring, before foliage, and are followed by spherical red fruit. Berries ripen in late summer through early fall. Likes full sun. Prefers limestone soil, but can tolerate a variety of sites. Height: 12 feet. Fully hardy. Zones 4 – 9.

Attracts *the hooded oriole and the ruby-throated, Anna's, and rufous hummingbirds, which come to eat the nectar of the vivid red-orange flowers in spring and summer.*

Attracts *many birds, including the ring-necked pheasant, American robin, cedar waxwing, and pine grosbeak, with the white berries, which are an important source of winter food.*

Attracts *at least 25 species that eat the red berries of the three-leaf sumac, including the evening grosbeak, American robin, northern bobwhite, and greater prairie-chicken.*

GROUNDCOVERS

CREEPING JUNIPER
Juniperus horizontalis

A prostrate or low-growing, creeping evergreen shrub with prickly needles that deter plant-nibbling deer, rabbits, and mice. There are many cultivars that do not have fruit, so look out for the small, blue juniper fruits on specimen plants. The prickly stems provide cover for ground-nesting birds. Likes full sun. Prefers well-drained soil. Height: to 12 inches. Hardy. Zone 4.

LITTLE BLUESTEM
Andropogon scoparius

This native, perennial grass of the prairies grows in tight clusters or bunches that form an excellent ground cover, and is suitable for both small patches and large areas in a backyard. Little bluestem has white seedheads that appear in fall, just as the foliage turns reddish amber. Likes full sun/partial shade. Prefers light, sandy, and well-drained soil. Height: to 12 inches. Hardy. Zone 4.

LOWBUSH BLUEBERRY
Vaccinium angustifium

Planted as the commercial blueberry of New England, this plant has great wildlife value, since no fewer than 37 species eat blueberries. A deciduous shrub, it usually grows in the dense, bushy form. In fall, the leaves turn a spectacular scarlet-orange before dropping. Likes full sun. Prefers acid, well-drained soil. Height: to 12 inches. Hardy. Zone 3.

Attracts *many birds, including the cedar waxwing, American robin, olive-backed thrush, and ring-necked pheasant, which favor the delicious small, blue juniper fruits.*

Attracts *sparrows and juncos, which often perch on the stalks and eat the white seedheads. The channels between bunches are also an excellent place for wildflowers to grow.*

Attracts *more than 37 species, and blueberries are a preferred food of 24 of these species, including the mockingbird, catbird, and thrush.*

OTHER GOOD PLANTS

EVERGREEN TREES

Juniperus ashei
OZARK WHITE CEDAR
This native is found in central to southwest Texas and is notable for its copious seed production, providing important food for the robin. *Height:* 6 – 20ft; likes sun. Prefers dry/sandy/gravel soil. The fruit appears all year round. *Fruit type:* blue berry. ZONE 7.

Juniperus monosperma
CHERRYSTONE JUNIPER
Rapid-growing for a juniper, this native provides excellent nesting cover. Only the female bears fruit, which is important food for the Gambel's quail and several species of songbird. *Height:* 20 – 30ft; likes sun. Prefers rocky soil. The fruit appears all year round. *Fruit type:* blue berry. ZONE 7.

Juniperus scopulorum
ROCKY MOUNTAIN JUNIPER
This drought-resistant native is similar in appearance to the eastern redcedar. It is not recommended for the eastern part of this region. *Height:* 30 – 40ft; likes sun. Prefers alkaline/dry/sandy soil. The fruit appears all year round. *Fruit type:* blue berry. ZONE 4.

Juniperus virginiana
EASTERN REDCEDAR
See Northeast region illus. listing, p.85.

Picea glauca var. densata
BLACK HILLS SPRUCE
Found on the northern plains, this native is more resistant to winter than the Colorado spruce (see page 92). *Height:* to 70ft; likes sun/half shade. Prefers moist soil. The fruit appears in fall. *Fruit type:* cone. ZONE 3.

Picea pungens
COLORADO SPRUCE
See Northeast region listing, p.92.

Pinus nigra
AUSTRIAN PINE
This exotic should only be planted where it will be protected from direct wind. It provides excellent cover and abundant seeds. Good for the northern plains.

Height: 70 – 90ft; likes sun/part shade. Prefers varied/sandy/poor soil. The fruit appears in fall through winter. *Fruit type:* cone. ZONE 4.

Pinus sylvestris
SCOTS PINE
This exotic is easy to grow in a variety of situations and produces good seed crops every 2 – 5 years. *Height:* 60 – 75ft; likes sun/half sun. Prefers a variety of drained soils. The fruit appears in early fall through late fall. *Fruit type:* cone. ZONE 3.

Tsuga heterophylla
WESTERN HEMLOCK
This native is an excellent choice for hedges or shady habitats. It has an abundant seed crop every 2 – 3 years, and is a preferred food of the pine siskin and chickadees. *Height:* 30 – 50ft; likes sun. Prefers dry/moist/drained soil. The fruit appears in fall. *Fruit type:* cone. ZONE 6.

Thuja occidentalis
EASTERN ARBORVITAE
See Northeast region listing, p.92.

DECIDUOUS TREES

Acer negundo
BOXELDER
See Northeast region listing, p.92.

Acer nigrum
BLACK MAPLE
The native black maple is closely related to the sugar maple (see page 86). The leaves have shallower sinuses than those of the sugar maple and the bark has deeper furrows. It flowers in spring. The fruits are readily eaten by the evening grosbeak, pine grosbeak, and bobwhite. *Height:* 75 - 100ft; likes sun. The fruit appears in fall. *Fruit type:* twin samara. ZONE 3.

Betula papyrifera
PAPER BIRCH
See Northeast region listing, p.92.

Betula nigra
RIVER BIRCH
See Northeast region listing, p.112.

Betula papyrifera var. humilis
ALASKAN PAPER BIRCH
This Alaskan variety is hardier and shorter than the eastern forms. Its seeds and buds are a favorite food of the ruffed grouse, pine siskin, and American goldfinch. *Height:* to 30ft; likes sun. Prefers

dry/moist soil. The fruit appears in late summer through early fall. *Fruit type:* samara. ZONE 1.

Carya illinoinensis
PECAN
See Southeast region listing, p.112.

Celtis laevigata
SUGAR HACKBERRY
See Southeast region illus. listing, p.107.

Celtis reticulata
NETLEAF HACKBERRY
The berries of this native are rich in calcium, and provide food for the Bullock's oriole, robin, roadrunner, and northern flicker. *Height:* to 21ft; likes sun. Prefers dry/moist/rich/drained soil. The fruit appears in spring. *Fruit type:* samara. ZONE 6.

Crataegus chrysocarpa
FIREBERRY HAWTHORN
A hardy native, it survives the harsh conditions of the northern plains well. As a group, hawthorns attract at least 36 species of fruit-eating birds, including the northern bobwhite, northern flicker, cedar waxwing, and robin. *Height:* to 13ft; likes sun. Prefers dry/moist/rocky soil. The fruit appears in early fall. *Fruit type:* red pome. ZONE 4.

Crataegus mollis
DOWNY HAWTHORN
A hardy native, it survives the harsh conditions of the northern plains well. *Height:* 15 – 25ft; likes sun. Prefers dry soil. The fruit appears in late summer through fall. *Fruit type:* red pome. ZONE 5.

Crataegus phaenopyrum
WASHINGTON HAWTHORN
This small, round-topped native is covered with white and pink flowers in spring, followed by an abundant crop of small red or orange fruits. Its dense, forked branches provide ideal nesting places for the robin, cardinal, blue jay, and other birds. The fruit is consumed by at least 18 species, including the cedar waxwing. *Height:* 20 – 30ft; likes sun. Prefers well-drained soil. Fruit appears late summer through late winter. *Fruit type:* red and orange pome. ZONE 5.

Crataegus succulenta
FLESHY HAWTHORN
This hardy native hawthorn survives the harsh climate conditions of the northern

plains. *Height:* to 15ft; likes sun. Prefers dry/moist/rocky soil. The fruit appears in early fall. *Fruit type:* red pome. ZONE 4.

Fraxinus pennsylvanica
GREEN ASH
See Northeast region listing, p.93.

Ilex decidua
POSSUM HAW
See Southeast region illus. listing, p.109.

Juglans nigra
BLACK WALNUT
See Northeast region listing, p.93.

Malus spp.
FLOWERING CRABAPPLE
See Northeast region illus. listing, p.85.

Malus pumila
COMMON APPLE
See Northeast region listing, p.93.

Morus microphylla
TEXAS MULBERRY
A thicket-forming native that does best in limestone soils. A male and female tree must be planted near each other to produce fruit successfully. A favorite of the Gambel's and harlequin quail and many species of songbird. *Height:* 10 – 20ft; likes sun. Prefers moist/drained soil. The fruit appears in spring. *Fruit type:* black compound drupe. ZONE 6.

Morus rubra
RED MULBERRY
See Northeast region illus. listing, p.86.

Populus deltoides
EASTERN COTTONWOOD
See Northeast region listing, p.93.

Populus sargentii
GREAT PLAINS COTTONWOOD
This native tree is frequently found along streams in western plains, and its buds are readily eaten by grouse. *Height:* 60 – 90ft; likes sun. Prefers moist soil. The fruit appears in spring through summer. *Fruit type:* capsule. ZONE 2.

Populus tremuloides
QUAKING ASPEN
See Northeast region listing, p.93.

Prunus pensylvanica
WILD RED CHERRY
See Northeast region listing, p.94.

Prunus serotina
BLACK CHERRY
See Southeast region illus. listing, p.104.

Quercus gambelii
GAMBEL OAK
This drought-tolerant native sometimes grows as a shrub. At least 63 species are known to eat acorns. *Height:* 15 – 35ft; likes sun. Prefers dry/drained soil. The fruit appears in fall. *Fruit type:* acorn. ZONE 6.

Quercus macrocarpa
BUR OAK
See Northeast region listing, p.93.

Quercus rubra
NORTHERN RED OAK
See Northeast region listing, p.93.

Quercus stellata
POST OAK
See Southeast region listing, p.113.

Salix amygdaloides
PEACH-LEAVED WILLOW
A native that provides excellent cover. Do not plant near underground plumbing since its roots may clog pipes. *Height:* 40 – 60ft; likes sun. Prefers moist soil. The fruit appears in spring. *Fruit type:* capsule. ZONE 5.

Salix discolor
PUSSY WILLOW
This native shrub is best known for its fuzzy catkins that add interest and color. It is extremely hardy. The buds are eaten by the pine grosbeak, wood duck, ruffed grouse, and redpolls. *Height:* to 25ft; likes sun/partial shade. Prefers wet or moist soil. The fruit appears in spring. *Fruit type:* capsule. ZONE 2.

Salix interior
SANDBAR WILLOW
Provides excellent cover, but do not plant near underground plumbing since roots may clog pipes. At least 23 species eat buds and tender twigs, including the ruffed, blue, spruce, and sharp-tailed grouse. *Height:* to 30ft; likes sun. Prefers moist/alluvial soil. The fruit appears in spring. *Fruit type:* capsule. ZONE 2.

Sorbus americana
AMERICAN MOUNTAINASH
See Northeast region illus. listing, p.84.

Sorbus aucuparia
EUROPEAN MOUNTAINASH
See Northeast region listing, p.94.

Sorbus decora
NORTHERN MOUNTAINASH
See Northeast region listing, p.94.

Ulmus rubra
SLIPPERY ELM
The buds of this native are eaten by many birds; its fruit is a favorite food of the purple finch and American goldfinch. *Height:* to 60ft; likes sun. Prefers moist soil. The fruit appears in spring through summer. *Fruit type:* capsule. ZONE 4.

EVERGREEN SHRUBS

Arctostaphylos pungens
MEXICAN MANZANITA
This native occurs as a creeping mat or shrub in the southwest mountains. It appears in dry, gravelly soils. Its fruit is eaten by grouse and quail. *Height:* 1 – 10ft; likes sun. Prefers dry/drained soil. The fruit appears in summer and spring. *Fruit type:* brown/dark red berry. ZONE 7.

Atriplex hymenelytra
DESERT HOLLY
This decorative shrub provides good cover for arid habitats. It is native to the southwest, and 29 species are known to eat saltbush fruit. *Height:* 2 – 5ft; likes sun. Prefers dry soil. The fruit appears in early fall. *Fruit type:* achene. ZONE 6.

Juniperus chinensis
CHINESE JUNIPER
See Northeast region listing, p. 94.

Juniperus communis
COMMON JUNIPER
See Southeast region illus. listing, p.111.

DECIDUOUS SHRUBS

Amelanchier alnifolia
SASKATOON SERVICEBERRY
See Pacific Coast region listing, p.164.

Amelanchier laevis
ALLEGHENY SERVICEBERRY
This multiple-trunked native shrub or small tree is an excellent choice for a backyard. It has spectacular displays of white flowers before the leaves emerge. *Height:* 25ft; likes full sun/partial shade. Prefers moist to well-drained soil. The fruit appears in early summer. *Fruit type:* red-purple berry. ZONE 3.

Amelanchier sanguinea
ROUNDLEAF JUNEBERRY
Serviceberries are eaten by at least 36 bird species, including the gray catbird and cardinal. This hardy native shrub has great potential for the backyard bird garden. *Height:* 8 – 12ft; likes sun/shade. Prefers well-drained soil. The fruit appears in summer. *Fruit type:* purple-black pome. ZONE 5.

Aralia spinosa
DEVIL'S WALKING STICK
See Southeast region listing, p.114.

Ceanothus fendleri
FENDLER CEANOTHUS
This native is useful for quail food and cover, and as a nest site for many species of songbird. *Height:* to 3ft; likes sun/shade. Prefers dry/drained soil. The fruit appears in late summer through early fall. *Fruit type:* red/brown capsule. ZONE 5.

Celtis reticulata
WESTERN HACKBERRY
This native shrub grows in dry, gravelly soils. Its fruits are eaten by at least 20 species, including the band-tailed pigeon, evening grosbeak, and roadrunner. *Height:* to 40ft; likes sun/shade. Prefers dry/moist/drained soil. The fruit appears in summer and winter. *Fruit type:* brown drupe. ZONE 6.

Cephalanthus occidentalis
COMMON BUTTONBUSH
See Aquatic Plants listing, p.73.

Cornus stolonifera
RED-OSIER DOGWOOD
See Northeast region illus. listing, p.90.

Cotoneaster horizontalis
ROCKSPRAY COTONEASTER
See Southeast region illus. listing, p.108.

Cotoneaster integerrimus
EUROPEAN COTONEASTER
An exotic shrub, it makes a good hedge shrub and provides excellent cover and fruit for many species, including the cedar waxwing and American robin. It is also an attractive landscaping plant. *Height:* to 5ft; likes sun. Prefers dry soil. The fruit appears in summer. *Fruit type:* red pome. ZONE 6.

Cotoneaster lucidus
HEDGE COTONEASTER
An exotic that provides good cover and nest sites for many birds in this region.

Height: 6 – 8ft; likes sun. Prefers dry soil. The fruit appears in early fall. *Fruit type:* black pome. ZONE 5.

Eleagnus commutata
SILVERBERRY
Livestock will not eat the silver leaves of this very hardy native shrub of the northern plains. It forms thickets, and provides food for the ring-necked pheasant and prairie chickens. *Height:* 3 – 8ft; likes sun/shade. Prefers varied soil. The fruit appears in summer through fall. *Fruit type:* silvery drupe. ZONE 2.

Euonymus alata
WINGED BURNING BUSH
See Southeast region listing, p.114.

Ilex decidua
POSSUM HAW
See Southeast region illus. listing, p.109.

Physocarpus opulifolius
NINEBARK
See Pacific Coast region illus. listing, p.159.

Prunus angustifolia
CHICKASAW PLUM
See Southeast region listing, p.113.

Prunus besseyi
SAND CHERRY
The fruit of this prostrate native shrub is eaten by the ring-necked pheasant and other birds. Its dense form provides excellent nesting cover. *Height:* to 2ft; likes sun. Prefers dry soil. The fruit appears in summer through early fall. *Fruit type:* black drupe. ZONE 3.

Quercus mohriana
MOHR OAK
Also called shin oak, this native sometimes grows to a small tree. *Height:* to 20ft; likes sun. Prefers dry soil. The fruit appears in fall. *Fruit type:* annual acorn. ZONE 7.

Rhus copallina
FLAMELEAF SUMAC
This native shrub has a dense form when young and then opens up, spreading to about 35ft. Its dark green leaves turn scarlet and crimson red in fall. Flowers form in spikes of yellowish-green blooms, in the shape of a pyramid. The flowers turn to 4 – 8-inch long woolly berries and persist through winter. The fruits are eaten by the American robin, red-winged blackbird, northern flicker, pileated woodpecker, and many others. *Height:*

20 – 35ft; likes full sun. Prefers well-drained soil. The fruit appears in summer. *Fruit type:* berry. ZONE 5.

Rhus glabra
SMOOTH SUMAC
See Northeast region listing, p.95.

Ribes cereum
WAX CURRANT
This native species of currant thrives in dry, rocky soils and prairies. Wild currants and gooseberries provide excellent cover and food for many song and gamebirds. At least 33 species eat the berries. *Height:* 2 – 4ft; likes sun. Prefers dry soil. The fruit appears in summer. *Fruit type:* red berry. ZONE 5.

Ribes missouriense
MISSOURI GOOSEBERRY
This native has prickly stems and large, abundant fruits. It also provides excellent cover. *Height:* 5 – 6ft; likes sun/shade. Prefers dry/moist/drained soil. The fruit appears in summer through early fall. *Fruit type:* purple-black berry. ZONE 5.

Ribes odoratum
BUFFALO CURRANT
A popular cultivated spine-forming shrub that is sometimes used in jams and jellies. It produces fragrant, bright yellow flowers in spring, followed by blackish purple berries. As soon as the berries ripen, they are eaten by many songbirds. *Height:* to 6ft; likes sun. Prefers dry/sandy soil. The fruit appears in early summer through early fall. *Fruit type:* black/purple berry. ZONES 5 – 8.

Rosa arkansana
PRAIRIE WILD ROSE
At least 38 species eat wild roses, including the northern cardinal and brown thrasher. This native prairie rose offers good shelter and food for the sharp-tailed grouse, ring-necked pheasant, and prairie-chickens. *Height:* 1 – 2ft; likes sun/light shade. Prefers drained soil. The fruit appears in summer. *Fruit type:* purple pome. ZONE 5.

Rubus spp.
HIGHBUSH BLACKBERRY
At least 63 species are known to eat the fruit of blackberries and raspberries. This native shrub also provides excellent cover. *Height:* 3 – 8ft; likes sun/half sun. Prefers dry/moist/drained soil. The fruit appears in summer. *Fruit type:* black berry. ZONE 6.

Rubus idaeus
RED RASPBERRY
See Northeast region illus. listing, p.88.

Rubus occidentalis
BLACK RASPBERRY
See Northeast region listing, p. 96.

Sambucus canadensis
AMERICAN ELDERBERRY
See Northeast region illus. listing, p.87.

Sambucus melanocarpa
BLACK-BEAD ELDER
This native shrub grows along mountain steams and canyons in the conifer belt from New Mexico to southern Alaska. *Height:* 3 – 6ft; likes sun/shade. Prefers moist soil. The fruit appears in late summer. *Fruit type:* blue berry. ZONE 6.

Sambucus pubens
SCARLET ELDER
See Northeast region listing, p.95.

Shepherdia argentea
BUFFALOBERRY
See Pacific Coast region illus. listing, p.157.

Shepherdia canadensis
BUFFALOBERRY
This extremely hardy native shrub is a good choice for mountain property backyards and those in northern climates. A deciduous native, it has yellow-red fruits which are eaten by the pine grosbeak, Swainson's thrush, northern flicker, ruffed grouse, California thrasher, hermit thrush, red-headed woodpecker, and rufous-sided towhee. *Height:* 2 – 12ft, and a spread of about 9ft; likes an open position. Prefers dry/sandy soil. The fruits appear in summer. *Fruit type:* berry. ZONE 2.

Vaccinium occidentalis
WESTERN BLUEBERRY
Native blueberries and huckleberries are very important wildlife foods, with at least 87 species known to eat their fruits. *Height:* to 4ft; likes sun. Prefers moist/drained soil. The fruit appears in late summer. *Fruit type:* blue berry. ZONE 6.

Viburnum prunifolium
BLACKHAW VIBURNUM
This native shrub has dark green leaves in summer which turn crimson red in fall. It has large, flat-topped, fragrant white flowers from late spring through early summer, followed by dark blue to black fruit on bright red stems. The fruits are eaten by the cedar waxwing, American robin, and olive-backed thrush. *Height:* 20 – 35ft. Prefers neutral to slightly alkaline soil. The fruit appears in early summer. *Fruit type:* berry. ZONE 3.

Viburnum trilobum
AMERICAN CRANBERRYBUSH
See Northeast region illus. listing, p.87.

VINES

Campsis radicans
TRUMPET VINE
See Southeast region illus. listing, p.110.

Celastrus scandens
AMERICAN BITTERSWEET
See Northeast region listing, p.97.

Lonicera ciliosa
ORANGE HONEYSUCKLE
This native deciduous vine provides attractive fruits for the Townsend's solitaire, thrasher, Swainson's thrush, wrentit, and towhees. Likes sun/shade. Prefers dry/drained soil. The fruit appears in summer through early fall. *Fruit type:* red berry. ZONE 6.

Lonicera sempervirens
TRUMPET HONEYSUCKLE
See Southeast region illus. listing, p.110.

Menispermum canadensa
COMMON MOONSEED
See Northeast region listing, p.96.

Parthenocissus inserta
WOODBINE
The fruits of this native vine are eaten by many species, including the vireo, warbler, robin, and woodpeckers. It clings to brick or stone, and is rapid-growing and drought-resistant. Likes sun/shade. Prefers moist/drained soil. The fruit appears in summer through fall. *Fruit type:* blue berry. ZONE 3.

Parthenocissus quinquefolia
VIRGINIA CREEPER
See Southeast region listing, p.115.

Smilax rotundifolia
COMMON GREENBRIER
See Northeast region listing, p96.

Vitis acerifolia
BUSH GRAPE
A native vine, it forms dense thickets and provides good nest sites for many species, including the cardinal and catbird. Likes sun. Prefers dry/drained/sandy soil. The fruit appears in summer. *Fruit type:* purple-black berry. ZONE 6.

Vitis labrusca
FOX GRAPE
See Northeast region listing, p.97.

Vitis mustangensis
MUSTANG GRAPE
This is a vigorous native grape that can survive great drought and heat. Likes sun/shade. Prefers moist/drained soil. The fruit appears in summer and often persists into winter. *Fruit type:* purple-black berry. ZONE 5.

Vitis riparia
RIVERBANK GRAPE
See Northeast region listing, p.97.

GROUNDCOVERS

Arctostaphylos nevadensis
PINE MAT MANZANITA
See Pacific Coast region illus. listing, p.161.

Arctostaphylos uva-ursi
COMMON BEARBERRY
See Northeast region illus. listing, p.91.

Cornus canadensis
BUNCHBERRY
See Mountains and Deserts region illus. listing, p.143.

Cotoneaster adpressus
CREEPING COTONEASTER
See Northeast region listing, p.97.

Fragaria spp.
STRAWBERRY
See Northeast region listing, p.97.

Vaccinium caespitosum
DWARF BILBERRY
A creeping native shrub that produces attractive berries. Among the many species that eat the berries are the cedar waxwing, northern flicker, hermit thrush, and pine grosbeak. Likes sun. Prefers dry/drained soil. The fruit appears in summer through early fall. *Fruit type:* blue berry. ZONE 2.

Vaccinium vitis-idaea
COWBERRY
See Northeast region illus. listing, p.91.

MOUNTAINS AND DESERTS REGION

A TYPICAL DESIGN for a garden in this area requires a diverse range of plants since the region includes climate zones from 2 – 9. Low-growing and drought-resistant groundcovers, small and dense fruiting shrubs, and nectar-producing flowers are ideal.

SIZE
5¼– 6½"

RED CROSSBILL

LOXIA CURVIROSTRA

Conifer seeds, including those of the rocky mountain juniper, are the crossbill's favorite food. It also eats the seeds of birch, alder, and willow.

SIZE
3¾– 4¼"

LESSER GOLDFINCH

CARDUELIS PSATRIA

Dripping water, such as in a small pond or a leaking garden hose, will bring this bird into the garden. It eats weed seeds, especially thistle.

Mesquite
Prosopis juliflora
Its principal value to birds is its thorny branches and foliage that provide good cover and nest sites. *(See page 140.)*

Wolfberry
Lycium spp.
A useful plant for poor soil areas that has berries in fall. *(See page 142.)*

Butterfly bush
Buddleia davidii
A favorite plant of hummingbirds, this is also an attractive border shrub. *(See page 140.)*

Wild strawberries
Fragaria spp.
These plants are an excellent groundcover. The fruit of the wild strawberry is smaller than that of cultivated berries and easier for a bird to swallow. *(See page 143.)*

Bunchberry
Cornus canadensis
A shade-loving groundcover with large white bracts that look like flowers. Its red fruit appears in late summer and is eaten by the warbling vireo and veery. *(See page 143.)*

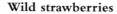

Prickly pear cactus
Opuntia spp.
This unique succulent can withstand the heat and drought of this region. Its fruits are very attractive to many birds. *(See page 142.)*

Rocky mountain juniper
Juniperus scopulorum
This evergreen tree is drought-resistant, and produces blue berries throughout the year. *(See page 139.)*

Buffaloberry
Shepherdia argentea
Separate male and female plants are needed to produce fruit. *(See page 157.)*

SIZE
6 – 6½"

CASSIN'S FINCH

CARPODACUS CASSINII

This bird is attracted to the seeds and buds of spruce and pine trees, and will visit flowering shrubs such as mesquite and wolfberry. It also eats salted soil.

Shrimp plant
Justicia brandegeana
Hummingbirds are attracted to the nectar of this shrub's white, tubular flowers, which appear from coppery bronze tracts. *(See page 142.)*

Quailbush
Atriplex lentiformis
In dry areas, this plant is deciduous. When pruned, it forms an excellent hedge. *(See page 145.)*

GARDEN FOR DRY REGIONS

Many of the colorful native shrubs and flowers used for this garden plan attract songbirds, hummingbirds, and other species. The evergreen trees produce abundant seed crops, and the small pond provides a supply of water for birds during summer.

A small pond
Water is an essential element of any garden in an arid climate zone. Not only does it provide drinking water, but it also provides a place for birds to bathe and clean their feathers. Insects also gather around water.

California fuchsia
Zauschneria californica
A clump-forming low shrub that likes a sunny spot. Evergreen in mild temperature zones; deciduous where winters are cold. It is visited by hummingbirds. *(See page 147.)*

COMMON BIRDS

THIS VAST and varied region includes birds of high mountain and lowland desert areas. In higher areas, and in the north, powerful winds and cold temperatures restrict the variety of birds. Here, birds such as the mountain chickadee, pygmy nuthatch, black-billed magpie, and bohemian waxwing occur throughout the year. These residents are sometimes joined by winter visitors such as the red crossbill and pine grosbeak that invade the lower areas when the northern conifer seed crops fail.

No fewer than 17 species of hummingbird occur in this region, frequenting gardens in the Southwest. These tiny birds are a gardener's delight. To attract them, create a landscape with native western hummingbird plants *(see page 28)* and a variety of other shrubs, vines, and trees that produce hummingbird-pollinated flowers, since these provide essential nectar for birds. A sugar-feeder also attracts hummingbirds; include water in a desert bird garden by making a drip above a pond *(see page 67)*.

SIZE 7 – 8"

YELLOW-BELLIED SAPSUCKER
Sphyrapicus varius

NEST *An unlined hole, excavated by the bird, in a tree, usually 8 to 40 feet above the ground. Aspens, in particular, are favorite nest trees.*
SONG *A mixture of several calls including churrring, mewing (catlike) notes, and squeals.*
ATTRACTED TO *coniferous and deciduous trees, shrubs, and vines; in all, 275 species are used. Horizontal holes are drilled into the tree to expose the inner bark and sap for consumption. The bird renews the holes each year. It also eats aspen buds, small berries, and suet, donuts, and sugar water from feeders.*

RUFOUS HUMMINGBIRD
Selasphorus rufus

NEST *A tiny, cottony plant-down cup, decorated with lichens, and usually built on conifer branches, 5 to 50 feet above the ground. Sometimes placed in vines or shrubs in treeless areas.*
SONG *A series of very buzzy and excited zeee-chuppity-chup.*
ATTRACTED TO *red flowers, including tiger lilies, columbines, penstemons, paintbrushes, and white flowers of madrone trees.*

SIZE 3¼ – 3½"

MOUNTAIN CHICKADEE
Parus gambeli

NEST *In a natural cavity or abandoned woodpecker hole, lined with fur or hair. May excavate its own nest in a rotted tree or stump. Usually sited 6 to 15 feet above the ground.*

SONG *Similar to the black-capped chickadee's chick-a-dee-a-dee-a-dee. Also has a soft whistle.*

ATTRACTED TO *poison ivy, sumacs, wild cherries, bayberries, acorns, beechnuts, serviceberries, blackberries, blueberries, and elderberries.*

SIZE
5 – 5³/₄"

VIOLET-GREEN SWALLOW
Tachycineta thalassina

NEST *Usually an old woodpecker cavity, rock crevice, or birdhouse. It may nest colonially where tree holes are abundant.*
SONG *A rapid twitter.*
ATTRACTED TO *flying insects, such as flies, ants, and wasps, during the nesting season. In winter and early spring, as much as one-third of the swallow's diet is berries, such as bayberry and dogwood, and seeds of sedges, bulrushes, and bayweed.*

SIZE
5 – 5¹/₂"

BLACK-BILLED MAGPIE
Pica pica

NEST *A substantial structure of sticks and twigs, lined with mud and plant material, and roofed with a loose dome of twigs. Usually built in a tree or tall shrub, although in some areas magpies nest on buildings or telephone poles.*

SONG *Common calls are a harsh kyack or a shak-shak-shak of alarm.*

ATTRACTED TO *insects, ticks from the backs of large animals, carrion, eggs and nestlings, and some fruit.*

SIZE
19"

BOHEMIAN WAXWING
Bombycilla garrulus

NEST *A flattish structure made of twigs, lichens, and grasses. Most often built in a conifer, between 5 and 40 feet above ground. Usually hidden in thick foliage.*
SONG *A nonmusical zir-r-r-r.*
ATTRACTED TO *a wide variety of tree fruits, including juniper, hawthorns, chokecherries, and mountainash; also may come to raisins, chopped apples, and currants at feeders. Insects are caught in summer and are the main food for young nestlings. May eat maple sap. When eating, the birds may gorge themselves until they are unable to fly.*

SIZE
7¹/₂"

PYGMY NUTHATCH
Sitta pygmaea

NEST *Usually an old woodpecker hole in a dead pine, lined with bark and fur, between 8 and 60 feet above the ground.*
SONG *A high-pitched ti-di, ti-di, ti-di, repeated quickly and often. While in flight utters a soft kit, kit, kit.*
ATTRACTED TO *pine seeds, cracking the nut with its powerful bill. Insects account for more than 80 percent of diet, including wasps, spiders, moths, and ants.*

SIZE
3³/₄ – 4¹/₂"

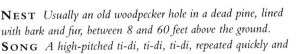

MOUNTAIN BLUEBIRD
Sialia currucoides

NEST *A cup of stems, grasses, rootlets, and pine needles, lined with hair and feathers. Built mostly by the male in a natural tree cavity or in a nestbox.*

SIZE
7"

SONG *The calls are a low chur and phew. The song is a clear, short warble. The mountain bluebird starts singing before dawn, then stops abruptly when the sun has risen.*
ATTRACTED TO *currants, raisins, grapes, elderberries, mistletoe, and hackberries, and.to insects caught on the ground. Through most of the year the mountain bluebird lives on a diet of insects, but this is supplemented by fruit when it is in season.*

BEWICK'S WREN
Thryomanes bewickii

NEST *A bulky, deep cup made from plant materials, feathers, and wool. Placed in natural cavities, fenceposts, and nestboxes.*
SONG *Reminiscent of song sparrow. Melodious, clear, and variable. Opening notes are high, then lowered, followed by a thin trill.*
ATTRACTED TO *tree limbs and shrubs, where it searches near the ground for caterpillars, ants, wasps, and other insects.*

SIZE
5 – 5½"

SAGE THRASHER
Oreoscoptes montanus

SIZE
8 – 9"

NEST *A bulky, twiggy cup, lined with finer materials. Built low to the ground in dense shrubs or on the ground.*
SONG *A high-pitched rally note and a blackbird kind of cluck.*
ATTRACTED TO *berries, grapes, wild currants, gooseberries, serviceberries, and also many kinds of insects, and other small animals found among dead leaves.*

CLIFF SWALLOW
Hirundo pyrrhonota

SIZE
5 – 6"

NEST *A jug-shaped mud structure with a tube-shaped opening. Built under building eaves and overhangs, or on sides of buildings and cliffs. Usually nests colonially.*
SONG *A low-sounding chrrr, and a series of harsh and creaking notes.*
ATTRACTED TO *flying insects, such as ants, wasps, and grasshoppers. If flying insects are scarce, insects are taken from leaves or the ground. Also partial to juniper berries.*

WESTERN TANAGER
Piranga ludoviciana

NEST *A loosely constructed dish of grasses, plant stems, and twigs built on the outer limbs of pines, oaks, and other trees, between 10 and 65 feet above the ground.*
SONG *Similar to scarlet tanager. Low-pitched, with short phrases.*
ATTRACTED TO *elderberries, cherries, and hawthorns. Also dried fruit or halved oranges at feeders, and insects.*

SIZE
7"

BLACK-HEADED GROSBEAK
Pheucticus melanocephalus

SIZE
7 – 8½"

NEST *A loose and flimsy structure of plant rootlets and twigs, built in thick, outer foliage of a deciduous tree or shrub, 4 to 25 feet above the ground.*
SONG *Rising and falling clear whistles with trills. Similar to a robin, but more fluid and sweeter.*
ATTRACTED TO *pine seeds, cherries, blackberries, strawberries, elderberries, and mistletoe. The black-headed grosbeak will also eat a wide variety of insects and bugs.*

GREEN-TAILED TOWHEE
Pipilo chlorurus

NEST *Sturdy cup of twigs and bark, lined with finer materials. Built on the ground or up to 2½ feet above. Usually found at the base of a sagebrush.*
SONG *Swings from a sweet to a burry-sounding call, weet-chur-cheeeee-churr.*
ATTRACTED TO *brushy areas, where it scratches around for insects and weed seeds.*

SIZE 6 – 7"

WHITE-CROWNED SPARROW
Zonotrichia leucophrys

SIZE
5½ – 7"

NEST *A bulky cup of mixed plant materials, usually located on or near the ground.*
SONG *Plaintive whistles and trills, similar to that of the white-throated sparrow. Sometimes sounds like more-wer-wetter-chee-zee.*
ATTRACTED TO *weed seeds and small seeds at feeders, such as white millet and fine-cracked corn.*

PINE GROSBEAK
Pinicola enlucleator

NEST *A bulky structure, loose and open, composed of mosses, twigs, lichens, and grasses. Usually positioned on a low conifer branch, between 6 and 30 feet above the ground.*
SONG *A whistled warble, with some trill notes. Similar to that of the purple finch, but not as long, nor as varied and strong.*
ATTRACTED TO *seeds and buds of maples, birches, larches, pines, firs, spruces, weed seeds, and also fruit and insects.*

SIZE
8 – 10"

BULLOCK'S ORIOLE
Icterus bullockii

NEST *A sock-like woven bag, suspended and drooping from a tree branch. May be 6 to 15 feet above the ground, although sometimes found as high as 50 feet. Constructed of plant fibers, hair, and string. Putting out short lengths of horsehair and odd pieces of yarn may entice orioles to nest nearby.*
SONG *A series of whistled notes, similar to that of the Baltimore oriole. The call is a loud skip.*
ATTRACTED TO *small fruits, including cherries, persimmons, hawthorns, elderberries, and insects. In winter, orioles are attracted to oranges, apples, and jelly. In summer, they visit sugar-water feeders that have perches.*

SIZE
7 – 8½"

137

RECOMMENDED PLANTS

PLANTS FOR this varied region should be selected according to their hardiness and water requirements.

Plants for the higher latitudes require ample water during the growing season, and must be hardy during the winter extremes of snowfalls and high winds.

Conifers are especially important for wintering birds because they provide shelter. Also, choose a variety of fruiting trees and shrubs to provide food throughout the seasons. Those that retain their fruits during winter and spring are of great benefit to the bird migrants that arrive early in the season.

It is essential to include a selection of drought-resistant plants in gardens in the south of the region. Here, it is especially important to replace those expanses of water-guzzling lawns with garden beds of native wildflowers, cacti, and other groundcovers that have proven drought-resistant. This will result in more bird visitors during the year.

If you cannot obtain some of the recommended plants at a local nursery, you can order them from the specialized mail-order nurseries. (See plant sources, pages 168–170.)

TREES

COLORADO SPRUCE
Picea pungens

This conifer produces good seed crops every 2 to 3 years. Excellent nesting site and protected roosting cover during extremes of summer and winter. Pine cones have papery scales. Likes full sun/light shade. Prefers well-drained soil. Height: 150 feet. Fully hardy. Zone 3.

Attracts *blue and spruce grouse, for which spruce needles are an important food. Many northern land birds eat the seeds, including the pine grosbeak, pine siskin, crossbills, and chickadees.*

HAWTHORN
Crataegus laevigata
'Crimson Cloud'

A deciduous, broadly spreading tree found in hedgerows. In late spring and early summer, the oval-toothed, glossy, dark green leaves set off a profusion of double crimson flowers. Rounded red fruits follow. It is particularly useful for growing in polluted urban areas, exposed sites, and coastal gardens. Likes full sun, but is suitable for many situations. Prefers a variety of soils, but not very wet soil. Height: 20 feet, and spreads to 20 feet. Fully hardy. Zones 5 – 8.

Attracts *the pine grosbeak, hermit thrush, black-headed grosbeak, purple finch, American robin, ring-necked pheasant, and Townsend's solitaire, which readily consume the fruit.*

ROCKY MOUNTAIN JUNIPER

Juniperus scopulorum

This slow-growing conifer is the western counterpart of the eastern redcedar. It is the most widely distributed juniper in the West. Produces abundant fruit crops every 2 – 5 years, with lighter crops in intervening years. Usually takes two years for the fruit to completely develop. An ideal tree for attracting birds since it provides good cover as well as food. Likes full sun. Prefers alkaline, dry soil. Height: 30 – 40 feet. Fully hardy. Zones 4 – 7.

Attracts *many species, which eagerly eat the fruit. The bright blue berries are a favorite of the Townsend's solitaire, mockingbird, pine grosbeak, and evening grosbeak.*

SHRUBS

BLUEBERRY ELDER

Sambucus caerulea

This broad, spreading shrub is an excellent choice for attracting songbirds. Produces yellowish white flowers from spring to summer, and abundant sweet, juicy fruits from late summer and sometimes as late as early winter. Grows best in low, moist areas. Likes sun. Prefers fertile, moist soil. Height: 30 – 40 feet. Fully hardy. Zone 6.

Attracts *many kinds of woodpeckers and quails, which favor the berries. Also eaten by the black phoebe, band-tailed pigeon, western kingbird, and black-headed grosbeak.*

BRITTLEBUSH

Encelia farinosa

An attractive, versatile, rounded shrub. Daisylike yellow flowers emerge in early spring through early summer. Fine white hairs cover the stems, giving a silvery green appearance. Provides a dramatic effect planted alone or against a backdrop of dark boulders or dark green plants. Irrigate when establishing brittlebush and during the summer. Additional water during hot, dry spells helps maintain its evergreen foliage. Overwatering can weaken the plant. Likes full sun. Prefers well-drained soil. Tolerates temperatures to 28°F. Height: 3 – 4 feet. Hardy. Zone 9.

Attracts *many birds to its abundant seeds, including the ground dove, mourning dove, sparrows, towhees, and quails.*

BUTTERFLY BUSH
Buddleia davidii

Also known as summer lilac. A vigorous, deciduous, arching shrub. Bears dense clusters of often fragrant, tubular, lilac to purple flowers with an orange eye from midsummer to fall. Leaves are long, lance-shaped, and dark green with white-felted undersides. Tolerates pollution and is good near the coast. May self-seed. Likes full sun. Prefers fertile, well-drained soil. Height: 15 feet, spreads to 15 feet. Hardy. Zones 5 – 9.

GOLDEN CURRANT
Ribes aureum

A native, spineless shrub commonly cultivated for its juicy fruit. Makes an excellent hedge and provides food and cover for birds. Named for its bright yellow flowers which appear from early spring, followed by fruits that vary in color from yellow to red to black. Young plants have yellow leaves. Aphids may attack young foliage. Likes sun/shade. Prefers moist and drained soil. Height: 3 – 8 feet. Fully to frost hardy. Zone 2.

MESQUITE
Prosopis juliflora

A common shrub or tree of the southwestern United States. Its main value to birds is its thorny branches and foliage, which provides excellent cover and nest sites. Because of its value as a cover plant, mesquite should be used in rocky soils, streamside habitats, and other property "corners" where few other woody plants will grow. Likes full sun. Prefers arid, dry soils. Height: 30 feet. Fully hardy. Zone 4.

Attracts *hummingbirds such as the ruby-throated hummingbird, and other songbirds, as well as the butterflies for which it is named.*

Attracts *at least 33 birds that eat the fruit, including the northern flicker, hermit and Swainson's thrushes, American robin, Townsend's solitaire, western bluebird, and quails.*

Attracts *many species, including Gambel's quail, scaled quail, and white-winged dove, which eat the seeds. The curve-billed thrasher and cactus wren nest in its dense cover.*

SHRIMP PLANT
Justicia brandegeana

An evergreen, rounded shrub grown mainly for its flowers. Has egg-shaped leaves and white, tubular flowers that appear from the coppery bronze, overlapping bracts, forming 3-inch spikes. An attractive choice for garden beds. Some species need regular pruning. Likes full sun/partial shade. Prefers fertile, well-drained soil. Height: 3 feet. Frost tender. Zones 9 – 10.

WESTERN THIMBLEBERRY
Rubus parviflorus

As with most members of the bramble group, this evergreen shrub is an important bird food. It is an especially prolific, spineless, fruiting species. Fragrant white flowers appear during early to mid summer, and are followed by red fruits that ripen during late summer. Likes full sun/light shade. Prefers well-drained, dryish soil. Height: 3 – 6 feet. Hardy. Zone 6.

WOLFBERRY
Lycium spp.

This group of native shrubs is characterized by its dense, spiny branches. Shown above is Lycium pallida. Forms thickets, providing cover and food for birds. Produces greenish yellow flowers in late spring, followed by multiple orange-red berries in fall. Best planted in a clump in hedgerows or as a barrier planting. Particularly useful for poor, dry soil and coastal gardens. Likes full sun/partial shade. Prefers well-drained soil. Height: 6 feet. Hardy. Zone 6.

Attracts *hummingbirds, including the ruby-throated and Anna's hummingbird, which eat the nectar of the white, tubular flowers. Water potted shrimp plants freely.*

Attracts *many species, including the red-headed woodpecker, western kingbird, gray catbird, cedar waxwing, northern flicker, and northern bobwhite, which consume the fruit.*

Attracts *many species, which readily consume the colorful berries, including the Gambel's quail and roadrunner. The shrub is at its most showy throughout the fall season.*

CACTI

PRICKLY PEAR CACTUS
Opuntia basilaris

Also known as the beaver-tail cactus. This succulent plant is adapted to withstand heat and drought. Its jointed branching stems have flattened segments called pads. It is ribless with tufts of spines and hooked glochids. Clump-forming. Grown for its decorative spines and colorful (though transient) flowers. Likes full sun. Prefers free-draining soil. Height: to 2 feet. Fully hardy. Zone 9.

PRICKLY PEAR CACTUS
Opuntia phaeacantha

The flowers of this attractive succulent plant generally appear in spring and summer, with the fruits forming in late summer to fall. It features jointed branching stems, in flattened segments called pads. It is ribless with tufts of spines and hooked glochids. Needs a little water in winter. Grows low and spreads. Has spines that measure 3/4 inch – 2 inches long. Likes full sun. Prefers free-draining soil. Height: to 3 feet. Fully hardy. Zone 9.

VINE

HONEYSUCKLE
Lonicera periclymemum

Known as the common honeysuckle, or woodbine, this vine is evergreen in the milder part of its range and deciduous elsewhere. Its flowers are 2 inches long and very fragrant. Some varieties have purple flowers with yellow centers. A profusion of red fruits are produced by fall. Likes full sun. Prefers well-drained soil. Height: to 22 feet. Fully hardy. Zone 2.

Attracts *the white-winged dove, curve-billed thrasher, golden-fronted woodpecker, cactus wren, wrentits, and quails, all of which eagerly consume the fruit.*

Attracts *many species, including the curve-billed thrasher, cactus wren, and white-winged dove, which welcome the fruit of this succulent on a hot, dry late summer day.*

Attracts *all nectar-feeding birds, including the ruby-throated, rufous, and Anna's hummingbirds, which find this plant irresistible. Feeding birds take pollen from one plant to the next.*

GROUNDCOVERS

BUNCHBERRY
Cornus canadensis

An attractive perennial deciduous groundcover with whorls of oval green leaves. In late spring and early summer it bears green, sometimes purple-tinged flowers, within large white bracts. These are followed by red berries in late summer. Makes an excellent front of the border planting. Likes shade. Prefers cool, moist, acid soil. Height: 4 – 6 inches. Hardy. Zones 2 – 7.

CORALBELLS
Heuchera sanguinea 'Red Spangles'

A semievergreen perennial that forms a dense mat of heart-shaped, hairy, purplish green leaves. It bears spikes of small, bell shaped crimson scarlet flowers in summer. Divide the plants every few years to ensure continuing good growth. Likes sun/partial shade. Prefers moisture-retentive but well-drained soil. Height: 12 inches, and a similar spread. Fully hardy. Zone 4.

STRAWBERRY
Fragaria spp.

Strawberry plants create a lush, spreading, evergreen mat of dark green glossy leaves, full of fruit for ground-feeding birds to eat in spring and summer. Plant rooted stolons in late spring; plants grown in flats can be planted at any time of the year. Strawberries produce white flowers in early spring, and produce sweet red fruits from early summer. Wild strawberries should be mown annually. Likes sun/partial shade. Prefers drained soil. Height: to 12 inches. Hardy. Zone 5.

Attracts *many ground-feeding and other species, including the Philadelphia vireo, warbling vireo, and veery, which normally forage for insects, and favor the red berries.*

Attracts *hummingbirds, with its colorful flowers that provide nectar. Hummingbirds also capture small spiders, ants, and other insects from within the hanging red flowers.*

Attracts *ground-feeding birds, including the Brewer's blackbird, California quail, California towhee, northern mockingbird, and black-headed grosbeak.*

OTHER GOOD PLANTS

EVERGREEN TREES

Abies concolor
WHITE FIR
At least 10 species feed on the needles and seeds of these large native evergreens. When planted in backyards, they provide important nest sites and cover. *Height:* 30 – 50ft; likes sun/shade. Prefers dry/moist/ drained soil. The fruit appears in fall. *Fruit type:* cone. ZONE 4.

Abies lasiocarpa
ROCKY MOUNTAIN FIR
Native. *Height:* 100 – 160ft; likes sun/shade. Prefers cool/moist/deep soil. The fruit appears in fall. *Fruit type:* cone. ZONE 3.

Fraxinus velutina
VELVET ASH
This native is a variable, drought-resistant, semievergreen tree. Ash seeds are eaten by at least 9 species, including evening and pine grosbeaks. *Height:* 20 – 30ft; likes sun. Prefers moist/drained soil. The fruit appears in fall. *Fruit type:* samara. ZONE 6.

Juniperus deppeana
ALLIGATOR JUNIPER
This is a native tree. *Height:* 30 – 35ft; likes sun. Prefers dry/rocky/sterile soil. The fruit appears in fall. *Fruit type:* blue–green berry. ZONE 7.

Juniperus monosperma
CHERRYSTONE JUNIPER
See Prairies and Plains region listing, p.128.

Juniperus occidentalis
SIERRA JUNIPER
These drought-resistant native junipers provide excellent cover and food; at least 26 species are known to eat juniper berries, including the pinyon jay and Townsend's solitaire. Plant male and female to provide a fruit crop. *Height:* 15 – 40ft; likes sun. Prefers dry/rocky soil. The fruit appears in fall. *Fruit type:* blue–green berry. ZONE 6.

Juniperus osteosperma
UTAH JUNIPER
Native. *Height:* to 20ft; likes sun. Prefers dry/rocky/sandy soil. The fruit appears in fall. *Fruit type:* blue–green berry. ZONE 5.

Picea engelmannii
ENGELMANN SPRUCE
This native spruce is the most shade tolerant in the northwest. Its berries are eaten by the ruffed grouse. *Height:* 20 – 50ft; likes sun/shade. Prefers moist/deep soil. The fruit appears in fall. *Fruit type:* red berry. ZONE 3.

Picea glauca
WHITE SPRUCE
See Northeast region listing, p.92.

Pinus albicaulis
WHITE-BARK PINE
Very resistant to wind, this native pine sometimes takes a prostrate or shrub form when under stress from strong, persistent wind. *Height:* 10 – 40ft; likes sun. Prefers dry/drained soil. The fruit appears in late summer through fall. *Fruit type:* cone. ZONE 4.

Pinus contorta var. *latifolia*
LODGEPOLE PINE
This tall native often falls in strong winds and is intolerant of pollution. *Height:* 70 – 150ft; likes sun. Prefers dry/moist/drained/sandy soil. The fruit appears in late summer through fall. *Fruit type:* cone. ZONE 5.

Pinus edulis
PINYON PINE
Slow-growing and drought-resistant, this native tree has seeds which are eaten by at least 9 species, including the Montezuma quail and wild turkey. *Height:* 10 – 40ft; likes sun. Prefers dry/drained soil. The fruit appears in fall. *Fruit type:* cone. ZONE 5.

Pinus lambertiana
SUGAR PINE
This native is the tallest pine, with enormous cones (26in). Its seeds are especially important to quail and grouse, but are also eaten by many species of songbird. *Height:* 175 – 200ft; likes sun. Prefers moist/drained soil. The fruit appears in fall. *Fruit type:* cone. ZONE 6.

Pinus monticola
WESTERN WHITE PINE
At least 54 species eat pine seeds, and this native tree is one of the most important seed-providers in this region. It is shade tolerant when young, but requires full sun when mature. *Height:* 90 – 200ft; likes sun. Prefers rich/moist/drained soil. The fruit

appears in fall through winter. *Fruit type:* cone. ZONE 6.

Pinus nigra
AUSTRIAN PINE
See Prairies and Plains region listing, p.128.

Pinus ponderosa
PONDEROSA PINE
See Prairies and Plains region illus. listing, p.123.

Pinus sylvestris
SCOTS PINE
See Prairies and Plains region listing, p.128.

Pseudotsuga menziesii
DOUGLAS FIR
This native thrives best on northern exposures. Its needles are important winter food for the blue grouse, but there are few other records of bird use. *Height:* 40 – 80ft; likes sun. Prefers dry/moist/drained soil. The fruit appears in fall. *Fruit type:* cone. ZONE 6.

Tsuga mertensiana
MOUNTAIN HEMLOCK
An excellent native choice for hedges or shady habitat. Its cones are a preferred food of the pine siskin and chickadees; abundant seed crops occur every two to three years. *Height:* 50 – 90ft; likes sun/shade. Prefers dry/moist/drained soil. The fruit appears in fall. *Fruit type:* cone. ZONE 5.

DECIDUOUS TREES

Acer glabrum
ROCKY MOUNTAIN MAPLE
Tolerant of poor soils, this native may appear as anything from a large tree to a shrub. Its buds are eaten by evening and pine grosbeaks. *Height:* 20 – 30ft; likes sun. Prefers dry/drained soil. The fruit appears in late fall. *Fruit type:* samara. ZONE 5.

Alnus oblongifolia
ARIZONA ALDER
Native. *Height:* 20 – 30ft; likes sun. Prefers moist/drained soil. The fruit appears in fall. *Fruit type:* nutlet in cone. ZONE 8.

Alnus rhombifolia
WHITE ALDER
Useful for planting along streams, ponds and other moist-soil habitats, this native tree provides excellent cover and nest sites for songbirds. Its seeds are important food

for the pine siskin, goldfinches, and redpolls. *Height:* 40 – 100ft; likes shade. Prefers moist soil. The fruit appears in fall through spring. *Fruit type:* nutlet in cone. ZONE 7.

Alnus tenuifolia
MOUNTAIN ALDER
Native. *Height:* 6 – 25ft; likes sun. Prefers moist/drained soil. The fruit appears in fall. *Fruit type:* nutlet in cone. ZONE 2.

Betula occidentalis
WATER BIRCH
The catkins and buds of this native tree are important food for grouse. Birch seeds are a favorite food of the pine siskin and redpolls. *Height:* 20 – 40ft; likes sun. Prefers moist/mineral soil. The fruit appears in fall. *Fruit type:* samara. ZONE 4.

Cornus nuttallii
PACIFIC DOGWOOD
See Pacific Coast region illus. listing, p.155.

Platanus wrightii
ARIZONA SYCAMORE
This native tree provides a favorite food of goldfinches; it is also eaten by the band-tailed pigeon. *Height:* 60 – 80ft; likes sun. Prefers moist/drained soil. The fruit appears in fall. *Fruit type:* achene. ZONE 7.

Populus angustifolia
NARROWLEAF COTTONWOOD
At least 10 species are known to eat cottonwood buds; they are especially important to the sharp-tailed grouse, evening grosbeak, and purple finch. *Height:* 50 – 70ft; likes sun. Prefers moist/drained soil. The fruit appears in spring. *Fruit type:* capsule. ZONE 3.

Populus balsamifera
BALSAM POPLAR
See Northeast region listing, p.93.

Populus fremontii
FREMONT COTTONWOOD
The native cottonwoods are fairly salt tolerant, especially Freemont cottonwood. *Height:* to 90ft; likes sun. Prefers dry/drained soil. The fruit appears in spring. *Fruit type:* capsule. ZONE 7.

Prosopis pubescens
SCREWBEAN
This spiny native grows in river bottoms and canyons, and a wide variety of soils, including gravel. It can vary from a large tree to a small shrub, depending on conditions, and it forms thickets. It provides food for the bobwhite, roadrunner, and Gambel's quail. *Height:* 15 – 30ft; likes sun.

Prefers dry/moist soil. The fruit appears in summer through fall. *Fruit type:* legume. ZONE 7.

Prunus emarginata
BITTER CHERRY
This native may appear as anything from a large tree to a shrub, and it forms dense thickets. It provides food for at least 9 species, including the Townsend's solitaire, mountain bluebird, and band-tailed pigeon. *Height:* 35 – 40ft; likes sun. Prefers dry/moist/drained soil. The fruit appears in spring through fall. *Fruit type:* drupe. ZONE 7.

Prunus serotina
BLACK CHERRY
See Southeast region illus. listing, p.104.

Quercus arizonica
ARIZONA WHITE OAK
Native. *Height:* to 40ft; likes sun. Prefers dry/drained soil. The fruit appears in fall. *Fruit type:* annual acorn. ZONE 7.

Quercus macrocarpa
BUR OAK
See Northeast region listing, p.93.

Salix exigua
COYOTE WILLOW
Native. *Height:* to 15ft; likes sun. Prefers moist/drained soil. The fruit appears in early summer. *Fruit type:* capsule. ZONE 2.

Salix lasiandra
PACIFIC WILLOW
This native tree stabilizes stream banks, and provides excellent cover and nest sites for many species of songbird. Its buds are eaten by grouse. *Height:* to 30ft; likes sun. Prefers moist/drained soil. The fruit appears in early summer. *Fruit type:* capsule. ZONE 5.

EVERGREEN SHRUBS

Acacia greggii
CATCLAW ACACIA
This thorny native sometimes grows as a small tree, and gives excellent cover. It is a preferred food of quails and doves. *Height:* to 20ft; likes sun. Prefers dry soil. The fruit appears in summer through spring. *Fruit type:* legume. ZONE 8.

Arctostaphylos patula
GREEN-LEAF MANZANITA
A dense native shrub that is attractive to grouse and quail. *Height:* 1 – 10ft; likes sun. Prefers dry/drained soil. The fruit appears all year round. *Fruit type:* brown berry. ZONE 7.

Atriplex lentiformis
QUAILBUSH
Growing in dense patches, this native shrub provides excellent cover for quails and other desert wildlife. When pruned, it forms excellent hedges for the arid-climate cities of the southwest and California. It is deciduous in dry areas. *Height:* 6 – 10ft; likes sun. Prefers dry soil. The fruit appears in fall through winter. *Fruit type:* achene. ZONE 6.

Celtis pallida
DESERT HACKBERRY
This native shrub provides valuable bird food and cover, and should be planted in the southern part of this region. Its fruits are eaten by the cactus wren, cardinal, pyrrhuloxia, scaled quail, and green jay. *Height:* 10 – 20ft; likes sun. Prefers dry soil. The fruit appears in summer through fall. *Fruit type:* yellow drupe. ZONE 7.

Mahonia nervosa
OREGON-GRAPE
The dense foliage of this native shrub offers excellent cover, and its berries are eaten by the ruffed and blue grouse. Several cultured varieties are available. *Height:* to 26ft, but often less than 2ft; likes sun/shade. Prefers dry/drained soil. The fruit appears in fall. *Fruit type:* berry. ZONE 6.

Quercus palmeri
PALMER OAK
This large, dense, native shrub sometimes grows as a tree and occurs in the grasslands and canyons of the Southwest. *Height:* to 15ft; likes sun. Prefers dry/drained/sandy soil. The fruit appears in summer. *Fruit type:* biennial acorn. ZONE 7.

Sambucus mexicana
MEXICAN ELDER
This semievergreen native shrub of the Southwest can grow to a small tree with up to a 12-inch-diameter trunk. It occurs in low, moist habitats, such as ditches, stream borders, and moist grasslands, and at least 12 species eat the fruit. *Height:* to 25ft; likes sun. Prefers moist soil. The fruit appears all year round. *Fruit type:* black berry. ZONE 7.

DECIDUOUS SHRUBS

Acacia constricta
MESCAT ACACIA
A common, native, spiny shrub of harsh soils in the extreme southern part of this

145

region. Its seeds are eaten by the scaled quail and white-winged dove. *Height:* 6 – 18ft; likes sun. Prefers dry/sandy soil. The fruit appears in summer. *Fruit type:* 4-inch black pods/legume. ZONE 7.

Amelanchier ralnifolia
SASKATOON SERVICEBERRY
See Pacific Coast region illus. listing, p.164.

Amelanchier utahensis
UTAH SERVICEBERRY
This is a native shrub of rocky soil and dry hillsides. As with other serviceberries, this is an important food for songbirds. *Height:* 4 – 16ft; likes sun. Prefers dry/drained soil. The fruit appears in summer. *Fruit type:* blue/black pome. ZONE 3.

Condalia lycioides
LOTEBUSH CONDALIA
This native is a very thorny, rounded shrub of the deserts and dry foothills in the Southwest. It provides an ideal nest site for songbirds, and important food for the scaled quail. *Height:* to 10ft; likes sun. Prefers dry/drained soil. The fruit appears in early summer. *Fruit type:* purple drupe. ZONE 7.

Condalia obtusifolia
LOTEWOOD CONDALIA
Native. *Height:* to 10ft; likes sun. Prefers dry soil. The fruit appears in early summer. *Fruit type:* black drupe. ZONE 7.

Condalia spathulata
KNIFE-LEAF CONDALIA
Native. *Height:* to 10ft; likes sun. Prefers dry soil. The fruit appears in early summer. *Fruit type:* black drupe. ZONE 7.

Cornus glabrata
BROWN DOGWOOD
Native. Brown dogwood forms dense thickets along mountain streams. *Height:* to 10ft; likes sun. Prefers moist soil. The fruit appears in late summer through fall. *Fruit type:* drupe. ZONE 8.

Cornus sessilis
MINER'S DOGWOOD
This native occurs as a large shrub or small tree that, along with other western dogwoods, provides important food for grouse, quails, woodpeckers, and bluebirds. *Height:* to 10ft; likes sun. Prefers moist soil. The fruit appears in late summer. *Fruit type:* drupe. ZONE 7.

Cornus stolonifera
RED-OSIER DOGWOOD
See Northeast region illus. listing, p.90.

Elaeagnus commutata
SILVERBERRY
See Prairies and Plains region listing, p.130.

Forestiera pubescens
HAIRY DESERT OLIVE
This native is a widely-distributed, spreading shrub of dry river bottoms in the Southwest. It provides the principal food of the scaled quail in Texas, and is also eaten by robins. *Height:* 6 – 10ft; likes sun. Prefers dry/moist/drained soil. The fruit appears in early summer through early fall. *Fruit type:* black drupe. ZONE 7.

Lonicera albiflora
WHITE HONEYSUCKLE
A thicket-forming shrub or climbing vine of the Southwest, this native occurs in thickets and on streambanks. It provides food for the bobwhite, catbird, robin, and hermit thrush. *Height:* to 9ft; likes sun. Prefers moist/drained soil. The fruit appears in fall. *Fruit type:* blue berry. ZONE 6.

Lonicera involucrata
TWINLINE HONEYSUCKLE
See Pacific Coast region illus. listing, p.160.

Lonicera utahensis
UTAH HONEYSUCKLE
The fruit of this erect, clump-forming native shrub is eaten by the hermit thrush, Townsend's solitaire, robin, and ring-necked pheasant. *Height:* to 5ft; likes shade. Prefers dry/drained soil. The fruit appears in summer through early fall. *Fruit type:* yellow/red berry. ZONE 6.

Lycium andersonii
ANDERSON WOLFBERRY
Tolerant of alkaline soils, this native shrub provides excellent cover. It is an important food for the verdin, gila woodpecker, and many other desert birds. The flower nectar is used by the black-chinned hummingbird. *Height:* 1 – 9ft; likes sun. Prefers dry/sandy soil. The fruit appears in spring. *Fruit type:* red berry. ZONE 6.

Prunus emarginata
BITTER CHERRY
This native can vary in size from a large shrub to a small tree, and it forms dense thickets providing good nest cover and food for at least 6 species. *Height:* 3 – 12ft; likes sun/shade. Prefers dry/moist/drained

soil. The fruit appears in spring and early fall. *Fruit type:* black drupe. ZONE 7.

Prunus virginiana
COMMON CHOKECHERRY
See Prairies and Plains region illus. listing, p.124.

Pyracantha coccinea
SCARLET FIRETHORN
See Northeast region listing, p.95.

Rhamnus alnifolius
ALDERLEAF BUCKTHORN
Dense foliage makes this plant good in border plantings. With its dark fruits and leaves, it is highly ornamental. Fifteen species eat the berries, including the mockingbird, pileated woodpecker, and brown thrasher. *Height:* 2 – 3ft; likes shade. Prefers damp soil. The fruit appears in late summer. *Fruit type:* black drupe. ZONE 2.

Rhamnus purshiana
CASCARA SAGRADA
See Pacific Coast region listing, p.164.

Rhus aromatica
FRAGRANT SUMAC
This drought-resistant, deep-rooted shrub makes an excellent shelterbelt planting. It earns its name from the strong smell that results from crushing its leaves. Its fruit is eaten by at least 25 species, including the evening grosbeak, robin, and bobwhite. *Height:* 8ft; likes sun. Prefers limestone soil. Hardy. The fruit appears in summer. *Fruit type:* red berry. ZONE 3.

Rhus glabra
SMOOTH SUMAC
See Northeast region listing, p.95.

Ribes cereum
WAX CURRANT
See Prairies and Plains region listing, p.129.

Ribes viscosissimum
STICKY CURRANT
This thornless native shrub has roots up to 4ft deep. At least 33 species eat the fruits of currants and gooseberries. *Height:* 1 – 4ft; likes sun/shade. Prefers drained soil. The fruit appears in late summer through early fall. *Fruit type:* black berry. ZONE 6.

Rosa woodsii
WOODS ROSE
This native is a widespread, thicket-forming rose found throughout the Rocky Mountains at an altitude of between 3,500 and 10,000ft. It has the largest flowers of

any western wild rose, and its fruits are eaten by the hermit and Swainson's thrushes, ruffed grouse, and other game birds. *Height:* to 3ft; likes sun/half sun. Prefers moist/drained soil. The fruit appears throughout the year. *Fruit type:* red hip. ZONE 4.

Rubus arizonensis
ARIZONA DEWBERRY
Trailing and very prickly, this native shrub provides excellent cover for songbirds. Its fruit is eaten by the cardinal, house finch, Steller's jay, bluebirds, and many other songbird species. *Height:* 2 – 3ft; likes sun. Prefers dry/moist/drained soil. The fruit appears in summer. *Fruit type:* red drupelets. ZONE 6.

Rubus deliciosus
ROCKY MOUNTAIN FLOWERING RASPBERRY
Native. *Height:* to 6ft; likes sun. Prefers dry/moist/drained soil. The fruit appears in summer through early fall. *Fruit type:* red/purple berry. ZONE 6.

Rubus idaeus
RED RASPBERRY
See Northeast region illus. listing, p.88.

Rubus leucodermis
WHITEBARK RASPBERRY
A plant of dry, rocky soils, this native shrub offers excellent cover and nest sites for the mockingbird. At least 146 species are known to eat the fruits of this important shrub. *Height:* to 5ft; likes sun. Prefers dry/moist/drained soil. The fruit appears in summer through early fall. *Fruit type:* dark purple berry. ZONE 4.

Sambucus microbotrys
BUNCHBERRY ELDER
The bunchberry elder is a small native shrub that occurs on the eastern slopes of the Rocky Mountains. At least 111 species are known to eat elderberry fruits. *Height:* to 5ft; likes sun/shade. Prefers moist/drained soil. The fruit appears in late summer. *Fruit type:* red berry. ZONE 6.

Sambucus pubens
SCARLET ELDER
See Northeast region listing, p.95.

Seriphidium tridentatum
BIG SAGEBRUSH
This native shrub is an indicator of alkaline-free soils and occurs widely in the West, growing in dry and stony soils in deserts and up to the timberline. It provides the principal food and cover for sage grouse. *Height:* 2 – 10ft; likes sun. Prefers dry/drained soil. The fruit appears in fall. *Fruit type:* achene. ZONE 4.

Shepherdia argentea
SILVER BUFFALOBERRY
See Pacific Coast region illus. listing, p.157.

Sorbus occidentalis
ALPINE MOUNTAINASH
A native that frequently forms dense thickets. At least 11 species readily eat the fruit, including the evening grosbeak, blue grouse, robin and Clark's nutcracker. *Height:* to 9ft; likes sun. Prefers moist/dry/drained soil. The fruit appears in late summer through winter. *Fruit type:* red pome. ZONE 6.

Sorbus scopulina
GREEN MOUNTAINASH
A native that forms thickets. *Height:* to 12ft; likes sun/shade. Prefers moist/drained soil. The fruit appears in summer through winter. *Fruit type:* red pome. ZONE 6.

Sorbus sitchensis
SITKA MOUNTAINASH
See Pacific Coast region illus. listing, p.156.

Symphoricarpos albus
COMMON SNOWBERRY
See Prairies and Plains region illus. listing, p.126.

Symphoricarpos longiflorus
LONGFLOWER SNOWBERRY
The fruit of all snowberries is eaten by at least 26 species, including the American robin, cedar waxwing, and pine grosbeak. *Height:* 3 – 4ft; likes sun. Prefers dry soil. The fruit appears in summer. *Fruit type:* white berrylike drupe. ZONE 7.

Symphoricarpos oreophilus
MOUNTAIN SNOWBERRY
Height: to 5ft; likes sun. Prefers dry/moist/drained soil. The fruit appears in late summer. *Fruit type:* white berrylike drupe. ZONE 6.

Symphoricarpos rotundifolius
ROUNDLEAF SNOWBERRY
Height: to 3ft; likes sun. Prefers dry/drained soil. The fruit appears in late summer. *Fruit type:* white berrylike drupe. ZONE 7.

Zauschneria californica
CALIFORNIA FUCHSIA
A clump-forming sub-shrubby perennial with clusters of bright scarlet flowers. *Height:* to 18in. Likes sun. Prefers well-drained soil. ZONES 8 – 10.

VINES

Celastrus scandens
AMERICAN BITTERSWEET
See Northeast region listing, p.97.

Lonicera interrupta
CHAPARRAL HONEYSUCKLE
This is a native evergreen vine which sometimes grows as shrub. Likes sun. Prefers dry soil. The fruit appears in summer and winter. *Fruit type:* berry. ZONE 8.

Lonicera sempervirens
TRUMPET HONEYSUCKLE
See Southeast region illus. listing, p.110.

Parthenocissus inserta
WOODBINE
See Prairies and Plains region listing, p.130.

Parthenocissus quinquefolia
VIRGINIA CREEPER
See Southeast region listing, p.114.

Vitis arizonica
CANYON GRAPE
This native deciduous vine grows in moist, sandy soils. It provides food for many birds, including the Gambel's and scaled quails. Likes sun. Prefers moist/drained soil. The fruit appears in summer and persists to fall. *Fruit type:* blue-black berry. ZONE 7.

GROUNDCOVERS

Gaultheria humifusa
ALPINE WINTERGREEN
Native. Likes sun/shade. Prefers drained soil. The fruit appears in late summer. *Fruit type:* berry. ZONE 6.

Gaultheria ovatifolia
BUSH WINTERGREEN
This small, native evergreen shrub forms mats that grow on sandy or other soils. At least 7 species are known to eat the fruit. Likes sun. Prefers drained soil. The fruit appears in late summer. *Fruit type:* berry. ZONE 6.

Vaccinium scoparium
GROUSEBERRY
This native is a creeping timberline shrub that produces highly attractive berries. Among the birds that eat these fruits are the cedar waxwing, ruffed grouse, northern flicker, hermit thrush, and pine grosbeak. Likes sun/shade. Prefers dry/moist soil. The fruit appears in summer. *Fruit type:* blue berry. ZONE 3.

PACIFIC COAST REGION

THE PRIORITY for a bird garden in this area is to select plants that can survive both dry coastal soil and the drought conditions, as well as provide food and cover for birds. Many native plants have adapted well to these conditions.

Mountain dogwood
Cornus nuttallii

A popular, native deciduou[s] flowering tree that produce[s] red fruit in fall. *(See page 155.)*

Sitka mountainash
Sorbus sitchensis

A deciduous shrub that forms dense thickets, and whose red fruits are a favorite of the robin, and pine grosbeak. *(See page 156.)*

SIZE
7½ – 8"

HOODED ORIOLE

ICTERUS CUCULLATUS

This bird gleans insects from the foliage of large trees and rarely descends to the ground. It also feeds on the berries of toyon and oregon grape.

SIZE
5 – 5¾"

HOUSE FINCH

CARPODACUS MEXICANUS

The house finch thrives around human habitation. It eats mainly weed seeds, including thistle and dandelion, as well as insects.

Oregon grape
Mahonia nervosa

This evergreen plant is a good choice since it provides good cover for many birds. Many varieties are available. *(See page 158.)*

Wild strawberries
Fragaria spp.

A border of strawberries offers a supply of food throughout the fruiting season. Its leaves will help make leaf litter. *(See page 143.)*

Flowering maple
Abutilon megapotamicum
Plant this evergreen shrub in front of a thicket of flowering currant for a more showy effect at the back of a shrub border. The purple finch and pine siskin eat its fruit. *(See page 158.)*

Western hemlock
Tsuga heterophylla
Plant this tall evergreen in the backyards of larger properties since it grows to 175 feet. It produces a seed crop every 2 – 3 years that is devoured by the pine siskin and chickadees. *(See page 128.)*

*SIZE
11 – 13"*

CALIFORNIA THRASHER
TOXOSTOMA REDIVIVUM

This bird rakes the ground with its long, curved bill as it searches for insects, berries, and seeds. It nests in dense, medium-sized shrubs.

Toyon
Heteromeles arbutifolia
A native evergreen shrub, its bright red or yellow fruits ripen from late summer through early spring. *(See page 156.)*

California lilac
Ceanothus spp.

A varied group of blue-flowered shrubs. Plant them in groups at the edge of a garden since they are fast-growing. *(See page 157.)*

Manzanitas
Arctostaphylos spp.
This is a groundcover plant that grows in a creeping manner. Some varieties produce white flowers and fruit that attract many species. *(See page 162.)*

Rough grass
Leave a small area of grass to grow longer, especially around the base of a tree or shrub, because birds will forage for insects and worms there.

COASTAL GARDEN

This garden plan includes native plants such as toyon and manzanitas that are usually overlooked for the backyard. They produce important food and cover for resident and migrant species all year round.

COMMON BIRDS

FROM THE COOL rainforests of coastal Alaska to the mild, moderate Mediterranean climate of southern California, the West Coast offers a variety of bird habitats. To the north of the region, backyards planted with conifers and fruiting shrubs will attract woodland birds such as the Stellar's jay, varied thrush, and hairy woodpecker throughout the year. Some resident birds such as the chestnut-backed chickadee and plain titmouse will frequent feeders throughout the most severe winters and nest in bird houses during the spring and winter. From central California to Mexico, bird gardeners will attract hummingbirds by planting colorful honeysuckle vines and fuchsias. Berry-eating species, such as the cedar waxwing and California towhee, will visit to eat fruit-bearing shrubs. The placement of a sugar-water feeder will appeal to orioles. In dry habitats, supply water.

*SIZE
3½ – 4"*

ANNA'S HUMMINGBIRD
Calypte anna

NEST *A tiny, lichen-covered cup of plant down is located 1½ to 30 feet above the ground in a shrub or small tree, usually in semishade near water.*
SONG *A squeaking, thin warble that is sung from a perch. The call is a chit.*
ATTRACTED TO *the flowers of eucalyptus, tree tobacco, century plant, fuchsias, and other hummingbird flowers (see page 28). Each day a single bird needs the nectar of about 1,000 blossoms. They also feed on sap from sapsucker holes and will come to sugar-water feeders.*

HAIRY WOODPECKER
Picoides villosus

NEST *Found in a tree cavity, 5 to 30 feet above the ground.*
SONG *A rolling and rattling series of notes, chikikikikikik....*
ATTRACTED TO *wild fruits such as blackberries and also acorns, hazelnuts, and beechnuts. They visit feeding stations for suet, peanut butter, meat scraps, cheese, apples, bananas, sunflower seeds, and cracked walnuts.*

*SIZE
9½"*

NORTHERN FLICKER
Colaptes auratus

SIZE
12 – 14"

NEST *A tree cavity with a round entrance hole that is 2 to 4 inches in diameter. It is usually found between 2 and 90 feet off the ground. Flickers will use a nestbox fixed to a pole among shrubs.*
SONG *A piercing flicka-flicka-flicka....*
ATTRACTED TO *a wide variety of fruits. Favorites include: dogwood berries, hackberries, blueberries, pokeberries, serviceberries, elderberries, and Virginia creeper. These make up about 25 percent of its diet — the remainder is insects, especially ants.*

BLACK PHOEBE
Sayornis nigricans

NEST *A mud and fiber structure, attached to the vertical wall of a cliff, or under eaves, or on ledges.*
SONG *A nasal rendition of fi-be, fi-be, usually with an upward or downward inflection.*
ATTRACTED TO *ants, bees, flies, and moths that can be taken from the air or the ground. It often feeds just above water and has been known to catch small fish.*

SIZE
6¼ – 7"

SCRUB JAY
Aphelocoma coerulescens

NEST *A thick-walled cup built in a low tree or bush, 2 to 12 feet above the ground.*
SONG *A varied repertoire which includes ike-ike-ike, kwesh-kwesh, or check-check-check....*
ATTRACTED TO *acorns, pine seeds, corn, cherries, raspberries, sunflower seeds, elderberries, manzanitas, and sumacs.*

SIZE
11 – 13"

STELLER'S JAY
Cyanocitta stelleri

NEST *Built of large sticks with a mud foundation, and lined with roots and pine needles, in the crotch or on a limb of an evergreen tree. The nests are often 8 to 15 feet up, though they are sometimes found as high as 100 feet. Steller's jays become very secretive during nesting.*
SONG *A loud and raucous, shook-shook-shook, or wheek-wek-wek. The song is similar to that of a robin. It also mimics the red-tailed hawk and eagles.*
ATTRACTED TO *acorns, sunflowers, corn, pine seeds, fruit, insects, and other tiny invertebrates. Small birds' nests and woodpeckers' caches are raided, and birds' eggs are occasionally eaten.*

CHESTNUT-BACKED CHICKADEE
Parus rutescens

SIZE
4½ – 5"

NEST *Found in a tree cavity, between 1 and 20 feet up, although sometimes as high as 80 feet above the ground.*
SONG *Sounds like tsick-i-see-see or, zhee-che-che, and is hoarser than the song of the black-capped chickadee.*
ATTRACTED TO *pine seeds, the fruit of poison ivy, apple, thimbleberry, and the fruit of California live oak.*

SIZE
12 – 13½"

PLAIN TITMOUSE
Parus inornatus

SIZE
5 – 5½"

NEST *Often in a disused woodpecker hole, but it will also excavate its own cavity in the rotting wood of a live tree and make use of welcoming nestboxes.*
SONG *A clear, whistling witt-y, witt-y, witt-y....*
ATTRACTED TO *pine seeds, acorns, cherries, and poison ivy berries.*

BUSHTIT
Psaltriparus minimus

SIZE 4"

NEST *A woven pouch suspended from a tree or bush, between 6 and 25 feet above the ground. The pouch is about 10 inches long, built of twigs, mosses, lichens, flowers, and oak leaves, and bound together with spider webs.*
SONG *A high-pitched twittering, tsit-tsit-tsit as they feed, but no song.*
ATTRACTED TO *insects mostly, but they also eat some fruits such as poison ivy berries.*

WESTERN BLUEBIRD
Sialia mexicana

NEST *Built in natural tree cavities or in nestboxes. Nestbox projects, known as bluebird trails, have reversed the decline of the bluebird in many areas.*
SONG *The call is a pew or a mew, similar in tempo to the song of a robin.*
ATTRACTED TO *blackberries, raspberries, elderberries, mistletoe berries, Canyon grapes, the fruit of the common fig, and the berries of the California pepper tree.*

SIZE
6 – 7½"

BROWN CREEPER
Certhia americana

NEST *Twigs, leaves, and moss located under loose bark on a mature tree, or sometimes in a natural tree cavity. Found between 5 and 15 feet above the ground.*
SONG *A thin, high-pitched see-ti-wee-tu-wee....* SIZE 5"
ATTRACTED TO *tiny insects, picked from tree bark. Also enjoys mixtures of peanut butter and cornmeal, placed in tree crevices.*

HERMIT THRUSH
Catharus guttatus

NEST *Typically on the ground, in a natural depression under a tree or bush. Occasionally found above the ground in a small tree, 2 to 5 feet up.*
SONG *Ethereal and flutelike, and considered by many to be one of the most beautiful birdsongs in North America.* SIZE 7"
ATTRACTED TO *fruits of hollies, dogwoods, serviceberries, sumacs, and grapes.*

GOLDEN-CROWNED SPARROW
Zonotrichia atricapilla

NEST *A cup-shaped nest of stems, sticks, grasses, and occasionally moose hair. Usually built on the ground at the base of a willow.*
SONG *Three, clear, whistling notes descending down the scale.*
ATTRACTED TO *millet and cracked corn at feeders, and weed seeds.*

SIZE
6 – 7"

CALIFORNIA TOWHEE
Pipilo crissalis

NEST *A bulky cup-shaped nest of twigs, stems, and grasses. Built in dense shrubs or a tree, usually between 3 and 12 feet above the ground.*
SONG *A rapid, chink-chink-ink-ink-ink....*
ATTRACTED TO *millet and cracked corn at feeders, and weed seeds.*

SIZE
8 – 10"

LAZULI BUNTING
Passerina amoana

NEST *A cup of dried grasses, lined with hair. Located in dense shrubs, vines, and weed stalks, or the crotch of a willow, rose, small pine, or scrub oak, between 1¹/2 and 4 feet off the ground.*
SONG *Rapid, loud phrases, sweet-sweet, or chew-chew.*
ATTRACTED TO *wild oats, weed seeds, and millets at feeders. They also feed on insects.*

SIZE
5 – 6"

CEDAR WAXWING
Bombycilla cedrorum

NEST *A cup-shaped nest of twigs, grasses, and fibers built into a tree fork or positioned on a branch, usually between 6 and 50 feet up. Occasionally colonial.*
SONG *A high, thin, zeee.*
ATTRACTED TO *fruits of cedar, mountainash, pyracantha, hollies, mulberries, serviceberries, hawthorns, crabapples, and other small fruits.*

Occasionally they may also be attracted to maple sap, raisins, and chopped apples.

SIZE
6¹/2 – 8"

FOX SPARROW
Passerella iliaca

SIZE
6³/4 – 7¹/2"

NEST *Made from plant material, and often lined with feathers. Found on the ground, in a shrub, or a small tree.*
SONG *Clear introductory notes, followed by sliding ones, often considered to be musical and joyful.*
ATTRACTED TO *Blueberries, elderberries, manzanita berries, and millet at feeding stations.*

RECOMMENDED PLANTS

FROM THE cool rainforests typical of Alaska and the Pacific Northwest to the Mediterranean climate of southern California, there is a tremendous variety of climates. As a consequence, there is also a wide array of bird-attracting plants from which to choose.

When selecting the plants, consider the hardiness zone and water tolerance first, then choose plants suitable to the microclimate conditions in your backyard, such as soil moisture and the availability of shade.

An understanding of local climate conditions is critical to the success of your gardening plans and your ability to attract birds. Hummingbirds in particular are abundant throughout the Pacific Coast region, and are especially common in the south, so consider planting a selection that will benefit these birds *(see page 28).*

As a general landscaping guide, place tall trees farthest from the house, with small trees and fruiting shrubs closer in medium-sized garden beds. Always plant in clumps to create large food patches and dense nesting places for resident birds. You will be amply rewarded.

TREES

CALIFORNIA LIVE OAK
Quercus agrifolia

This large evergreen is adaptable to normal garden conditions. Bears rigid, spiny-toothed, glossy, dark green leaves. Produces an acorn crop each year. Likes sun. Prefers dry, well-drained soil. Height: 75 feet, spread to 130 feet. Fully hardy. Zone 9.

Attracts *many birds, which eat the acorns of this large native oak, including the California quail, jays, woodpeckers, the chestnut-backed chickadee, and the plain titmouse.*

DESERT OLIVE
Forestiera neomexicana

This native, spreading, deciduous small tree has lush green leaves that have pointed tips. It is fast-growing, and an ideal choice for a screen or border hedge. Produces blue-black fruits in early summer through fall. Likes full sun. Prefers dry, well-drained soil. Height: 6 – 10 feet. Hardy. Zone 7.

Attracts *many species, including the ruffed grouse, pine grosbeak, and American robin, which all use its blue-black drupes as their principal source of nourishment.*

GIANT ARBORVITAE

Thuja plicata

This tree is native to the Pacific slope. Its foliage provides a good source of food for insect-eating birds. The trees do not start fruiting until they are 70 years old (they live to 800 or more years), but then produce massive seed crops about every third year. Smaller specimens can be pruned back and are suitable as living fences in the backyard. Likes partial shade. Prefers moist soil. Height: 50 – 70 feet. Fully hardy. Zones 5 – 7.

MADRONE PACIFIC

Arbutus menziesii

This native evergreen, spreading tree is grown for its leaves, clusters of small, urn-shaped white flowers, and strawberrylike fruits, which are edible but tasteless. Has smooth, reddish bark, and oval, dark green leaves. Produces orange or red berries in summer that persist through early winter. Likes full sun. Prefers fertile, well-drained soil. Height: 20 – 100 feet. Frost hardy. Zones 7 – 9.

MOUNTAIN DOGWOOD

Cornus nuttallii

This native, deciduous tree produces inconspicuous clusters of yellow-green flowers, surrounded by 4 – 6 white bracts, in late spring. Has oval, dark-green leaves. Fruit clusters ripen in fall, and consist of 30 – 40 bright red, berrylike drupes. The tree's fall color is as attractive as its spring show, because the leaves turn a brilliant burgundy red. It is a popular cultivated tree. Likes full sun/partial shade. Prefers fertile, well-drained soil. Height: 10 – 40 feet. Fully to half hardy. Zone 9.

Attracts many species, including thrushes, the pine grosbeak, and the red-breasted nuthatch, which consume the massive seed crops. Its foliage also provides excellent nesting places.

Attracts at least 5 species that eat the clusters of orange or red berries, including the band-tailed pigeon and wild turkey.

Attracts the band-tailed pigeon, northern flicker, hermit thrush, cedar waxwing, warbling vireo, purple finch, and pileated woodpecker, all of which eat its fruits, which follow the flowers.

SITKA MOUNTAINASH
Sorbus sitchensis

Named for its site of discovery in Sitka, Alaska, this graceful, small, deciduous tree is spectacular when set against a backdrop of taller conifers, since it makes a dramatic display in spring, producing large masses of creamy-white flowers. By late summer through early fall it produces abundant clusters of shiny, orange-red fruits. Likes sun/partial shade. Prefers fertile, moist soil. Height: can grow to 30 feet, but 15 feet is more common. Fully hardy. Zone 5.

TOYON
Heteromeles arbutifolia

In southern California, toyon is also known as Christmas berry or California holly because its fruits ripen from early fall through winter. This evergreen, shrublike tree has stiff, leathery, deep-green leaves. Broad, flat heads of small, 5-petaled, white flowers appear in summer. These mature into bright red or yellow berries during the winter. Likes full sun/partial shade. Prefers fertile, well-drained soil. Height: 6 – 10 feet, or grows to a small tree, 35 feet tall. Frost hardy. Zone 8.

BIRD OF PARADISE
Caesalpinia gilliesii

This fast-growing, deciduous, open shrub is grown for its foliage and colorful flowers, making it an excellent border plant. Has finely divided, dark green leaves and bears short racemes of yellow flowers with long, red stamens from mid- to late summer. Propagate by softwood cuttings in summer or by seed in fall or spring. Likes full sun. Prefers fertile, well-drained soil. Height: 15 feet, spreading to 20 feet. Frost tender to frost hardy. Zone 10.

Attracts *at least 11 species which eat its fruit, including the evening and pine grosbeaks, American robin, western bluebird, hairy woodpecker, and Clark's nutcracker.*

Attracts *many birds that eat the toyon fruit, including the wrentit, northern flicker, hermit thrush, western bluebird, American robin, northern mockingbird, and cedar waxwing.*

Attracts *hummingbirds, including the rufous, Anna's, ruby-throated, and black-chinned, which feed on the nectar, as well as songbirds.*

BUFFALOBERRY
Shepherdia argentea

A deciduous, bushy, often treelike shrub grown for its foliage and fruit. Bears tiny, inconspicuous yellow flowers amid oblong silvery leaves in spring. Followed in summer by small, egg-shaped, bright red berries. Separate male and female plants are needed to obtain fruits. Can be grown in areas too dry, salty, or alkaline for other shrubs. Likes full sun/partial shade. Prefers dry, well-drained soil. Height: 3 – 7 feet. Fully hardy. Zone 2.

CALIFORNIA LILAC
Ceanothus spp.

This varied group of 60 species of shrubs and groundcovers has great value as bird-attracting plants, and gives good choice in finding plants to meet specific needs. About 40 species occur in this region. They include Point Reyes creeper (C. gloriossus). Height: 4 – 20 inches, spread of 5 feet. Zone 8. Tree ceanothus (C. arborea) *can grow to 20 feet. Zone 10. Most of the California lilacs are evergreen, although a few are deciduous. All species like full sun/partial shade and prefer dry soil.*

EUROPEAN RED ELDER
Sambucus racemosa

This deciduous, bushy shrub is also known as red-berried elder, and is grown for its foliage, flowers, and fruit. Its gray-green leaves have 5 oval leaflets, and do not change color before they drop in fall. In midspring, star-shaped, creamy-yellow flowers are borne in dense, conical clusters, followed by spherical, red berries. Likes full sun. Prefers moist, well-drained soil, but plants are drought-tolerant. Height: 10 feet, and spreads to 10 feet. Fully hardy. Zones 4 – 7.

Attracts at least 12 birds common to this region, which eat the cheerful red fruits of the buffaloberry. It is a preferred food of the American robin and sharp-tailed grouse.

Attracts many species, including the California towhee, white-crowned sparrow, song sparrow, and western bluebird, which eat its small fruit capsules.

Attracts many birds that eat the berries, including the robin, western bluebird, California towhee, and gray catbird. Shown above are berries of the American elder.

FLOWERING MAPLE

Abutilon megapotamicum

An evergreen shrub grown for its flowers and foliage. Its long, slender branches are usually trained against a wall. Dark green leaves are oval, with heart-shaped bases. Yellow-and-red flowers appear from late spring through fall. White-breasted nuthatches often nest in cavities of mature trees. Insect-eating birds such as orioles and wrens glean insects from the foliage. Likes full sun/partial shade. Prefers fertile, well-drained soil. Height: 10 feet, and spreads to 10 feet. Half hardy. Zones 8 – 10.

LANTANA

Lantana 'Spreading Sunset'

This lovely evergreen, rounded to spreading shrub is grown for its attractive flowers. Has finely wrinkled, deep green leaves. Bears tiny, tubular flowers in a range of colors, carried in rounded, dense heads from spring to fall. Likes full sun. Prefers fertile, well-drained soil. Height: 3 feet, spreads to 4 feet. Frost tender. Zones 9 – 10.

MAHONIA

Mahonia pinnata

A native, evergreen shrub with crinkly, spine-tipped leaves that show bronze, red, and orange colors on new growth. Yellow, bell-shaped flowers are followed by full clusters of berries. This mahonia can grow taller and does better in drought conditions than Oregon grapeholly (Mahonia aquifolium). Requires water occasionally in summer. Likes partial shade. Prefers fertile, well-drained soil. Height: minimum 6 feet. Half hardy. Zone 7.

***Attracts** many birds that eat the ripe seeds in summer, including pine and evening grosbeak. Shown above is the flower of A. pictum 'Thompsonii'.*

***Attracts** many species, including the lazuli bunting, western bluebird, yellow-breasted chat, ash-throated flycatcher, and western kingbird, all of which consume the fruit.*

***Attracts** many birds that eagerly consume the berries of this shrub, including the cedar waxwing, varied thrush, hermit thrush, American robin, and northern mockingbird.*

NINEBARK
Physocarpus opulifolius

This deciduous, arching, dense shrub (the variety 'Dart's Gold' is seen above) is grown for its foliage and flowers. It has peeling bark and broadly oval, toothed, and lobed, green leaves. Clusters of tiny, shallow cup-shaped, white or pale pink flowers are produced in early summer. Fruit clusters of 3 – 5 reddish pods form in fall. Likes full sun. Prefers fertile, acid soil; does not grow well in shallow, chalky soil. Height: 10 feet, and spreads to 15 feet. Fully hardy. Zones 2 – 8.

OREGON GRAPEHOLLY
Mahonia aquifolium

This evergreen shrub is the state flower of Oregon. Excellent bird-attracting plant for low-light conditions, or as a screen between properties. Young leaves are purple or bronze, and change to dark green and wine red in winter. Bears clusters of white flowers in spring that mature to blue-black fruit with a gray bloom from early fall. Likes shade/partial shade. Prefers fertile, well-drained soil. Height: 1 – 6 feet. Fully to half hardy. Zones 6 – 9.

RED SAGE
Salvia greggii

This native, erect, evergreen shrub is also known as autumn sage. Its leaves are narrowly oblong, and matt, deep green. Starts blooming in spring, and to a lesser extent in summer, with a final burst of flowers in fall. Well adapted to western gardens from Mexico to northern California. Likes partial shade. Prefers fertile, well-drained soil. Height: 2 – 3 feet. Frost tender. Zone 8.

Attracts *many species, including the American goldfinch, yellow warbler, and flycatchers, which nest in the foliage of the native ninebark shrub.*

Attracts *many birds that eat the fruit of this close relative of the barberry, including the cedar waxwing. It occurs from British Columbia to northern California.*

Attracts *hummingbirds, including rufous and Anna's hummingbird, which are drawn by the loose spikes of the 1-inch-long magenta flowers.*

SUGAR BUSH
Rhus ovata

This is an excellent choice for low-rainfall plantings and thrives in dry, rocky soil. Has white or pinkish flowers from spring to early summer. Its reddish, hairy ¼-inch fruits are covered with a sweet, waxy coating and ripen in summer. Grows as a rounded evergreen shrub or small tree. Needs extra water in low, desert areas. Likes full sun/partial shade. Prefers well-drained soil. Height: 10 feet. Hardy. Zone 9.

TWINLINE HONEYSUCKLE
Lonicera involucrata

Also known as fly honeysuckle, this deciduous shrub is an excellent choice since both the fruit and flowers are important to birds. It produces yellow, funnel-shaped flowers that are paired on long stalks in summer. These develop into paired blackish berries by late summer. Likes partial shade. Prefers moist, calcareous soil. Height: 2 – 3 feet, occasionally 10 feet in ideal conditions. Hardy. Zone 9.

WAX MYRTLE
Myrica cerifera

Also known as southern bayberry, southern wax myrtle, and candleberry. A large evergreen, its yellowish green leaves are oval, slender, and tooth-edged. Male and female flowers develop in catkins on separate plants, so plant both sexes. The fruit matures in fall, persisting through winter. Excellent as a screen or hedge plant, and is an attractive ornamental. Salt-tolerant. Likes full sun/partial shade. Prefers moist but well-drained soil. Height: to 20 feet. Hardy. Zone 7.

Attracts *at least 15 species of western birds, including the golden-crowned sparrow, yellow-rumped warbler, northern flicker, hermit thrush, and roadrunner.*

Attracts *many hummingbirds because its flowers are an excellent food source. The fruits are also eaten by the Townsend's solitaire, robin, wrentit, and thrashers.*

Attracts *more than 80 species, including the black-capped chickadee, bobwhite, brown thrasher, hermit thrush, scrub jay, and downy woodpecker.*

GROUNDCOVERS

MANZANITA
Arctostaphylos spp.

There are about 50 species in this large group of western shrubs. Most of the species are evergreen, producing white or pink flower clusters from early spring and persistent red fruits that begin to ripen in early summer. Likes full sun/partial shade. Tolerates a variety of soils. Growth forms vary greatly from tall shrubs to prostrate groundcovers. Hardy. Zones 4 – 9.

Attracts many ground-feeding birds that consume the red manzanita fruits, including the fox sparrow, and the California and rufous-sided towhees.

LANTANA
Lantana montevidensis

This evergreen, trailing, and mat-forming shrub with serrated leaves makes an ideal groundcover in full sun situations. Produces attractive rose-purple flowers with yellow centers. Blooms intermittently throughout the year, but most flowers occur in summer. Will tolerate temperatures down to 50°F. Red spider mite and whitefly may be troublesome. Likes full sun. Prefers fertile, well-drained soil. Height: 3 – 4 feet, and spreads to 5 feet. Frost tender. Zone 10.

Attracts a wide variety of birds, including the lazuli bunting, western bluebird, yellow-breasted chat, western kingbird, and ash-throated flycatcher.

SALAL
Gaultheria shallon

This is a low-growing, spreading shrub with an open growth form. It is an evergreen with shiny, green foliage that forms a dense groundcover, and is an excellent plant for coastal gardens. Produces pink flowers in the spring that mature into fruits from midsummer. Salal spreads rapidly by sending out wandering roots, so give it lots of room. Likes shade. Prefers acid soil. Height: 1 – 2 feet, occasionally up to 8 feet. Hardy. Zone 7.

Attracts many birds that consume the purple-black fruit, and it is a favorite food source of the wrentit and ring-necked pheasant. It is an ideal songbird nesting habitat.

OTHER GOOD PLANTS

EVERGREEN TREES

Abies concolor
WHITE FIR
See Mountains and Deserts region listing, p.144.

Abies lasiocarpa
ROCKY MOUNTAIN FIR
See Mountains and Deserts region listing, p.144

Abies magnifica
SHASTA RED FIR
Native to the Oregon Cascades, this tree has good ornamental value. It produces an abundant seed crop every 2 – 3 years, and is the preferred food of the blue grouse, pine grosbeak, and many other species. *Height:* 60 – 200ft; likes sun. Prefers drained soil. The fruit appears in early fall. *Fruit type:* Cone. ZONE 6.

Abies procera
NOBLE FIR
Native to the Cascade Mountains of Oregon and Washington, this long-lived tree is notable for its rapid growth. Its seeds provide food for chickadees, jays, nuthatches, and many other species. *Height:* 60 – 225ft; likes sun. Prefers drained soil. The fruit appears in fall. *Fruit type:* cone. ZONE 6.

Ilex aquifolium
ENGLISH HOLLY
This ornamental, which is native to Europe and Asia, is a multibranched tree. The berries are eaten by at least 32 species. Frost hardy. *Height:* 70ft; likes sun/half sun. Prefers moist/drained soil. The fruit appears in fall and persists through the winter. *Fruit type:* red berry. ZONE 7.

Juniperus californicus
CALIFORNIA JUNIPER
This native provides excellent cover for dry soils. Its berries are eaten by at least 10 species, including the mockingbird and varied thrush. *Height:* 10 – 30ft; likes sun. The fruit appears all year round. *Fruit type:* blue-green berry. ZONE 8.

Juniperus occidentalis
SIERRA JUNIPER
See Mountains and Deserts region listing, p.144.

Juniperus scopulorum
ROCKY MOUNTAIN JUNIPER
See Mountains and Deserts region illus. listing, p.139.

Juniperis virginiana
EASTERN REDCEDAR
See Northeast region illus. listing, p.85.

Pinus contorta var. latifolia
LODGEPOLE PINE
See Mountains and Deserts region listing, p.144.

Pinus jeffreyi
JEFFREY PINE
This native occurs naturally high in the mountains. Its cones sometimes grow to 15in long. *Height:* 60 – 200ft; likes sun. Prefers drained soil. The fruit appears in fall. *Fruit type:* cone. ZONE 6.

Pinus monticola
WESTERN WHITE PINE
See Mountains and Deserts region listing, p.144.

Pinus ponderosa
PONDEROSA PINE
See Prairies and Plains region illus. listing, p.123.

Pinus radiata
MONTEREY PINE
A native that is commonly planted in backyards in the coastal zone near San Francisco. Its cones occur every 3 – 5 years. *Height:* 40 – 100ft; likes sun. Prefers drained soil. The fruit appears on exposure to heat. *Fruit type:* cone. ZONE 7.

Pinus sabiniana
DIGGER PINE
The dry foothills of northern and central California are the native habitat of this pine. *Height:* 40 – 80ft; likes sun. Prefers dry/moist/drained soil. The fruit appears all year round. *Fruit type:* cone. ZONE 8.

Pinus torreyana
TORREY PINE
Native to coastal southern California, its dense foliage and often twisted trunk gives this tree value as an interesting ornamental. It also provides cover and food for coastal landbirds. *Height:* 20 – 40ft; likes sun. Prefers drained soil. The fruit appears all year round. *Fruit type:* cone. ZONE 7.

Prunus lyonii
CATALINA CHERRY
Often cultivated as an ornamental tree. The fruit is readily eaten by many species

of songbird. *Height:* 15 – 35ft; likes sun. Prefers dry/drained soil. The fruit appears in late summer through early fall. *Fruit type:* purple/black drupe. ZONE 8.

Pseudotsuga menziesii
DOUGLAS FIR
See Mountains and Deserts region listing, p.144.

Quercus douglasii
BLUE OAK
Native. Many birds eat the acorns, including jays. *Height:* 20 – 60ft; likes sun. Prefers dry/drained soil. The fruit appears all year round. *Fruit type:* annual acorn. ZONE 7.

Quercus engelmannii
ENGELMANN OAK
Its acorns are eaten by the band-tailed pigeon, quails, jays, and many other species. *Height:* 20 – 50ft; likes sun. Prefers dry/drained soil. The fruit appears all year round. *Fruit type:* acorn. ZONE 7.

Thuja occidentalis
EASTERN ARBORVITAE
See Northeast region listing, p.92.

Tsuga heterophylla
WESTERN HEMLOCK
See Mountains and Deserts region listing, p.144.

Tsuga mertensiana
MOUNTAIN HEMLOCK
See Mountains and Deserts region listing, p144.

Umbellularia californica
CALIFORNIA BAY LAUREL
Depending on growth conditions, this native laurel may appear as a shrub, tree, or creeping groundcover. It provides food for the Steller's jay and Townsend's solitaire. *Height:* 20 – 75ft; likes sun/shade. Prefers moist/drained soil. The fruit appears in fall. *Fruit type:* Drupe. ZONE 7.

DECIDUOUS TREES

Acer glabrum
ROCKY MOUNTAIN MAPLE
See Mountains and Deserts region listing, p.144.

Acer negundo var. californicum
CALIFORNIA BOXELDER
This native tree is extensively cultivated for street and park plantings. Its seeds are eaten by at least 4 species, including the evening grosbeak. *Height:* 20 – 40ft; likes

sun/shade. Prefers dry/moist soil. The fruit appears in summer through fall. *Fruit type:* samara. ZONE 3.

Alnus rhombifolia
WHITE ALDER
See Mountains and Deserts region listing, p.145.

Alnus rubra
RED ALDER
Native along coastal stream banks and shore flats, its seeds are eaten by the American goldfinch, pine siskin, bufflehead, green-winged teal, and American wigeon. *Height:* 40 – 80ft; likes sun/shade. Prefers moist/drained soil. The fruit appears in fall through winter. *Fruit type:* nutlet in cone. ZONE 6.

Alnus sinuata
SITKA ALDER
A useful native planting in moist soil areas. Alders provide excellent cover and nest sites for songbirds. The seeds are important for the pine siskin, goldfinches, and redpolls. *Height:* 20 – 30ft; likes sun. Prefers moist/drained soil. The fruit appears in fall. *Fruit type:* nutlet in cone. ZONE 1.

Alnus tenuifolia
MOUNTAIN ALDER
See Mountains and Deserts region listing, p.145.

Arbutus menziesii
MADRONE
See Pacific Coast region illus. listing, p.155.

Betula papyrifer
PAPER BIRCH
See Northeast region listing, p.92.

Cephalanthus occidentalis
COMMON BUTTONBUSH
See Aquatic Plants listing, p.73.

Crataegus crus-galli
COCKSPUR HAWTHORN
See Prairies and Plains region illus. listing, p.122.

Crataegus phaenopyrum
WASHINGTON HAWTHORN
See Prairies and Plains region listing, p.128.

Fraxinus oregona
OREGON ASH
This tree is native along stream banks and moist valley bottoms from British Columbia to southern California. Plant both male and female for a seed crop. It is a favorite of the evening grosbeak. *Height:* 30 – 70ft; likes sun. Prefers moist/drained

soil. The fruit appears in fall and may persist for a year. *Fruit type:* samara. ZONE 7.

Malus diversifolia
OREGON CRABAPPLE
Native to the Pacific coast from Alaska to northern California, and sometimes occurs as a shrub. The fruit is a favorite food of the robin and ruffed grouse. Many cultivated varieties are also available; some other flowering crabapple species and varieties hardy to Alaska include 'Japanese Hopa', 'Radiant', 'Pink Cascade', 'Sparkler', and 'Dolgo'. *Height:* 10 – 30ft; likes sun. Prefers moist/drained soil. The fruit appears in fall. *Fruit type:* purple pome. ZONE 3.

Morus rubra
RED MULBERRY
See Northeast region illus. listing, p.86.

Platanus racemosa
WESTERN SYCAMORE
This native grows along streams and adjacent floodplains in central and southern California. Its seeds are a favorite food of goldfinches. *Height:* 40 – 90ft; likes sun. Prefers drained/moist soil. The fruit appears in fall through winter. *Fruit type:* achene. ZONE 10.

Populus balsamifera
BALSAM POPLAR
See Northeast region listing, p.93.

Populus fremontii
FREMONT COTTONWOOD
See Mountains and Deserts region listing, p.145.

Populus tremuloides
QUAKING ASPEN
See Northeast region listing, p.93.

Populus trichocarpa
BLACK COTTONWOOD
A fairly salt-tolerant native, the fruit of this tree is eaten by at least 10 species, including the evening grosbeak and purple finch. *Height:* to 100ft; likes sun. Prefers moist/sandy/gravelly soil. The fruit appears in spring. *Fruit type:* capsule. ZONE 5.

Prunus emarginata
BITTER CHERRY
See Mountains and Deserts region listing, p.145.

Quercus garryana
OREGON OAK
Native. *Height:* 35 – 60ft; likes sun. Prefers dry/drained soil. The fruit appears all year round. *Fruit type:* acorn. ZONE 7.

Quercus lobata
VALLEY WHITE OAK
The acorns of this native tree are an important food for the band-tailed pigeon, Lewis' woodpecker, and ring-necked pheasant. The Oregon white oak often occurs as a shrub. *Height:* 40 – 125ft; likes sun/shade. Prefers dry/drained soil. The fruit appears in fall. *Fruit type:* annual acorn. ZONE 9.

Salix scouleriana
SCOULER WILLOW
This native is excellent for stablizing stream banks on large properties. At least 23 birds, especially grouse and quail species, are known to eat the tender buds and twigs of willows. *Height:* 4 – 30ft; likes sun. Prefers dry/moist/drained soil. The fruit appears in summer. *Fruit type:* capsule. ZONE 6.

Sorbus americana
AMERICAN MOUNTAINASH
See Northeast region illus. listing, p.84.

Sorbus aucuparia
EUROPEAN MOUNTAINASH
See Northeast region listing, p94.

EVERGREEN SHRUBS

Acacia greggii
CATCLAW ACACIA
See Mountains and Deserts region listing, p.145.

Arctostaphylos manzanita
PARRY MANZANITA
This native shrub and the similar summer-holly (*A. densiflora*) occur along the California coast and in the coastal mountains of southern California. The fruit is eaten by at least 8 species, including the scrub jay, band-tailed pigeon, fox sparrow, wrentit, and mockingbird. *Height:* 12 – 15ft; likes sun. Prefers dry/drained soil. The fruit appears all year round. *Fruit type:* red berry. ZONE 7.

Atriplex hymenelytra
DESERT HOLLY
See Prairies and Plains region listing, p.129.

Atriplex lentiformis subsp. *brewerii*
BREWER SALTBUSH
This semievergreen native is salt-tolerant, provides excellent cover for dry habitats, and makes good windbreaks and hedges (with pruning). *Height:* 1 – 5ft; likes sun. Prefers dry soil. The fruit appears in early fall. *Fruit type:* achene. ZONE 8.

Atriplex polycarpa
DESERT SALTBUSH
Plant both male and female of this semievergreen native, which can spread to 6ft, providing excellent cover. *Height:* to 6ft; likes sun. Prefers dry soil. The fruit appears in fall. *Fruit type:* achene. ZONE 5.

Isomeris arborea
BLADDERBUSH
This semievergreen native usually grows in alkaline soils. It gives good cover throughout the year, and can spread to 6ft. *Height:* to 7ft; likes sun. Prefers loamy soil. The fruit appears in summer through fall. *Fruit type:* capsule. ZONE 9.

Juniperus chinensis
CHINESE JUNIPER
See Northeast region listing, p.94.

Lycium andersonii
ANDERSON WOLFBERRY
See Mountains and Deserts region listing, p.147.

Mahonia nervosa
CASCADES MAHONIA
This native forms dense, low thickets and gives excellent cover. It is resistant to black stem rust. *Height:* to 2ft; likes sun/shade. Prefers dry/drained soil. The fruit appears in late summer. *Fruit type:* berry. ZONE 6.

Myrica californica
CALIFORNIA WAX MYRTLE
A large native evergreen shrub or small tree with dark green, glossy foliage and a dense form. It is a popular choice for a specimen tree or pruned hedge. The purplish, waxy, nutlet fruits appear in summer and persist over the winter until the following summer. These fruits are an important food for many species, including the northern flicker, tree swallow, chestnut-backed chickadee, wrentit, yellow-rumped warbler, and towhees. *Height:* 10 – 35ft; likes sun. Prefers moist/sand soil. *Fruit type:* purple nutlet. ZONE 8.

Opuntia spp.
PRICKLY PEAR CACTUS
See Mountains and Deserts region illus. listing, p.142.

Prunus ilicifolia
HOLLY-LEAVED CHERRY
Also known by its Indian name, Islay. It is resistant to drought and fire. Holly-leaved cherry has small white flowers in spring and produces sweet, dark red or purple fruits that are often available until early winter. The fruit is eaten by many species, including the hairy woodpecker, scrub jay, and

Swainson's thrush. Its dense foliage provides excellent protection for bird nests. *Height:* 6 – 25ft; likes sun. Prefers sand/loam/clay soil. The fruit appears in late spring. *Fruit type:* berry. ZONE 7.

Rhamnus californica
CALIFORNIA BUCKTHORN
This native shrub, also known as the coffeeberry, provides food for at least 7 species, including the band-tailed pigeon. *Height:* to 8ft; likes sun. Prefers dry soil. The fruit appears in early fall. *Fruit type:* drupe. ZONE 7.

Rhus aromatica
FRAGRANT SUMAC
See Mountains and Deserts region listing, p.146.

Rhus integrifolia
LEMONADE SUMAC
A native with thick evergreen leaves that produce dense shade and endure salt, extreme heat, and drought. At least 6 species eat its fruit, including the wrentit. *Height:* to 30ft; likes sun. Prefers dry/drained soil. The fruit appears in late summer. *Fruit type:* red drupe. ZONE 9.

Rhus laurina
LAUREL SUMAC
Thick, evergreen leaves provide dense shade and endure salt, extreme heat, and drought. At least 6 species eat the fruit. Native. *Height:* 10 – 20ft; likes sun. Prefers dry/drained soil. The fruit appears in early fall. *Fruit type:* red drupe. ZONE 9.

Ribes aureum
GOLDEN CURRANT
See Mountains and Deserts region illus. listing, p.140.

Rubus parviflorus
WESTERN THIMBLEBERRY
See Mountains and Deserts region illus. listing, p.141

Symphoricarpos albus
COMMON SNOWBERRY
See Prairies and Plains region illus. listing, p.126.

Vaccinium ovatum
CALIFORNIA HUCKLEBERRY
This native shrub provides important food for the blue grouse and many songbird species. At least 87 other species are known to eat huckleberries and blueberries. *Height:* to 10ft; likes sun/shade. Prefers moist/drained soil. The fruit appears in late summer. *Fruit type:* black berry. ZONE 7.

DECIDUOUS SHRUBS

Amelanchier alnifolia
SASKATOON SERVICEBERRY
A hardy serviceberry which varies in growth form depending upon the soil and water availability. In rich, moist soils it forms dense thickets. In hard, dry soils, it often grows prostrate. Its fragrant white flowers appear in early summer, and are followed by juicy fruits. *Height:* 6 – 12ft. Likes sun/shade. *Fruit type:* purple-black pome. ZONE 6.

Amelanchier florida
PACIFIC SERVICEBERRY
This native shrub provides important food for at least 10 western species, including the northern flicker, house finch, cedar waxwing, western tanager, and evening and black-headed grosbeaks. *Height:* 3 – 20ft; likes sun. Prefers dry/moist drained soil. The fruit appears in late summer. *Fruit type:* blue pome. ZONE 2.

Cornus glabrata
BROWN DOGWOOD
See Mountains and Deserts region listing, p.146.

Cornus sessilis
MINER'S DOGWOOD
See Mountains and Deserts region listing, p.146.

Cornus stolonifera
RED-OSIER DOGWOOD
See Northeast region illus. listing, p.90.

Osmaronia cerasiformis
INDIAN PLUM OSOBERRY
The fruits of this native shrub are readily eaten by many species. *Height:* to 12ft; likes shade. Prefers well-drained soil. The fruit appears in late summer. *Fruit type:* purple-black drupe. ZONE 4.

Prunus virginiana
CHOKECHERRY
See Prairies and Plains region illus. listing, page124.

Rhamnus purshiana
CASCARA SAGRADA
This small tree or shrub is best known for the medicinal qualities of its bark. Its juicy berries are eaten by many species including the evening grosbeak, purple finch, pileated woodpecker, Steller's Jay, robin, and western tanager. *Height:* 20 – 40ft; likes sun. Prefers rich moist soil. The fruit appears in late summer. *Fruit type:* black berry. ZONE 7.

Rosa californica
CALIFORNIA ROSE
This native shrub has pink flowers. It provides excellent cover, and food for the ruffed and blue grouse, Swainson's thrush, Townsend's solitaire, ring-necked pheasant, bluebirds, and possibly other species. *Height:* to 10ft; likes sun. Prefers dry/ drained soil. The fruit appears in fall. *Fruit type:* red hip. ZONE 6.

Rosa gymnocarpa
WOOD ROSE
This native deciduous shrub produces pink flowers and provides excellent cover and food for many birds. *Height:* to 3ft; likes sun. Prefers dry/drained soil. The fruit appears in fall. *Fruit type:* red hip. ZONE 6.

Rosa rugosa
RUGOSA ROSE
See Northeast region listing, p.96.

Rubus leucodermis
WHITEBARK RASPBERRY
See Mountains and Deserts region listing, p.147.

Rubus macropetalus
CALIFORNIA BLACKBERRY
This climbing or shrublike native bears fruits that are readily consumed by at least 12 species. *Height:* to 6ft; likes sun. Prefers dry/ moist/drained soil. The fruit appears in late summer. *Fruit type:* black drupelets. ZONE 8.

Rubus spectabilis
SALMONBERRY
This native shrub provides food for the robin, cedar waxwing, pine and black-headed grosbeaks, band-tailed pigeon, and blackbirds. *Height:* to 6ft; likes sun. Prefers dry soil. The fruit appears in summer. *Fruit type:* yellow/red drupelet. ZONE 6.

Sambucus caerulea
BLUEBERRY ELDER
See Mountains and Deserts region illus. listing, p.139.

Sambucus callicarpa
PACIFIC RED ELDER
The prolific fruit of this native shrub are eaten by at least 8 species, including the California quail, robin and Swainson's thrush. *Height:* to 20ft; likes sun/half sun. Prefers rich/moist/drained soil. The fruit appears in late summer through early winter. *Fruit type:* red berry. ZONE 8.

Sambucus melanocarpa
BLACK-BEAD ELDER
See Prairies and Plains region listing, p.130.

Seriphidium tridentatum
BIG SAGEBRUSH
See Mountains and Deserts region listing, p.147.

Shepherdia argentea
SILVER BUFFALOBERRY
See Pacific Coast region illus. listing, p.157.

Sorbus occidentalis
ALPINE MOUNTAINASH
See Mountains and Deserts region listing, p.147.

Sorbus scopulina
GREEN MOUNTAINASH
See Mountains and Deserts region listing, p.147.

Symphoricarpos oreophilus
MOUNTAIN SNOWBERRY
See Mountains and Deserts region listing, p.148.

Symphoricarpos rotundifolius
ROUNDLEAF SNOWBERRY
See Mountains and Deserts region listing, p.148.

VINES

Lonicera ciliosa
ORANGE HONEYSUCKLE
See Prairies and Plains region listing, p.130.

Lonicera hispidula
PINK HONEYSUCKLE
This native is an evergreen vine that sometimes grows as a 12-foot shrub, and has white or purple flowers. Its fruits are eaten by the Townsend's solitaire, robin, wrentit, and towhees. Likes sun. Prefers dry/drained soil. The fruit appears in summer and persists through winter. *Fruit type:* red berry. ZONE 7.

Smilax californica
CALIFORNIA GREENBRIER
This native is a smooth or prickly vine that often spreads by rootstocks. Its fruits are eaten by the mockingbird, robin, Swainson's thrush and thrashers. Likes sun/shade. Prefers moist/drained soil. The fruit appears in summer through fall. *Fruit type:* berry. ZONE 7.

Vitis californica
CALIFORNIA GRAPE
The fruits of this tall, native vine are favorites of many birds, including the mockingbird, wrentit, western bluebird, and cedar waxwing. Likes sun. Prefers moist/drained soil. The fruit appears in summer through fall. *Fruit type:* purple berry. ZONE 7.

GROUNDCOVERS

Arctostaphylos nevadensis
PINE-MAT MANZANITA
This native forms a creeping evergreen mat with white flowers and persistent fruit. It provides excellent food into winter for the band-tailed pigeon, grouse, and jays. Likes sun. Prefers dry/drained soil. The fruit appears in summer through early fall. *Fruit type:* red berry. ZONE 7.

Arctostaphylos uva-ursi
BEARBERRY
See Northeast region illus. listing, p.91.

Cornus canadensis
BUNCHBERRY
See Mountains and Deserts region illus. listing, p.143.

Fragaria bracteata
WOOD STRAWBERRY
A perennial herb, this native occurs in prairies and open, dry woods. At least 9 species are known to eat its fruit, including the cedar waxwing, ruffed grouse, song sparrow, robin, and pine and black-headed grosbeaks. Likes sun/half sun. Prefers dry/moist/drained soil. The fruit appears in spring. *Fruit type:* red berry. ZONE 5.

Fragaria californica
CALIFORNIA STRAWBERRY
At least 7 species eat strawberries, including the California quail, mockingbird, California towhee, robin, and black-headed grosbeak. Likes sun. Prefers moist/drained soil. The fruit appears in spring through early summer. *Fruit type:* red berry. ZONE 7.

Gaultheria humifusa
ALPINE WINTERGREEN
See Mountains and Deserts region listing, p.148.

Mitchella repens
PARTRIDGEBERRY
See Northeast region listing, p.97.

Rosa spithamea
GROUND ROSE
This low-growing native bush provides good cover and fruit for ground-feeding birds. Likes sun. Prefers dry/drained soil. The fruit appears all year round. *Fruit type:* red hip. ZONE 7.

Vaccinium uliginosum
BOG BILBERRY
See Northeast region listing, p.97.

IMPORTANT WEEDS AND GRASSES

WILD PLANTS are among the most important foods for birds. An excellent way to encourage the growth of these plants, and to attract birds, is to establish a small wild food patch in your backyard *(see page 26)*. By definition, a weed is just an unwanted plant. Most are nonshowy, tenacious, and prolific seeders. They adapt to trampling, pulling, and poisoning. Weeds are survivors. The act of displacing them usually improves the soil for the following generation.

To understand the importance of weeds for attracting birds, let a group of plants in a back corner grow to seed, or expose a small

DOVEWEEDS
Croton spp.

Doveweeds are important wild bird foods in the prairie and southern states. Their common name comes from their popularity as a preferred food for mourning, ground and white-winged doves. Doveweed seed is also favored by the bobwhite, cardinal, and many other ground-feeding birds. Most doveweeds are annual, but some, like Gulf croton, are perennial. Likes full sun. Prefers well-drained soil. Height: 2 – 4 feet. Hardy. Zones 5 – 9.

POLYGONUM
Polygonum campanulatum

A member of the knotweed family, a diverse group of mostly moist habitat plants, this is an ideal herbaceous annual border plant. It has a spreading habit (to 3 feet), and soft, green pointed leaves that feature 2 – 3-inch panicles of small pink bell flowers appearing in early summer through fall. Favored by many ground-feeding birds and at least 39 other species. Likes sun/shade. Prefers moist soil. Height: to 3 feet. Hardy. Zones 1 – 9.

POLYGONUM
Polygonum milettii

A member of the knotweed family, this plant is a good groundcover and forms large clumps when planted close to other polygonums. Its deep green, narrow leaves, and spikes of rich crimson flowers all summer, make it a favorite of ground-feeding birds, including the rosy finch, and McCown's longspur, as well as lark and white-crowned sparrows. At least 39 other species eat the seeds. Likes sun/shade. Prefers moist soil. Height: to 2 feet. Hardy. Zones 1 – 9.

patch of bare soil at the rear of your backyard. The natural supply of dormant seeds will soon result in a crop of seed-producing amaranth, bristlegrass, ragwood, lamb's quarters, and many more varieties from the surrounding environment. The birds will follow.

The huge quantities of seed produced by the weeds far exceed the comparatively meager amounts of commercial grain that are available at backyard feeders. Weeds are clearly the staple food for most common seed-eating birds such as the dark-eyed junco, pine siskin, American tree sparrow, red-winged blackbird, goldfinch, and red-breasted nuthatch. A wider recognition of the value of weeds to birds might lead to a more tolerant view of these abundant, useful plants. Plant a few of the plants listed here and you will notice an increase in the number and variety of birds that visit the backyard.

PANIC GRASS
Panicum capillare

At least 160 species grow in North America; above is witchgrass, a tuft-forming annual with broad leaves and hair-covered stems. An important food for ground-feeding birds. At least 61 bird species eat the seeds, including the bobwhite, red-winged blackbird, brown-headed cowbird, and blue grosbeak, as well as the lark, and clay-colored, song, and white-crowned sparrows. Likes full sun. Prefers moist soil. Height: 2 − 3 feet. Hardy. Zones 1 − 9.

SHEEP SORREL
Rumer acetosella

This small member of the dock family is naturalized from Europe. It spreads its seeds by creeping perennial rootstock. The seeds are its principal value to birds. At least 29 bird species are known to eat sheep-sorrel seed, including many game and songbirds. Sheep-sorrel seed is also a food source for the red-winged blackbird, and hoary redpoll, as well as song, tree, and white-crowned sparrows. Prefers acid, low-fertility soil. Height: to 12 inches. Hardy. Zones 1 − 9.

SUNFLOWER
Helianthus spp.

Its cultivated varieties are one of the most important bird foods. It is also a good annual for screens and temporary hedges. The common sunflower has heart-shaped leaves, can have a single daisy flower of up to 14 inches across, and is a prolific seed producer. Chickadees, nuthatches, and titmice prefer sunflower seeds to all other seeds. At least 43 other species eat its seeds. Likes full/partial sun. Prefers well-drained soil. Height: 3 − 10 feet. Zones 5 − 8.

PLANT SOURCES

The code beneath the plant name refers to the nursery from which the plant can be obtained.

Abutilon megapotamicum
FLOWERING MAPLE
LG

Acer saccharum
SUGAR MAPLE
BS, TE, MI, WI

Aesculus pavia
RED BUCKEYE
CG, AF,

Ajuga reptans
CARPET BUGLE
CG, KB

Amelanchier arborea
DOWNY SERVICEBERRY
FF, SC

Andropogon scoparius
LITTLE BLUESTEM
WN

Arbutus menziesii
PACIFIC MADRONE
TP, CS

Arctostaphylos
MANZANITA
CV

Arctostaphylos uva-ursi
BEARBERRY
EP, FF, EG, LP

Buddleia davidii
BUTTERFLY BUSH
CG, FF, EG

Caesolpinia gilliesii
BIRD OF PARADISE
CS

Callicarpa americana
AMERICAN BEAUTYBERRY
AP, EE, FS, TN

Campsis radicans
TRUMPET VINE
AP, EE, FS, GI, CM

Carya ovata
SHAGBARK HICKORY
MI, FF, BR

Ceanothus spp.
CALIFORNIA LILAC
EG

Celtis laevigata
HACKBERRY, NETTLE
TREE
FF, AP, EE, TN, SI

Celtis occidentalis
COMMON HACKBERRY
FF, BS, TE, MI

Cephalanthus occidentalis
COMMON BUTTONBUSH
TN, SI, LF, GI, FS

Chilopsis linearis
DESERT WILLOW
LP, CS

Cornus alternifolia
PAGODA DOGWOOD
AF, FF, MN, BS

Cornus canadensis
BUNCHBERRY
FF, CG, EP

Cornus florida
FLOWERING DOGWOOD
FF, MI, CG, CM

Cornus nuttallii
PACIFIC DOGWOOD
FF, CS, BR, EG

Cornus racemosa
GRAY DOGWOOD
FF, MN, WI, AF, EG

Cornus stolonifera
RED-OSIER DOGWOOD
FF, EG, VN, MN

Cotoneaster franchettii
FRANCHET
COTONEASTER
SC

Cotoneaster horizontalis
ROCKSPRAY
COTONEASTER
FF, CS, EG

Crataegus crus-galli
COCKSPUR HAWTHORN
FF, MN, WI, VN

Crataegus laevigata
HAWTHORN
CG, MI, MN

Crataegus phaenopyrum
WASHINGTON
HAWTHORN
FF, MI, WI, MN, CS

Diospyros virginiana
COMMON PERSIMMON
AP, EE, GI, LF, SI

Encelia farinosa
BRITTLEBUSH
LP, TP, CS, MS

Forestiera neomexicana
DESERT OLIVE
FF, LP

Fouquieria splendens
OCOTILLO
SW

Fragaria spp.
STRAWBERRY
FF, CV, CG, LP

Gaultheria procumbens
WINTERGREEN
FF, CG, MI, CM

Gaultheria shallon
SALAL
FF, LP, TP, CM

Heteromeles arbutifolia
TOYON
FF, LP, CS, EG

Heuchera spp.
CORALBELL
EG, FF, CG

Ilex decidua
POSSUM HAW
EE, SI

Ilex glabra
INKBERRY
FS, TN, LF, GI

Ilex opaca
AMERICAN HOLLY
EE, LF

Ilex verticillata
WINTERBERRY
CG, FF

Ilex vomitoria
YAUPON HOLLY
AN, AP, EE, FS, LF

Juniperus communis
COMMON JUNIPER
FF, MI, VN

Juniperus horizontalis
CREEPING JUNIPER
CG, MI, MN

Juniperus scopulorum
ROCKY MOUNTAIN
JUNIPER
FF, AL, CG

Juniperus virginiana
EASTERN RED CEDAR
FF, EG, MI

Justica brandegeana
SHRIMP PLANT
LG

Lantana spp., var.
'Spreading Sunset'
LANTANA
MN

Lantana montevidensis
LANTANA
LG

Lindera benzoin
COMMON SPICEBUSH
FF, MI, CG

Liquidambar styraciflua
AMERICAN SWEETGUM
SI, LF, GI, EE, TN

Lonicera involucrata
TWINLINE HONEYSUCKLE
FF, LP

Lonicera sempervirens
TRUMPET HONEYSUCKLE
AN, EE, FS, GI, LF

Lycium spp.
WOLFBERRY
MS

Magnolia grandiflora
SOUTHERN MAGNOLIA
AN, EE, FS, AP

Mahonia aquifolium
OREGON GRAPEHOLLY
CG, MI, FF, TP, CS

Mahonia pinnata
MAHONIA
YA, YB

Malus spp.
(small-fruited varieties)
CRABAPPLE
FF, CG, BS

Malus sargentii
SARGENT CRABAPPLE
CG, WI, MN, FF, AF

Morus rubra
RED MULBERRY
FF, CM

Myrica pensylvanica
NORTHERN BAYBERRY
FF, EG, AF, MI

Nyssa sylvatica
BLACK TUPELO
TN, SI, AN, FS, GI

Opuntia spp.
PRICKLY PEAR CACTUS
CG, TP

Physocarpus opulifolius
NINEBARK
FF, BS, CG, WI

Picea pungens
COLORADO SPRUCE
WI, MI, AL, TE

Pinus ponderosa
PONDEROSA PINE
FF, TP, LP, VN, MI

Pinus taeda
LOBLOLLY PINE
AN, EE, LF, SI, TN

Prosopis juliflora
MESQUITE
TP, CS, MS

Prunus americana
AMERICAN PLUM
BS, MN, FF

Prunus serotina
BLACK CHERRY
FF, EG, VN, MN

Prunus virginiana
COMMON CHOKECHERRY
WI, FF

Pyracantha coccinea
SCARLET FIRETHORN
MI, CS, CG, FF

Quercus agrifolia
CALIFORNIA LIVE OAK
FF, LP, CS, EG

Quercus alba
WHITE OAK
FF, AF, TE, MI, WI

Quercus laurifolia
LAUREL OAK
TN, FS, AP, EE

Rhus aromatica
FRAGRANT SUMAC
FF, WI, MN

Rhus ovata
SUGAR BUSH
LP, CS, TP, EG

Rhus typhina
STAGHORN SUMAC
FF, MN, TE, BS

Ribes aureum
GOLDEN CURRANT
VN, AL, BC, LP, EG

Ribes sanguineum
FLOWERING CURRANT
LP, EG, CM

Rosa spp.
ROSE
FF, EG

Rubus parviflorus
WESTERN THIMBLEBERRY
CV, FF, BC

Sabal minor
DWARF PALMETTO
AN, TN, SI, LF, GI

Salvia greggii
RED SAGE
EG, LG, MS

Sambucus caerulea
BLUEBERRY ELDER
FF, VN, BC, LP, BR

Sambucus canadensis
AMERICAN ELDERBERRY
FF, MI, LP

Sambucus racemosa
EUROPEAN RED ELDER
FF, BC, AL

Sassafras albidum
SASSAFRAS
AN, SI, AF, MI

Shepherdia argentea
BUFFALOBERRY
FF, MI, TE, MN, VN

Sorbus americana
AMERICAN
MOUNTAINASH
AF, AL, MN, MI, TE

Sorbus sitchensis
SITKA MOUNTAINASH
FF

Symphoricarpos albus
SNOWBERRY
FF, MI, CG, VN, LP

Symphoricarpos orbiculatus
CORALBERRY
FF, CG

Thuja plicata
GIANT ARBORVITAE
FF, LP, TP, CM

Vaccinium corymbosum
HIGHBUSH BLUEBERRY
EE, TN

Vaccinium vitis-idaea
COWBERRY
FF, MI, CM

Viburnum dentatum
ARROWWOOD VIBURNUM
FF, MI, WI, CS

Viburnum lentago
NANNYBERRY
FF, VN, WI, MN

Viburnum trilobum
AMERICAN CRANBERRY
BUSH
VN, MN, BS, TE, AL

Weigela florida
WEIGELA
CG, MN, FF

Zauschneria californica
CALIFORNIA FUCHSIA
FF, EG, MS

MAIL-ORDER NURSERIES

Code

AP AMERICAN NATIVE
PRODUCTS
PO Box 2703
3455 Johns Road-Scottsmoor
Titusville, FL 32781
407-383-1967

AN APALACHEE NATIVE
NURSERY
Route 3, Box 156
Monticello, FL 32344
904-997-8976

AF ARBORVILLAGE FARM
NURSERY
PO Box 227
Holt, MO 64048
816-264-3911

AL AUBIN NURSERIES, LTD.
Box 1089, Carman
Manitoba, R0G 0J0
Canada
204-745-6703

BS BERGESON NURSERY
Route 1, Box 184
Fertile, MN 56540
218-945-6988

KB BLUEMEL, KURT, INC.★
2740 Greene Lane
Baldwin, MD 21013
410-557-7229

BR BURNT RIDGE NURSERY
432 Burnt Ridge Road
Onalaska, WA 98570
206-985-2873

CG CARROLL GARDENS ★
444 East Main St., PO Box 310
Westminster, MD 21158
410-848-5422

CS CARTER SEEDS
(WHOLESALE)
475 Mar Vista Drive
Vista, CA 92083
800-872-7711

CM CLOUD MOUNTAIN
NURSERY
6906 Goodwin Road
Everson, WA 98247
360-966-5859

CV COLVOS CREEK FARM
PO Box 1512
Vashon, WA 98070
206-441-1509

EG CORNFLOWER FARMS,
INC.
PO Box 896
Elk Grove, CA 95759
916-689-1015
916-689-1968 (FAX)

EE ENVIRONMENTAL
EQUITIES, INC.
12515 Denton Ave.
Hudson, FL 34667
813-862-3131

FS FLORIDA SCRUB
GROWERS
730 Myakka Road
Sarasota, FL 34240
813-322-1915

FF FORESTFARM ★
990 Tetherow Road
Williams, OR 97544
503-846-6963

GI GREEN IMAGES
1333 Taylor Creek Road
Christmas, FL 32709
407-568-1333

LP LAS PILITAS NURSERY★
Star Route BX 23X
Las Pilitas Road
Santa Margarita, CA 93453
805-438-5992

LG LOGEE'S GREENHOUSES★
141 North St.
Danielson, CT 06239
203-774-8038

LF THE LINER FARM, INC.
PO Box 701369
4020 Packard Ave.
Saint Cloud, FL 33770-1369
407-892-1484

MN MCKAY NURSERY CO. ★
PO Box 185
Waterloo, WI 53594
414-478-2121

MI MELLINGER'S INC.
2310 W. South Range Road
North Lima, OH 44452
216-549-9861

MN MONROVIA NURSERY
CO. (WHOLESALE)★
18331 E. Foothill Blvd.
Azusa, CA 91702
818-334-9321

MS MOUNTAIN STATES
NURSERY (WHOLESALE)
PO Box 33982
Phoenix, AZ 85067
602-247-8509

N THE NATIVES
2929 JB Carter Road
Davenport, FL 33837
813-422-6664

SC SCHUMACHER F.W. CO.
INC. (WHOLESALE)
36 Spring Hill Road
Sandwich, MA 02563
508-888-0659

SW SOUTHWESTERN
NATIVE SEEDS★
PO Box 50503
Tucson, AZ 85703

SI SUPERIOR TREES, INC.
PO Box 9225
US Highway 90 East
Lee, FL 32059
904-971-5159

TE TEC
PO Box 539
Osseo, MN 55369

TP THEODORE PAYNE
FOUNDATION
10459 Tuxford Street
Sun Valley, CA 91352
818-768-1802

VN VALLEY NURSERY
PO Box 4845,
2801 N. Montana Ave.
Helena, MT 59604
406-442-8460

WI WEILER, ARTHUR, INC.
12247 Russell Road
Zion, IL 60099
708-746-2393

YA YA-KA-AMA NATIVE
PLANTS
6215 Eastside Road
Forestville, CA 95436
707-887-1541

YB YERBA BUENA NURSERY
19500 Skyline Blvd.
Woodside, CA 94062
415-851-1668

WN WILDLIFE NURSERIES INC.
PO Box 2724
Oshkosh, Wisconsin, 54903-2724
414-231-3780

★ Accept a Chargecard

NATIVE PLANT SOURCE DIRECTORIES

Andersen Horticultural Library's Source List of Plants and Seeds★
This excellent book contains a plant list of 40,000 species available by mail-order from North American nurseries. *AHL, Minnesota Landscape Arboretum, 3675 Arboretum Drive, Box 39, Chanhassen, Minnesota 55317*
612-443-2440

Hortus Northwest
A magazine-style directory of 1,000 plants and seeds of native species of the Pacific Northwest. It is published biannually.

Hortus Northwest, PO Box 955, Canby, OR 97013
503-266-7968

New England Wild Flower Society – Sources of Propagated Native Plants and Wildlife
Lists 45 nurseries that propagate at least 30% or collect from the wild no more than 5% of their native stock. *New England Wild Flower Society, Garden in the Woods, Hemenway Road, Framingham, MA 01701*
508-877-7630

Nursery Sources For California Native Plants
Lists California native plants and nearly 100 dealers that supply them.

Department of Conservation, Publications Office, 801 K Street, MS 14-33, Sacramento, CA 95814-3529

Plant and Service Directory★ Florida Native Nurseries, Inc.
Excellent directory of Florida native plants and nursery sources.
PO Box 436, Melrose, FL 32666
1-800-293-5413

Taylor's Guide to Specialty Nurseries
Published by Houghton Mifflin Company, it lists mail-order nurseries for many plants that are hard to find.

AQUATIC AND BOG PLANT SOURCES

WILDLIFE NURSERIES, INC.
PO Box 2724
Oshkosh, WI 54903-2724

NICHE GARDENS★
Dept. AUD
1111 Dawson Road
Chapel Hill, NC 27516
919-967-0078
($3.00 for catalog)

MARYLAND AQUATIC NURSERIES★
3427 N. Furnace Road
Jarretsville, MD 21084
410-557-7615

National
Audubon
Society

NATIONAL AUDUBON SOCIETY

THE MISSION of the NATIONAL AUDUBON SOCIETY is to conserve and restore natural ecosystems, focusing on birds and other wildlife for the benefit of humanity and the earth's biological diversity.

In the vanguard of the environmental movement, AUDUBON has 560,000 members, 14 regional and state offices, and an extensive chapter network in the United States and Latin America, plus a professional staff of scientists, lobbyists, lawyers, policy analysts, and educators.

Through our nationwide sanctuary system we manage 150,000 acres of critical wildlife habitat and unique areas for birds, wild animals, and rare plant life. Our award-winning *Audubon* magazine, published six times a year and sent to all members, carries outstanding articles and color photography on wildlife and nature and presents in-depth reports on critical environmental issues, as well as conservation news and commentary. Other publications include the newsjournal,

Audubon Activist; *Audubon Field Notes*, a journal reporting bird sightings continent-wide; and *Audubon Adventures*, a bimonthly children's nature newsletter reaching 600,000 elementary school students.

Our acclaimed *World of Audubon* television specials, airing on the Turner Broadcasting System, deal with a variety of environmental themes; companion books and educational computer software give viewers the opportunity for further in-depth study of the subjects covered by the television series.

Audubon's travel program sponsors many exciting trips every year to exotic places such as Alaska, Antarctica, Baja California, Galapagos, Indonesia, Japan, and Patagonia.

For information about how you can become a member, please write or call:
NATIONAL AUDUBON SOCIETY Membership Dept. 700 Broadway, New York, New York 10003. Telephone: 212-979-3000

INDEX

ACKNOWLEDGMENTS

I could not have written this book without the help and enthusiastic encouragement of many people. I especially thank Donna Ramil, whose patience and thorough research helped me assemble many of the details presented in this edition. I also thank Lynn Bryan of The BookMaker, and Jill Hamilton, my editor at Dorling Kindersley, for their meticulous care to detail and design, and Christine Rista for the picture research. The manuscript also benefited greatly from the helpful comments of many colleagues who reviewed text, recommended plants, and made useful suggestions. For their generous assistance, I thank Bruce Barbour, Kate Beck, Norm Brunswick, Kimball Garrett, Jesse Grantham, Beth Huning, Stephen Lewis, Pete Salmansohn, Dan Savercoll, Dale Shank, Gregg Starr, Tim Smith, Sarah Stein, and Rick Thom.

All illustrations by Elizabeth Pepperell.

PHOTOGRAPHY
Abbreviations: bj= back jacket, b = bottom, c = center, fj= front jacket, if= inside flap, l= left, r= right, t= top

All special photography by Mark Gatehouse 47, 50, 51, 54

Dorling Kindersley
6, 7, 8, 10, 11, 20t, 33t, 34, 35, 36, 37, 38, 39, 41b, 44, 45, 46, 49tl, 52c, 53, 59tl, 61, 62, 63c, 65r, 66tc, 66br, 71, 72l, 72c, 73tl, 73tc, 73bl, 73bc, 80bl, 81cl, 83cl, 84br, 85tl, 85tc, 85bl, 85bc, 86br, 89br, 90bc, 98t, 98b, 101tl, 101cr, 101bl, 103tr, 105tc, 105bc, 106tl, 106bl, 107bl, 107bc, 107br, 111bc, 116tl, 119tr, 119br, 120tr, 120br, 121cl, 123bl, 123br, 124tl, 124bl, 125tr, 127bl, 132tl, 138tr, 138br, 139bl, 140bl, 141bl, 143tl, 143bl, 143bc, 152cr, 154bl, 155tr, 155br, 158tl, 158tc, 158bc, 159tl, 159tc, 161, 166r, 167l, 167r.

Agencies and Photographers
Aquila N.J. Bean 81cr, 101tr, S. and B. Craig 13r, Kevin Carlson 82tr, 152br, Mike Lane 119tl, Wayne Lankinen fjtl, fjtr, half title, 17, 30t, 30l, 31br, 75br, 78tl, 79, 80br, 81tl, 81tr, 81bl, 81br, 82tl, 82cr, 82bl, 82br, 83tl, 83tr, 83bl, 99,100l, 102tl, 102br, 103tl, 103cl, 103br, 116bl, 119bl, 120tl, 120bl, 134l, 134r, 135br, 136tl, 137bl, 148tl, 148bl, 150l, 150r, 151tl, 151br, 153br Mike Wilkes 78bl, 100r, 117, 119cl, 135cl **Bruce Coleman Ltd.** fjbr, Bob and Clara Calhoun 126bc, John Cancalosi 57r, Patrick Clement 15tl, 72r, 157br, Eric Crichton 9tl, 13l, 18, 29b, 88tl, 166c, Peter Davey 166l, Sir Jeremy Grayson 9tr, Stephen J. Krasemann 140br, Joy Langsbury 86bl, John Markham 167c, Dr. Scott Nielsen 83br, Hans Reinhard 2, 64, Leonard Lee Rue 55l, 106tc, Frieder Sauer 65l, 73br, John Shaw 55r, 87bl, Konrad Wothe 15r **Mike Dirr** 89bc, 108br, 109tc, 109bc, 160tr **Christine Douglas** 89tl **Earth Scenes** R.F. Head 122bl, Breck P. Kent 138bl, Liz Leszyczynski 157tr, C. C. Lockwood 109tl, 160br, Patti Murray 106br, Maresa Pryor 86tc, Richard Shiell 27br, 105tl, 125bc, Fred Whitehead 110tl, Jack Wilburn 154tl **Steven Foster** 84tr, 87tr, 87br, 88bl, 88bc, 90br, 104br, 105tr, 105bl, 107tl, 107tr, 109bl, 110bl, 123bc **Garden Picture Library** John Glover 142tr, Michael Howes 143tr, Gary Rogers 143br, Didier Willery 142br **Russell C. Hansen** fjtc **Jerry Harpur** 21b, 32, 86tr designer Sonny Garcia, San Francisco 16, designer Oehme and van Sweden 21t, designer Mark Rios 24t **Grant Heilman Photography** John Colwell 105br, Jane Grushow 87tl, Hal Harrison 88tr, Larry Lefever 104bl, Lefever/Grushow 85tr, 104tl, Runk/Schoenberger 86bc, 88br,

Jim Strawser 86tl, 108tr **Beth Huning** 156tc, 156bc **Dency Kane** fjc **Stephen Kress** 85br, 106tr, 109tr, 109br, 123tc, 124bc **Frank Lane Picture Agency** Ron Austing bjif, 43r, S. Maslowski 23 **Jeff Lepore** 88tc **Charles Mann** 28, 41t, 87tc, 90tr, 90bl, 91tl, 91bl, 122tl, 123tl, 124tc, 125tc, 126tl, 126tc, 126tr, 126bl, 126br, 127tc, 127bc, 139tl, 139tc, 140tl, 140tc, 140bc, 141tc, 141tr, 141br, 142tc, 142bc, 154tc, 154br, 156tr, 156br, 157tl, 157bl, 159tr, 160tl, 160bl **A & E Morris** 26tr, 59br, 69t, 118l, 118r, 119cr, 120cl, 120cr, 121tl, 121tr, 121bl, 121br, 137cl, 153tr, 153bl **NHPA** Stephen Krasemann bjcr, Susan Schubel, bjif **Clive Nichols** 69b, 108tc, 108bc, 111tl, 111bl, 125tl, 125bl, 143tc, 159bc **Oxford Scientific Films** Deni Bown 110tr, 110br, Martyn Chillmaid 91br, J. A. L. Cooke 140tr, Jack Dermid 73tr, 106bc, David Fox 91bc, Terry Heathcote 125br, Geoff Kidd 90tl, Richard Kolar 14l, G. A. Maclean 26bl, Frithjof Skibbe 91tr, Mills Tandy 157bc, David Thompson 142tl **Jerry Pavia** 12, 19, 22, 27tr, 84tl, 84bl, 87bc, 89tr, 108tl, 108bl, 111tr, 111br, 122br, 127tl, 138tl, 139tr, 139br, 141tl, 141bc, 142bl, 155tc, 155bl, 156tl, 156bl, 157tc, 158tr, 158bl, 158br, 160bc **Joanne Pavia** 139bc, 155bc **PhotoResearchers Inc.** Leonard Lee Rue 48t **Photos Horticultural** 90tc, 91tc, 104tr, 107tc, 110tc, 110bc, 111tc, 122tr, 123tr, 124tr, 124br, 127tr, 127br, 155tl, 159bl, 160tc **Gregory Scott** fjbl **Hugh P. Smith** 14r, 20b, 24b, 27bl, 29t, 31tr, 33l, 43l, 48l, 48br, 49br, 56, 57l, 58t, 58b, 59br, 63b, 66bl, 67, 68, 74, 75tl, 132bl, 133, 135tl, 135tr, 135bl, 136tr, 136c, 136bl, 136br, 137tl, 137tr, 149, 151tr, 151c, 151bl, 152tl, 152tr, 152bl, 153tl, 153cl **Greg Starr** 159br **Robert A. Tyrell** fjif **VIREO** H. Cruickshank 52b, R. English 42, Sam Fried 103bl, S. J. Lang 25, A. Murphy 101br, B. Schorre 70, 102tr, J. R. Woodward fjcrb, 102c, 102bl **F. R. Wesley** 89tc, 89bl.